Relations of Literary Study

Relations of Literary Study

ESSAYS ON INTERDISCIPLINARY CONTRIBUTIONS

EDITED BY JAMES THORPE

Modern Language Association of America

62 Fifth Avenue

New York, N.Y. 10011

Contents

Introduction

If we can imagine that there once was a golden age of literary studies, we can also suppose that it was a time of perfect integration. Each reader must then have possessed within himself the power to respond, in balanced harmony, to all of the various appeals with which the literary work is endowed.

German philologists of the nineteenth century have, along with their reputed successors, historically-minded American pedants of the twentieth, often been credited with the destruction of this happy state of felicity, or with the commission of original sin. But that golden age must have ended a very long time before. As early as the first century A.D., literary scholars were apparently gathering a harvest of thorns and thistles.

They were already fair game for the witty and the wise: Seneca made great fun of the scholars who were busy converting Homer into a philosopher of one persuasion or another, and he laughed at specialized topics with the disdain of a reader of titles of doctoral dissertations that do not stir his interest. "It is," Seneca wrote in Letter 88, "no more to the point, of course, for me to investigate whether Homer or Hesiod was the older poet, than to know why Hecuba, although younger than Helen, showed her years so lamentably. What, in your opinion, I say, would be the point in trying to determine the respective ages of Achilles and Patroclus? Do you raise the question, 'Through what regions did Ulysses stray?' . . . We have no leisure to hear lectures on the question whether he was sea-tost between Italy and Sicily, or outside our known world. . . . Why try to discover whether Penelope was a pattern of purity, or whether she had the laugh on her contemporaries? Or whether she suspected that the man in her presence was Ulysses, before she knew it was he?"

Seneca's laugh is on all manner of scholars, those who devote themselves to biographical detail, to facts about characters, to the relation between fiction and reality, and to careful analysis of the work of art to understand (or to create) its obscure sense. All these subjects and many more seemed irrelevant to Seneca, who thought that the only valid use of literature was as a model for conduct. We should read about Ulysses' wanderings to prevent ourselves from going astray; we might study Penelope to learn what purity is.

It is true that the topics which Seneca scorned may be irrelevant if they are detached from the work of art and never brought back in touch with it; likewise, factitious emphasis on any part may distort our understanding of the whole. It is also true that Seneca's special preoccupation with morality revealed only one dimension (though admittedly a very important dimension) of the literary work and therefore distorted his own understanding of art.

All of these incomplete and fragmented forms of literary study seem to belong to the time after the fall. But we will have to give up our little fancy of a golden age of literary studies. There has never been a time, I presume, when literary studies represented a perfect integration of all human responses, and perhaps never a golden age in any sense except the mythic or symbolic.

We may sometimes revel in our nostalgia for the past, or think that there were giants in the earth in those days. But when we look back on the work of earlier literary scholars in the light of common day, we generally feel that their supposed supremacy must have been caused by force of personality, or reputation, or our own impressionable spirits. Their work may offer perpetual benediction, but the visionary gleam is fled. Such is never the case with poetry, at least not permanently with great poetry, and we ought not to forget this essential distinction between art and scholarship. We are sometimes urged to see to it that our contributions to scholarship become works of art. So far as this advice is merely an exhortation to good writing, it is innocent enough and always timely; but so far as it seeks to give permanent importance to the literary study for its own sake, it generally represents a misunderstanding: the work of scholarship is secondary, exhaustible, and replaceable, while the work of art is primary, inexhaustible, and permanent. I have put the matter bluntly to make the point. In principle, art and scholarship can meet on some grounds, as in certain examples of biography (as Leon Edel argues later in this volume), in some kinds of historical criticism (as Robert E. Spiller has argued elsewhere), and perhaps in other forms of discursive writing. Not usually, however, and the ground on which they are made to meet often will not support the more valuable qualities of either art or scholarship. So, in practice, anyone who goes into scholarship to satisfy his intimations of immortality has generally chosen the wrong mystery.

I believe that there has never been a time like the present for the production of rewarding and penetrating literary studies. I will not try to convince others that there are individuals today whose work is more perceptive and more useful than that of the great literary students of the past whose names come to mind—though I myself think that there are. I do want to assert that there has been continued progress in literary studies, that is to say in understanding the theory and practice of literature. This progress has been accumulative whenever previous work has been reasonably accessible, and the process is one of assimilating the positions and the methodologies as well as the facts and insights of our predecessors. Hence our sensation about the scholarship of the past. The literary studies by Thomas Warton and by Hippolyte Taine are now interesting mainly, or only, for historical reasons; whatever they had to say of permanent value has long since become a part of our common knowledge and methods, and the same will undoubtedly be true in due course of scholars of our own time. Thus graduate students can refer to notable scholarship of an earlier decade with tolerant superiority or sometimes with amused contempt.

If there is progress in literary studies, then, rather than descent from some golden age of the past, one may wonder how improvement has in fact taken place. Commonly, it seems, through fragmentation or specialization. A mind stored with a considerable knowledge of literary works comes to the study of literature from some fresh perspective, or with a governing theory about the nature of certain kinds of literary works, or with a new body of facts. Most of the time, alas, this confrontation results in nothing worthy of report. Occasionally, it leads to an understanding of one poem, say, ampler than had previously existed, and very rarely it supplies a key which unlocks many doors that had previously been locked.

George Lyman Kittredge's work on Shakespeare may serve as one example of the methods and results of literary scholarship, far enough in the past to be seen in perspective. When Kittredge began his intensive study of Shakespeare in the 1880's in order to give an undergraduate course at Harvard—in succession to his mentor, Francis James Child— he brought to his task a wide knowledge of Elizabethan plays and cultural and intellectual backgrounds, to be sure, but also a detailed familiarity with comparative grammar, with lexicography and semantics, and with general linguistics, all based on a ranging study of ancient and modern European languages and a critical reading of contemporary linguistic scholarship. From this perspective, Kittredge tried to understand Shakespeare's precise meaning in each word, line, sentence, and speech: from the historical perspective of language, that is, he was always trying to answer the question "Exactly what did Shakespeare mean by this?"

Naturally enough, the solution to most problems involved some special knowledge of Elizabethan belief or convention or fact, like demonology or costume or canon law. When Kittredge could bring all of his powers to bear on a difficult passage, the result was a succinct paraphrase of the meaning, couched in admirably lucid prose. His method was both successful and influential. Arthur Colby Sprague has said that Kittredge was, in his time, "the foremost influence on Shakespearean criticism in America," and Irving Ribner has maintained that Kittredge was "the teacher who for almost half a century had dominated and shaped the direction of Shakespearean study in America." Perhaps this is why his explanatory notes—first published almost thirty years ago, but thought out or recorded as much as fifty years before then—do not now seem very remarkable. The rudiments, at least, of his method have for so long been a part of every student's equipment that it may seem laughable to talk about it under the lofty name of scholarship. Moreover, the similarities (as well as the differences) are obvious between Kittredge's method and such other forms of literary study as the nineteenth-century way of teaching Latin and Greek, explication de texte, and the more recent "close reading."

We might pause to notice that Kittredge's method was, for all of his knowledge, extremely one-sided and incomplete. Paraphrase itself, however luminous, can hardly be said to exhaust the meaning of literature. Kittredge rarely considered the plays as performances on the stage, or in relation to problems of production, either in Shakespeare's or in any other theater; he had almost no interest in the symbolic nature of imagery; he had only a perfunctory acquaintance with analytical bibliography. Each of these ways of approaching Shakespeare—and the number could be increased in various directions—was the basis for a method which came into prominence during the latter part of Kittredge's career. The problems of production and staging were at the center of studies by, for example, H. Granville-Barker and E. E. Stoll; Caroline Spurgeon and G. Wilson Knight dealt with matters of imagery in the plays; and J. Dover Wilson developed his method for interpreting Shakespeare out of the materials of analytical bibliography. These three methods (and several others) have all been productive, whatever the shortcomings or excesses of some practitioners.

Kittredge made no effort to integrate what he discovered with what other people were finding out. (It could be argued that it was his duty to have done so as a teacher, if not as a scholar—but that is another subject.) He made, in his own terms, a tremendous contribution to the study of literature. When the productive scholar himself does undertake to synthesize the results of research in the area of his own achievements, the result is often (and perhaps naturally enough) an account in which the peaks are sliced off and the valleys filled in, all except for that one range in which he has personally found gold.

Generally, it is left for us as students and readers to balance and harmonize all that we have learned. We have to make our own golden age of literary studies: one of the crucial steps is in sharing the vision that comes from each new perspective.

II

This is a book about some new perspectives for the study of literature. Our first hope is that literary students will be able to extend their vision by looking at literature from a series of vantage points. If we try them out, one after another, in a certain sequence, it is possible that a stereoscopic view will result which can lead to a truer understanding of the nature of literature. That is one form of vision, the vision of some of the infinite complexity and some of the beautiful integration which is the work of art. Another form of vision is perception into depth, into the beautiful mystery which is also the work of art. Each of these perspectives is accessible because the form of scholarship on which it depends has been built up through a great deal of specialization and fragmentation. These perspectives are "new" in the sense that they have been established, in something like their present form, within the last generation or two at most, within the last decade or two at least. Once you can say that positions have been established, or views consolidated, however, you can hardly consider them new in the sense of being unusual; it will remain for others, hopefully for readers of this book, to move on into unexplored territory.

We call the essays which make up this book by the name of "relations" of literary study in order to suggest that they represent members of a family. The entire family would be a big one, because literature has a lot of relatives by blood and by marriage, sisters, cousins, double in-laws, and all the rest, in a more complex order than the language of genealogy can sort out. So it would be a mistake to insist on the exact kinship even of those seven members who have been invited to make an appearance here. A few words about the kinds of relations that they represent may be desirable, however, as a form of introduction in this mixed company.

History. Since a past can be conceived of for everything, history is everybody's sister. History is an intellectual discipline, it is true; but, more basically, the act of being can be said to create a history. On this assumption, every work of art has its history (or histories), as well as every person, idea, society, and intellectual discipline. Thus it is appropriate for this volume to begin with Rosalie L. Colie's essay on Literature and History, and face, at the outset, what is implied in the relational questions that we ask about art. Under her guidance we explore the historical dimension of the work of art, particularly through intellectual history, and consider what kinds of assistance have been made available to literary students by several different forms of historical study.

Myth. The complexity of the relations between myth and literature is of a different sort. Myths are themselves works of literary art when they appear as stories in undeveloped cultures, and they continue as literature in their elaboration into a mythology; myths also have cultural importance of a religious nature; and the myths of one culture are re-ordered into the substance of art in later cultures. The study of myth (or myth criticism) has other complications: it parallels the study of literature, and at the same time it *is* a form of the study of literature; it is also an important branch of the social sciences, particularly in anthropology and comparative religion. Northrop Frye's essay on Literature and Myth clarifies these relations, moves on to a consideration of the allegorical and the archetypal responses to (and interpretation of) myth, and proposes that myth criticism is a study of the structural principle of literature itself.

Biography. The relation of Literature and Biography is, as Leon Edel describes it in his essay, extremely intimate because the essence of the writer is in his work. Since an understanding of the author's imaginative life is the ultimate goal of literary biography, literary criticism and literary biography are complementary ways of analyzing his writings. Literary biography is thus an integral form of literary study, it supplies an important check on conclusions reached in other ways, and at best it reveals the inner symbolic world of the writer.

Psychology; *Sociology.* The relations of these subjects to literature are similar; both are something like first cousins to the study of literature. The subject of literature is human experience—potentially, every sort and variety of human experience that there is. When any special type of human experience is systematized in conceptual terms and made the subject of formal study, it can be called a "discipline," whatever else it may also be. Each of these disciplines (like psychology and sociology) puts into its kind of order one of the forms of human experience that literature digests into a different kind of order. Take alienation as a form of human experience, for example. Sociology analyzes it, classifies those who are subject to it, and studies the social and individual problems that accompany or give rise to it; literature represents it, in many guises and in assorted company, under such titles as *Victory* and *Sons and Lovers* and *Lucky Jim.* The literary student may hope that he can increase his understanding of the literary work (or perhaps of literature as a whole) by applying the insights that are characteristic of another discipline.

In Literature and Psychology, Frederick C. Crews points out that psychology has seriously changed our way of reading literature by offering a theory of motives which can give an account of the inner action of the artist and of his work. In a review of the grievances often voiced against psychology, Crews speaks of the successes and failures of the past; in the process, he also defines the relationship more precisely and suggests attitudes and methods that will increase the returns for literary students in the future.

In Literature and Sociology, Leo Lowenthal outlines the kinds of modern sociological work that may be of special interest and use to literary scholars, particularly in studying contemporary literature. They include work on the basic problems of modern civilization, on people, and on sociological methodology. He speaks of the main tasks confronting the contemporary sociologist of literature, and concludes with a survey of the relevant scholarly studies which have an important bearing on literary scholarship.

Religion. In Literature and Religion, J. Hillis Miller focuses on the relational problems that are inevitably involved in the interpretation of literary works which treat religious themes, however indirectly. There are distortions that result from the confrontation of the work by the critic, each with commitments of one sort or another. There are other dangers for the critic and for the reader in deciding what the important context is for the given work of art. No clear answers are visible for any of these questions—indeed, many of the easy answers lead to great difficulties for criticism; but the first step at the present time is to observe the pitfalls.

Music. The relation between Literature and Music is different from all of the others in this volume. Literature is one of the arts, along with (at least) music, painting, and sculpture. All of the arts are capable of creating the human experience called aesthetic pleasure, each in its own characteristic way, literature through a formal ordering of language, and music through a formal ordering of sounds. As Bertrand H. Bronson reminds us in his essay, poetry and music used to be thought of as sisters; until recently they lived together in harmony. The formal patterns and technical devices of music generally have only an elementary relevance to literature, but some musical analogies are promising for future literary studies. It is when poetry and music are united (as in song) that their mutual assistance, their multifarious interconnections, and the opportunities for rewarding study of the relations all become evident.

III

This book is sponsored by members of the Committee on Research Activities in the Modern Language Association of America. It is one of a series on subjects that need to be discussed, we think, in the interest of improving the scholarly health of the profession of letters. It is addressed to younger scholars, primarily; we particularly hope that it will prove valuable to graduate students.

Each of the essays included was written expressly for this volume.

We appealed to distinguished scholars for their views on one of their own special interests, and they responded generously. Our original plan envisioned several other essays, which were carried to various stages of completion; but illness or other misfortune has unhappily prevented their appearance. Since we never intended a comprehensive collection of essays on every possible relation of literary study, these absences are regrettable but not disabling to our plan.

We realize that these essays may be misunderstood and misapplied by anyone who seeks a short and easy way to success as a literary scholar. They are not a substitute for any of the first conditions of being a scholar. Not a substitute for reading very widely in literature, nor for studying many literary works intensively, structurally, devotedly. Not a substitute for the basic forms of literary study: the kinds discussed in the MLA pamphlet entitled *The Aims and Methods of Scholarship in Modern Languages and Literatures,* which contains an essay on Linguistics by William G. Moulton, one on Textual Criticism by Fredson Bowers, one on Literary History by Robert E. Spiller, and one on Literary Criticism by Northrop Frye. These basic methods must still be understood and mastered, at least in principle. It is only then, we believe, that the relations of literary study can be wisely exploited as forms of useful scholarship—and we hope that this exploitation will take place, more and more. The way to get the greatest reward from any one of these relations is, of course, to practice the appropriate type of literary scholarship.

We hope that these essays will offer some fruitful insights and valuable perspectives to all readers. We would be glad if they suggest, to some readers, profitable ways that they may follow in the effort to become better scholars.

James Thorpe
Chairman, Committee on Research Activities

Literature and History

By Rosalie L. Colie

If one begins with the assumption (as I do) that a work of art—a painting, a poem, a drama, a fugue, a dance—does not exist *an sich* only, and
is not solely an "ontological" entity, then one is willy-nilly committed to
consider its "history," or, as I prefer to say, its histories. For literary
purposes, history, past or present, is what is implied in the relational
questions we ask about a work of art: e.g., what is the relation of that
work to its creator, its audience, its genre, its time, its place, its particular language? What can be said about this work of art in relation to its fellows, to the taste of its time, and to the history of style or styles? For the
fun of it, let me briefly (and inadequately) answer some of these questions, out of order, in relation to *one* literary work, a taxing experiment
bound to fail. Thence, referring to this work and to many others, I will
go on to discuss certain kinds of history that have helped to elucidate
certain literary works, beginning with the most obvious, literary history;
next considering, all too briefly, political, economic, and cultural history;
and ending with a rather longer discussion of the branches of intellectual
history in relation to literary study.

As my text, let me choose a book many of my most perceptive colleagues (though not my friends) regard as a prodigious bore, Robert
Burton's *Anatomy of Melancholy*. Even more than *Paradise Lost*, Burton's life-work may seem to be a monument to dead ideas; it is certainly
a book peculiarly of its age, though by examining it, we may be able to
see how little it is merely that. First of all, what is the relation of this
book to its creator, its audience, its genre, its time, its place, its particular language? Its creator, Robert Burton, Student of Christ Church,
Clerk of the Market at Oxford, etc., etc., wrote very little else in his life
besides this book which in its six ever-longer editions was his life-work

and perhaps the love of his life. He made it "his"—choosing a pseudo-
nym appropriate to his task, Democritus Junior, he broke up the world,
as well as the books he read, into fragments of experience, into atoms of
perception, and reorganized those fragments, those atoms, into a whole
global world which, like his satirical namesake, he then twirled about in
his hand, to observe and to smile at every corner of it. Robert Burton
was a tricky author: though so thoroughly identified with his book, he
signed it only in its first edition. His name did not appear on the title page
(though his portrait did, unmistakably copied in his funerary bust in the
Oxford Cathedral). Without actually setting his name to the book,
though, he signed it again and again—he told his readers where he lived,
what he did there, what his profession and particular tasks were, what
livings he held for what patrons, the name of his father, mother, and
brother, the name of their family seat, the title of the only book (and the
only book of its kind) that his brother wrote. He sought anonymity only
apparently, providing clues to his identity all too easy to read in the limited world of seventeenth-century English gentry families. As for his audience, Burton was highly conscious of them. Like Montaigne, he took a
pose of utter unconcern for his readers' reaction to his work, but the suc-
cessive revisions even of his most casual passages demonstrate his care
to remain informal and readable—to seduce, really, his "rejected" reader
into feeling that the book *was* written for him personally. As for time
and place, the book bears marks of both—Burton could "only," as we too
often say, be an English seventeenth-century writer. "English" because
of course he wrote in English, in many styles from colloquial to magnilo-
quent; "seventeenth-century" because of his mastery of the vocabularies
and styles offered writers at that rich period. As for place, Burton clearly
had to be writing where books on many subjects were available to him—
as the habitat of Democritus Junior, we might postulate Oxford, blessed
by the Bodleian and the college libraries, if he had not saved us the
effort of guessing by telling us exactly where he lived and what libraries
he used. His profession, his scholarly cast of mind, his preferences for
learning, speak out clearly from the pages, too: he was a divine, we learn
at once, whose concern was for the cure of souls. Because he was literally concerned with the soul's cure, he turned to psychology and thus to
melancholy; as comparison with contemporary and earlier medical texts
makes evident, Burton made himself master of psychological and medical theory and practice. He was a humanist, too, in both the modern
sense of the word—that is, concerned with human life, its joys and mis-
eries; and in the old sense, a reader of ancient texts and a moral re-crea-
tor, from those texts, of a world of his own. His method of quoting is
"humanistic," out of context, like Erasmus' *Adagia,* or atomistic, like
Democritus: whatever fragment of wisdom or information appealed to

him he combined with whatever other fragments he had already extracted from the books he had read.

His book bears a clear relation to its fellows, other books of medical and moral theory and casuistry: much of Burton's material overlaps
with books which none but the specialized scholar can nowadays bear to
read. The *Anatomy of Melancholy* can be read as a medical text or a
moral disquisition, for it is both of those things; but it is far more than
either of them. If we look sharply at Burton's book, a great many more
sorts of literature, genres with their appropriate styles, suddenly appear
in it: the satirical preface, with its utopia; two *consolationes philosophiae*
(indeed, the whole book can be perceived under this rubric); a love-dia-
logue turned inside-out, to show the discomforts attendant upon climbing
the Platonic ladder of love; a collection of sermons and moral tales; an
"anatomy" or analysis of a medical condition; jeremiads here and there,
especially directed against the Roman Church; an imaginary voyage, the
"Digression on Air," but a voyage imaginary in other senses as well, including a voyage around the imagination, an internal picaresque in
which the *picaro* is, quite naturally, a rogue, flawed by original sin like
all God's men and women but in hopes of ultimate grace. Burton's book
belongs in two traditions hallowed by classical scholars: it is a macaronic
of style and genre; and it is a paradox. Both forms mix modes, genres,
and styles, as Democritus Junior, seeking to match his book to the
tumultuous world he perceived, governed by a contradictory disease,
well knew; the mixture of mode, genre, and style is the decorum appropriate to Burton's philosophical notion of melancholy. The book is a
paradox because it belongs, in part anyway, to a "kind" now well-recog-
nized, the praise of folly, in this case, the protective and creative lunacy
of melancholy; it is a paradox also because it does exactly what it says it
does not do. Burton is subtlest in this respect: though the author appears
to accept the terms of humoral psychology, as his title and subject suggest, we learn by the end of the book that he has rejected the categories
implied by the humors, and attributed to melancholy *all* that is in human
experience, good and bad, painful and beautiful, ill and healthy. Like
Montaigne's great *Apologie,* pretending to be an apology for an old idea,
Burton's book demolishes the system from within which it seems to
speak. For all these reasons, the *Anatomy* is naturally a "stylistic museum," keeping us off-balance by its variety and variation, matching its
subject, melancholy, with all its variety and variation; it manages at once
to be an encyclopedia of "all" knowledge and an idiosyncratic reorgani-
zation of that knowledge. Ultimately we can see why this book appealed
to readers of its time, seduced both by its ponderous thoroughness and
by its irresponsible iconoclasm, impressed by its solidity and organization (witness the splendid scholastic schemata at the beginning of each

3

section) and enchanted by its disjunctive informality. The history of taste enters, too; two generations after Burton, Swift parodied the whole digressive style in his *Tale of a Tub,* his "Digression upon Digressions" marking the end of discursive informality in favor of a dominant sense of literary order. From time to time wayward literary men (Johnson, Lamb) have loved the *Anatomy,* but it has taken twentieth-century concern for psychopathology to revive the book for non-scholarly readers. For it *is* a monument to dead ideas, undeniably; though in more important respects, Burton's book is a powerful exercise in the modern kind, with one man's imagination bending extremely recalcitrant material to fit his private view of the world.[1]

To some extent the historian, of letters as of all else; refuses to accept that intention is a "fallacy"; he attempts some re-creation in himself, of the author's point of view, assuming that intellectual understanding will not detract from, and may even deepen, aesthetic pleasure. What "histories" are legitimately involved in the study of literature? First of all, the history of language, of words, of usage, of semantics. Renaissance humanists believed that to understand ancient texts, one had to know what the words meant, singly and in grammatical context, at the time they were put together: for them, the beginning was, literally, the word. For us, the *Oxford English Dictionary* is a monument to that conviction. From the specialized study of language and vocabulary, of grammar and grammars, has flowed not only the wealth of classical literature now in our possession, but also our discipline of modern letters. Those of us brought up on Germanic paradigms may not have carried away a particularly lively impression of the values of historical philology, but to its grey discipline we owe many of our most valued texts. That philology's dry bones may be made to live has been demonstrated in the spry work of Leo Spitzer, who resurrected the method in his historical-linguistic scrutiny of texts so familiar as to defy new conclusions, or to texts not hitherto illuminated by linguistic study. A fine example in the first category is his essay on Diderot, where he demonstrates the cross-purposes deliberately brought out in Diderot's stylistic manipulations; an example in the second is his work on American advertising.[2]

---

[1] See my *Paradoxia Epidemica* (Princeton, 1966), Chap. xiv, for a fuller account of these points.

[2] "The Style of Diderot," in *Linguistics and Literary History* (New York, 1962); "American Advertising Explained," *Essays on English and American Literature* (Princeton, 1962). Two other important studies in stylistics are Marie Boroff, Sir Gawain and the Green Knight: *A Stylistic and Metrical Study* (New Haven, 1962), and Joan Webber, *Contrary Music: The Prose Style of John Donne* (Madison, Wis., 1963).

Spitzer's work stresses history, not chronology; but even lowly chronology can serve history. When we try to date a work of art, when we collect material on the printing history of a work or compile a bibliography of critical works about our author and his work, we use chronological data for a larger interpretative purpose. Like any institution, literature has its special histories—national literatures, genre, form, style, metrics. In tracing change in any of these categories, "mere" chronology does count: what happens before may have some influence on what happens later, though the reverse is rarely the case. Within the history of style, mode, genre, and technique, a work of art may, perhaps must, be "sited."[3] Our aesthetic chronology is in fact built up largely from our assumptions about the histories of style and type: if we were to find a perfect sonnet written in Attic Greek, we would tend to suspect our text, or to look for its origins in the poetic compositions of a university like Oxford; on the other hand, we would take seriously a Sicilian sonnet dated a decade or so before our present knowledge of "earliest" sonnets, without suspecting forgery or imitation. Our notions of the stylistic and generic norms of literature (as of the other arts) are deeply dependent upon established chronology, and upon the "taste" associated with particular dates. To one eighteenth-century critic, *Lycidas* may have seemed artificial and cold; but when that poem is sited within its context of renaissance stylistic and generic criteria, we cannot fail to see it as a substantial exercise within a demanding and complicated artistic tradition. Seen against the various individual pastorals and pastoral traditions of its own past, the poem speaks out as the massive climax of a form difficult precisely because of its artificiality, its "low" style, and the light tone with which it officially treats its subjects. Milton's particular talent for transmuting his sources can be read not only from the various elements of the pastoral tradition that he manages to exploit in the course of the poem, but also from his daring excursions out of the pastoral into the heroic mode, expanding a traditional frame to hold more than it had ever held before. This is not to say that *Lycidas* must be read historically to seem beautiful: on the contrary, it offers its own authentic aesthetic experience. But when it is seen "historically," against its intellectual and aesthetic referents, the poem's artistry becomes apparent in a professional way. So with Burton: the degree of his control over many ways of writing, concealed by the informality and the thickness of his styles, deepens one's realization of his talent and imagination.

It is from our ideas of literary history that we, and all readers, ad-

[3] On the "situs" of a work of art, see René Wellek and Austin Warren, *Theory of Literature* (New York, 1956), pp. 142-157; and George Kubler, *The Shape of Time* (New Haven, 1962), pp. 96-122.

5

just our expectations to the alternatives possible to an artist or writer working at a given time and place.[4] We do not expect Milton to have written like Arnold, but we are expected to recognize when, and why, Arnold occasionally wrote like Milton. From our knowledge of the variations, nuances, and range of any particular genre or style, we can read more clearly the particular signature of a given artist: we learn to tell apart, as my students beginning a course invariably say they cannot, the works of Elizabethan sonneteers or metaphysical poets. Conversely, we learn from studying genre and style that many a writer is less original than we once thought—that Donne, for example, was a far more conventional writer in subject, theme, persona, and imagery than he was considered by critics in the nineteen-thirties. Further, we can come to realize the many different meanings of "originality"—as an earlier critical vocabulary put it, of "invention"—by an artist within his chosen tradition. By this sort of study, our sensibilities can become sharpened to something like an author's own professionalism. When we know what and whom to expect in, say, a Deposition from the Cross, we note the peculiarities in particular Depositions—the shift from one side of the cross to the other of St. John, or the presence of a man holding the sheet between his teeth, to leave his arms free to move the body. We come to recognize such things as the bird-watcher recognizes spring warblers or fall ducks: we know what to expect in a given milieu and what salient characteristics to look for in individual instances. We know the range of ecological possibilities and compare, almost unconsciously, the particular against a set of norms. The scholar who has achieved such customary comfort in some aspect of a period other than the one in which he lives has become, whether he knows it or not, an historian, re-creating a past alive.

The historian studies change: to study style or genre is also to study change, both within and beyond the particular boundaries of the subject. Within a working tradition, we note the effort of a particular writer to "ring" or "band" his work as unmistakably his own, to master his tradition so that, as Shakespeare said of his own sonnets, "every word doth almost tell my name." One can then admit a legitimately developmental concept within the local limits of style and genre: style and genre impel, press individual artists to greater technical experience and display than the tradition had hitherto presented. French medieval towns vied with one another in building churches ever higher; Brunelleschi deliberately "outdid" antiquity by building his cupola bigger than that of the Pan-

[4] I take much of the material in this and adjacent paragraphs from E. H. Gombrich, *Art and Illusion* (London and New York, 1960); see also his "Art and Scholarship," in *Meditations on a Hobby-Horse* (London, 1963), pp. 106-119. Gombrich's 1961 lectures at Princeton, on primitivism in the visual arts, are a model for the systematic study of style; these await publication.

theon; Michelangelo followed classical canons of taste in his David, carved, to make things as difficult as possible, from an immense and immensely flawed block of marble. Milton's boast at the beginning of *Paradise Lost,* that he was about to undertake "things unattempted yet in prose or rhyme," is interesting because of how much it says about working from within a tradition. In the first place, the statement is a variant upon an almost obligatory epic *topos;*[5] in the second, as Milton well knew, it is in some sort a lie, since men had written epics before he wrote his, and the various materials in his poem had been attempted, both in prose and rhyme, many times between the Book of Genesis and his enterprise. But, miraculously, in the third place, the boast is also true, for before Milton, no one had managed to put "everything" into one epic poem—all time with its history from the Creation to the Judgment; eternity, before, during, and after the tract of human time; as well as the whole imaginable cosmos, with its chaos.[6] Milton's epic has a pitch of arrogance which came off, as Addison observed, comparing *Paradise Lost* to the great epics of antiquity. Milton had outdone, had overgone, his mighty predecessors.

Sometimes a style or genre impels an artist past the limits officially set for itself. Once again, *Lycidas* is a case in point: as the poet deliberately said, should readers miss what he has done, a "higher tone" entered his pastoral, a mode conventionally set in the "low style," sung to the "oaten flute," the simple shepherd's pipe. When genres and styles cross and intermix, we have an historical marker, as when the picaresque and pastoral, twin modes of ancient romance, join with a third, the medieval courtly romance, in *Don Quixote.* Or in the hands of Bembo, Tasso, Della Casa, and (once more, o ye laurels!) Milton, the sonnet, traditionally a small form concerned with mortal and spiritual love, takes heroes and heroism as its subjects.[7] *Gargantua and Pantagruel,* gigantic in more than one respect, elaborates on a scale thitherto unimagined the macaronic, mixing languages, styles, themes, literary elements so as to include epic, romance, farce, fairy-tale, fabliau, fable, sermon, etc., etc.[8] To take a modern instance, Hesse's and Virginia Woolf's novels have been demonstrated to be part of a subgenre dependent for its techniques and point of view as much on lyric poetry as on conventional modes of narrative.[9] Half the fun of reading works of this sort lies in our

[5] Ernst Robert Curtius, *European Literature and the Latin Middle Ages,* tr. Willard R. Trask (New York, 1953), pp. 85-89.

[6] See *Paradoxia Epidemica,* Chap. v.

[7] See F. T. Prince, *The Italian Element in Milton's Verse* (Oxford, 1954).

[8] I try to deal with *genera mixta* in *Paradoxia Epidemica,* Chaps. i and xiv; for *genre* and influence, see the forthcoming study by Adrian Jaffe.

[9] Ralph Freedman, *The Lyrical Novel* (Princeton, 1963).

familiarity with the range of possible alternatives from which a given author may have chosen, in our ability to understand the author's professional situation and to appreciate the ingenuity with which he met his professional problems.

These observations are by no means designed to leave the impression that, even technically, the arts must get better and better just because styles and techniques develop and cross-fertilize: as an art historian remarked in a stimulating essay, "in art there is no progress, but only change."[10] That is, though there are technical improvements in any art—linear perspective, fast colors, cantilever construction, stream-of-consciousness technique, and the like—the value of any given work cannot be measured by its technical virtuosity alone. Rogier van der Weyden's Crucifixion in Philadelphia has not been displaced by Dali's in New York, though there is no doubt which painter shook more tricks from his sleeve. We do not cease to read Balzac because Stendhal was a greater virtuoso, nor abandon the simpler Hardy because of the stylistic innovations of *Finnegans Wake*. Styles change, after all, and in any given period no style, however dominant, is immune to competition. There are radical leaps in style—sometimes a style breaks through thick layers of convention, as Vasari believed Cimabue to have done; sometimes a style manages to leap both forward and backward, as Manet did in his *Déjeûner sur l'herbe* and *Olympe*, treating with a style "radically new" subjects borrowed, in the one case, from High Renaissance Venetian painting and, in the other, from Goya. Recollections of past styles, whether deliberate or accidental, sometimes have as by-product the increased critical reputation of a dead artist: the Impressionists' success brought Rembrandt to critical attention once more, and T. S. Eliot did at least as much for the metaphysical poets as they for him. But recollections of a past style are no guarantee of success: Van Gogh's blue-and-gold evocations of Rembrandt and Millet are not regarded as among his best work, nor do his Vesalian quotations alone make Leonard Baskin's woodcuts so impressive. Opinion is divided about the outspoken relation of *The Waste Land* to its sources; and though Spenser's archaisms in *The Shepherds' Calendar* and *The Faerie Queene* seemed to have pleased his contemporaries and to be acceptable to us, Auden's metrical experiment in *The Age of Anxiety* was criticized as meaninglessly artificial. Archaism, or quotation from an older stage of a style, is significant in context but never for itself alone: its success or failure is bound up with aesthetic, not historical, judgment.

Traditions of style and genre are, actually, discontinuous, rather than an unbroken series. As Maurice Mandelbaum expressed it in a

[10] James S. Ackerman, "Science and Visual Art," in *Seventeenth Century Science and the Arts*, ed. Hedley Howell Rhys (Princeton, 1961).

searching article,[11] the particular problems of examining a discontinuous tradition involve the care with which one should approach the subject with a developmental bias. As he says, "any series of events may show a developmental pattern in certain respects, while it displays alternation or randomness in others; in the second place, even when there has been no pattern of development in a series of events taken as a whole, there may be such a pattern within one segment of that series." Literary historians, or historians of any art, may profit from Mandelbaum's pluralism in approaching their subject, because of course the history of any literary theme or form must of necessity be discontinous—as, for example, certain institutional traditions are not, such as that of the Roman Catholic Church or the Internal Revenue Service. The fact is that there is necessarily always some randomness in artistic work within any given genre, form, or style; naturally enough, no artist can have mastered all of the past tradition of his art—as, say, we pretend the Ph.D. candidate ought to do—but will have formed his stylistic and thematic habits from rational and irrational samplings of the tradition, which he transmutes or mutes according to his own preference and talent.

Literary history depends upon an assumption of relative chronology—that the time when a thing was written has something to do with its nature. Any date is by itself insignificant, of course; but the use of dates (in life as in scholarship) is to establish relationships. For these reasons, then, it is often illuminating to know something of "public" or "general" history as well as about the relevant special history to which a work of art belongs. For the professional historian, political history is the substratum of whatever else he wishes to study; for the literary historian, this is not necessarily the case. In some periods of literature, political history is of the utmost importance, when the subject matter of politics overlaps, or is, the subject matter of literature. In a general way, thoughts about politics are often relevant: Kantorowicz's reading of *Richard II* against the background of medieval theory of kingship enriches both the play and his technical study;[12] so also there is much to be learnt about Machiavellianism as an idea and a style of life from *Richard III,* but not much about Machiavelli. There have been critics who insisted that most of Shakespeare's work was a political allegory, though such a view nowadays seems eccentric. England under the later Stuarts provides us with a pure example of the topical importance of politics to literature: the new edition of *Poems on Affairs of State*[13] contributes to "history"

[handwritten: *Political History*]

[11] "The History of Ideas, Intellectual History, and the History of Philosophy," *History and Theory,* Beiheft 5 (1965), pp. 33-66.

[12] E. H. Kantorowicz, *The King's Two Bodies* (Princeton, 1957).

[13] *Poems on Affairs of State: Augustan Satirical Verse,* ed. George de F. Lord, et al. (New Haven, 1963—).

and is also properly parasitic upon the work of professional historians. To take a more evidently literary figure than the authors of most of the poems in that edition, Dryden's great discursive poems must be known not only in their unique and particular integrity, but also in connection with the poet's changing intellectual and spiritual biography, which in turn is linked to the poet's attitude to events in the public life of his time. A crude view of Dryden is that he was a very gifted pamphleteer; even for those who admire him far more than that phrase implies, his work requires siting within the political world. Satire is of course a genre, or mode, particularly dependent upon topicality—a knowledge of Swift's political likes and dislikes helps to deepen the meaning of his permanent satires. We do not need to know for the satire who the "cushion" was by which Flimnap's fall was broken; but the fact that that "cushion" had a great name and more than one local habitation helps to show us how sharp Swift's feelings and his satire were. That MacHeath "was" Walpole is in itself interesting, and makes MacHeath a far more significant figure than just the hero of a ballad-opera; it tells us something as well about Walpole's astonishing security, that such an opera, so satirical and so successful, should have been harmless to the man.

In other literary periods (e.g., the Romantic period in France and England; the *Risorgimento* in Italy; the interwar period in Europe and America), politics, so obviously important in men's lives, also formed the subject matter of the arts. It is idle to try to comprehend much of Brecht's, Malraux's, or Sartre's work without knowing something of political history, both as the "background" of which literary students so maddeningly speak, and as the foreground and setting of the texts themselves. Sometimes great political upheavals produce odd effects that nonetheless make sense—Trakl's disjunctive lyric style, for example, has been attributed to his perception of the horribly disconnecting effect upon him of his experiences in the First World War. Certainly some of the poignancy of Wilfrid Owen's awkward verse makes us realize one result of that war—that a young man trying to find new ways of writing poetry appropriate to an unpoetic world of horror should have been cut off by death and thus wasted, as young men never before had been wasted, before he could finish his difficult experiment or find his proper speech. Sometimes what is interesting is that great events are *not* worthily represented in the arts—the literature of the European Resistance is usually technically inept, and concentration-camp literature and art, though extremely moving, is rarely so for its aesthetic success. If we take the example of Tolstoy as normative, then we can expect to wait a long time before the significance of an overwhelming historical event, such as the Second World War, can be proportioned into art.[14]

---

[14] But see Frederick J. Hoffman, *The Mortal No* (Princeton, 1964).

But disjunctions between an active political period and its literature are curious, too: why in other periods, equally "political," such as the English Commonwealth, are *belles-lettres* untouched by the political questions of such obvious magnitude debated in national life and so evident in the subliterary production of the period? The answer to the puzzle of why politics did not enter "high" literature of that period lies not so much in the realm of literature as in the realm of social history, with the whole culture of the Commonwealth forming the subject of investigation.

Social History

Though political history may or may not be directly relevant to literature, social history is another matter. Indeed, social history is somehow part of all literature, and all literature is part of it. There are scholars and critics who assert that they can derive from a literary or artistic work the social attitudes of its author and the class to which it was directed, sometimes also the social motives which brought the work into being. This talent is claimed chiefly by Marxist critics, and from Lenin to Lukács one can certainly learn a great deal from this attitude to literature.[15] To take a more neutral example, the considerable reputation of Lionel Trilling as an interpreter of literature rests partly on his insights into the social attitudes, the social milieu, and the social morality of, among others, Jane Austen, Henry James, and Mark Twain;[16] his epigoni work industriously in the literature particularly fruitful for such investigations, that of nineteenth-century England and America. Lenin, Lukács, Trilling, Irving Howe take political commitment seriously; their preference is for writers involved in the task of social criticism and comment, direct or implied. James, Conrad, Hardy, Lawrence, Faulkner, Camus, Sartre, all offer obvious subjects for this sort of concentration, but writers less overtly concerned with political and social questions can be related to their milieu as well. A case in point is e.e. cummings: the experimental forms of his verse say something about his audience, or about the toleration and even demand for poetry of unconventional shapes and constructs.

There is a gross sense, of course, in which almost all literature can imply something about social life and society. So private and so apparently accidental a lyric as the anonymous

> O western wind, when wilt thou blow?
> The small rain down can rain:
> Christ, that my love were in my arms
> And I in my bed again!

[15] See George Lukács, *Realism in our Time: Literature and the Class Struggle* (New York, 1964); *Studies in European Realism* (London, 1950).

[16] Lionel Trilling, *The Liberal Imagination* (New York, 1950); *The Opposing Self* (New York, 1955).

looks frightfully simple; but such a reduced production is in fact very sophisticated, and depends upon the charged meaning of endless love-accounts and fantasies in chivalric romance and other courtly lyrics. To take an opposite instance, Burns's beautiful "simplicities" are extremely literary renderings of folk-themes, folk-ballads, folk-meters, artificial when compared with their originals. But Burns's fancifications of local tradition tell us something about romantic yearnings for the "simple," the "natural," the "sincere," as reactions against the formality and artificiality, real or supposed, of dominant literary standards. Such yearning is an event of social as well as of literary significance.

To shift to another area altogether, it is difficult to read the Homeric epics more than once without being driven to consider traditional society; faced with the paucity of records from so distant a period, the Homeric epics themselves are a kind of "historical" source, to be used with caution, but to be used with gratitude.[17] It is difficult to read chivalric romance without trying to identify the assumptions of "feudal" society, or to read the body of Provençal lyrics without trying to relate that literary phenomenon to the social structure from which it sprang. At first meeting, all *précieuses* may seem *ridicules,* but before long we find ourselves obliged to comprehend something of the society that produced so deformed a subculture as that of the salon coterie. Some authors (like the *précieux*) initially address an audience made up of the segment of society about which they write—Balzac, Tolstoy, Henry James are cases in point; others, such as Zola and the expressionist Döblin, address an audience totally different in social make-up from the people of whom they write. The author's conception of the relation of his book and his audience raises important questions, to which part of the answer lies in our capacity for social re-creation. Though Bouvard and Pécuchet may have read *Bouvard et Pécuchet,* they could hardly have enjoyed that experience as "we" do, so smugly critical of "them"; on the other hand, the Julien Sorels of Stendhal's society were supposed to recognize themselves and to mend their ways, or at least to take the consequences of them, as a result of Stendhal's preaching. Balzac wrote for, at, and against the bourgeois society he portrayed at such length and with such bitter, grudging understanding. To be interesting, the social statements of literary works need not be cosmic: for the literary student, the milieu of the Bennett family is as important as that of Fabrice del Dongo, the social assumptions of Karenin and Vronsky as important as those of Levin and Pierre Bezukhov, or the absence of any such ideas from the heads of Russian generals.

[17] Moses I. Finley, *The World of Odysseus* (New York, 1954); see also Michael Ventris and John Chadwick, *Documents in Mycenaean Greek* (Cambridge, Eng., 1956).

economic history [handwritten marginal note]

When we study history, we study economic history as well, though we may not have the exchange-rates or corn-tables in our heads. It is important to know what the economic situation is of any given writer, and of writers as a class in any given time or place. It makes a difference that Petrarca did not have to live by his pen, that Machiavelli thought he did, and that Dickens in fact did. The "freedom" of a writer, especially in modern times, is not entirely unrelated to his financial situation: and Grub Street can take gilded forms. That Shakespeare lived to make himself into a gentleman by his pen may seem a major triumph of literature over social stratification: actually, it only means that a man with a certain sum of money, got however might be, was able to buy the credentials of gentility in late Renaissance England. Donne was a skilful poet and a popular preacher, but his pen did not make his fortune. Swift turned a pretty penny from time to time, but his letters record his discontent with the returns of genius. The work of men like John Toland, or Daniel Defoe, can and must be related to the author's financial situation; Defoe's subjects, too, are interesting in part because of his preoccupation with economic matters.

As in the case of politics, some literary works deal directly with economics, some only indirectly. For some critics, economic context is crucial to the interpretation of works of art, but most of us take a less extreme view. Though a great deal about the economics of the Mediterranean world can be deduced from the *Odyssey,* it is not fair to say that economics is the subject of that book, as it is, for instance, of *The Grapes of Wrath* or *The Pit. The Fable of the Bees* is a document in economic as well as in literary history, but *The Merchant of Venice,* another work about commercial transactions, is so only incidentally. Swift offers a good case in point of the range of economic knowledge necessary to interpret a text: without knowing something of the political-economic relation of Ireland to England, and without knowing who Wood was and what his scheme was, it would be impossible now to make sense of the *Drapier's Letters. A Modest Proposal,* however, stands independently as satire and can be read without knowing either the horrifying social effects of mercantilist policy upon underdeveloped areas, or the quantitative stylistics of the statistical arguments put forward by the new economists of Swift's time: the meaning emerges from the satire itself. If one does happen to know something about the background of Swift's pamphlet, his satire cuts far deeper, mortally deep, in historical as well as in moral terms.[18]

These examples, from literary history itself, from the interrelations

[18] Louis A. Landa, "A Modest Proposal and Populousness," *MP,* XL (1942), 161-170; George Wittkowsky, "Swift's *Modest Proposal*: The Biography of an Early Georgian Pamphlet," *JHI,* IV (1943), 75-106.

of literary works with political, social, and economic history, might all be gathered under the rubric of cultural history, which on the face of it has close relations with all the arts, perhaps most of all with literature. One great cultural historian has remarked that although cultural history is made up of various special histories, it is by no means equivalent to the mere sum of those special histories.[19] The cultural historian must seek to find some pattern in the varied materials he treats, some indications of the values and ideals of the society he investigates. Huizinga's *The Waning of the Middle Ages*[20] is an example both of the "intuitive" selected reconstruction of the consistencies and contradictions of a whole society and of the service literature particularly renders the social historian. In his reconstruction of the Burgundian period, Huizinga drew heavily upon its high and its low literature, in various languages and from various milieux, precisely because he thought that from literature characteristically full of legitimated fantasy one could educe the values, observed or imaginary, of a given culture. Turning back to gather in my remarks upon the history of taste, I should like to suggest that records of "taste" are properly part of cultural as of social history: that they involve the rhetorical problem of a consuming audience and thus enter into the realm of social value.

In dealing with taste, I want to leave aside "low" art—chapbooks, comics, women's magazines, soap-operas, pornography, historically important though all those subjects are—and consider simply "high" art, a very small element in popular consumption. Taste in such matters is set by people the sociologist R. K. Merton calls "influentials," men and women regarded as models by others. E. H. Gombrich has demonstrated the importance of one taste-setter, Niccolò Niccolì, in the Florentine Renaissance;[21] such "influentials" as the Earl of Leicester, the Earl of Arundel, the Cardinal de Richelieu, and Louis XIV left their mark on the arts of their time because of their personal preferences and their power to make those preferences known. Roman values in late eighteenth- and early nineteenth-century France gave us literary and visual works of art, to say nothing of styles in dress, imitative of both republican and imperial styles. In some cases—the Elizabethan stage is an obvious one, with its "public" and "private" theaters—audience expectation had real influence upon the plot, form, and language of literary works. The establishment of a novel-reading public made it easier to publish Dickens', Thackeray's, and other novelists' work serially—and serial

[19] Johan Huizinga, "De taak van cultuurgeschiedenis," *Verzamelde Werken,* ed. Leendert Brummel, et al., 9 vols. (Haarlem, 1948-53), VI, 71-84; translation in Fritz Stern, ed., *Varieties of History* (New York, 1960).

[20] London, 1927.

[21] Gombrich's article on Niccolò Niccolì will soon appear in a *Festschrift.*

publication then altered the structure of novels by its peculiar demands. Sometimes there seem to be "waves" of literature and art bearing similar themes—the short-lived pop, the abortive op; novels of black humor following on Heller's and Harington's books, or the sensational plays of the Jacobean stage—which evidently answer to some consuming demand difficult to define precisely; it is worth noting, however, that Huizinga tried to read from just such widespread literary and artistic preoccupation with death the psycho-social "set" of his fifteenth-century Lowlands society. The study of "taste" is technically difficult, and involves knowing a great deal about distribution (publication, in literary works); however speculative it remains, though, it inevitably links the arts to their society in mutual interaction.

There is a whole polemical literature on the autonomy and interrelations of the disciplines called cultural history, intellectual history, and the history of ideas, a subject with which for the rest of this essay I will deal. Quite obviously, these categories flow into one another. All are, in one way or another, subdivisions of social history, the history of collective behavior, public, private, conscious, and unconscious, of any society. Though the categories overlap, at the same time they observe conventional limits: empirically, at least, one can draw some distinctions among the disciplines. Jacob Burckhardt, for instance, parent of the discipline of cultural history, was less interested in intellectual content than in the form it took: less interested, for example, in Ficino's philosophical system than in the neoplatonic predilections of the men gathered around the great Medici. For him, the reflection of Ficino's Neoplatonism in literature and the visual arts was proof of the idea's cultural importance: or, aesthetic manifestation validated intellectual constructs.[22] Following Burckhardt's model, Huizinga related the public displays, secular and religious, of the Netherlands to the hypothesized spiritual and aesthetic impulses among the participants and the spectators. The self-conscious products of any period or place are the natural sources for the study of the cultural historian; in turn, his formulations provide useful norms against which the literary historian may apply the particularities of his subject.

Intellectual history is more concerned than cultural history with the ideas themselves, and assumes their importance, both as cultural manifestations and as agents in the culture. Unlike the historian of philosophy, the intellectual historian concerns himself with "minor" as well as "major" ideas, especially if the minor idea (or, in a useful phrase, the "failed" idea) was widely-referred to in the time and place he studies. One might say, among much else, that the intellectual historian concerns

[22] Jacob Burckhardt, *The Civilization of the Renaissance in Italy* (London, 1944).

himself with taste in ideas and tries to find explanations for such taste in any given period or place. Intellectual history is an inclusive and a systematic study, involving chiefly a willingness on the part of its practitioner to read widely in texts often in themselves uninteresting. Oddly enough, such reading can produce interesting results: the sum of such parts is far less than the whole they produce. Before talking of intellectual history in the large, let me turn to one of its sub-disciplines, very influential in literary study, the history of ideas. The term was made famous by a group of scholars around A. O. Lovejoy, particularly Marjorie Hope Nicolson and George Boas, whose contributions to literary study have been influential. Lovejoy's books and articles have had considerable impact upon the scholarly world as a whole, and the *Journal of the History of Ideas* is a monument to the man and his method. Originally, Lovejoy advocated studying any idea, major or minor, successful or failed; he extracted "unit-ideas," as he called them, tracing their development over time, in all their mutations, their legal and morganatic marriages, their affairs and alliances with other ideas. His classic study in this genre, *The Great Chain of Being* (Cambridge, Mass., 1936), exists to demonstrate how one major idea, now obsolete, worked in various times, ways, and contexts, an idea at once structurally fundamental and seminal of variation, an idea informing men's views of their place in the world and in society. That particular book made extensive use of literary evidence and in turn its formulations have contributed much to students of literature.

Lovejoy's personal range of competence was extraordinary, and he fearlessly recommended a similar range to his students—which in part explains why there are so few scholars of his sort in the world. The study of ideas, he recommended, should reach from the history of philosophy, the history of science, the history of religion and religions, into folklore, ethnography, the history of language and languages (especially semantics), literary history (especially "comparative literature"), the histories of the arts, of changes of taste in the arts; the history of all kinds of theory, political, economic, educational, etc.; the historical part of sociology, especially the sociology of knowledge.[23] Such a program is not for the pusillanimous, since it breaches so many different barriers and boundaries—between disciplines, between languages, between cultures, even between methods.

Like most intellectual historians, Lovejoy took a democratic attitude toward ideas of the past, though there is some value-choice involved in his selection of "unit-ideas." The method of the unit-idea has

[23] Lovejoy, *Great Chain*, pp. 7-23; "The Historiography of Ideas," *Essays in the History of Ideas* (Baltimore, 1948), pp. 1-13.

been criticized, especially for its isolative tendencies.[24] I once heard a student of seventeenth-century English literature say to a friend, "Say, Sam, what's Hobbes's view of original sin?" What then mattered to that student was *only* that portion of the philosopher's thought, quite unrelated to his other ideas or to his system: it is true that the pursuit of one idea across time may encapsulate it fatally from its fellow-ideas, though such studies as Martin Foss's *Idea of Perfection* (Princeton, 1946) and Benjamin Nelson's *Idea of Usury* (Princeton, 1949) are elegant examples of a major idea's being taken, as Ariadne's thread, through an otherwise impenetrable maze of "related ideas."

Lovejoy himself was irresistibly drawn to "related ideas," as his work with George Boas, *Primitivism and Related Ideas in Antiquity* (Baltimore, 1935), shows. This is a *Gestalt*-study, one might say, and Boas' subsequent workings-out of aspects of primitivism are examples of using both *Gestalt* and unit-idea approaches.[25] Lovejoy's handling of romanticism presents us with the contradictions and anomalies involved in a covering-term of that sort; in spite of Wellek's heroic attempt to recover the term's unity, many students shy away from the word as a cow from an electric fence.[26] A different kind of study is Lovejoy's "Deism and Classicism" article,[27] which brought into meaningful parallel salient features of two contemporaneous but quite different movements. For literary students, his "Milton and the Paradox of the Fortunate Fall"[28] affords a particularly happy model: puzzling out the structural and ideational meaning of Adam's speech on being vouchsafed a vision of the Crucifixion, Lovejoy went through the long history of the orthodox paradox, *felix culpa,* illuminating at once the tradition from and to which Adam spoke, and also Milton's arrangement of events in his epic.

As a discipline, the history of ideas owes its existence to Hegel, and there are one or two caveats to enter against Hegelian assumptions, or their tautological implications. For Hegel, ideas existed and went their inexorable way, regardless of whether men thought them, or thought about them; furthermore, they worked themselves out in the stuff of

[24] See Herbert Weisinger, "On the History of Ideas," *History of Ideas Newsletter,* I, iii (1955), 4-8; George Boas, "On the History of Ideas," ibid., I, iv (1955), 5-7.

[25] George Boas, *The Happy Beast* (Baltimore, 1933); *The Cult of Childhood* (London, 1966); and the forthcoming study of *vox populi.*

[26] Lovejoy, "On the Discriminations of Romanticism," *Essays,* pp. 228-253; René Wellek, "The Concept of Romanticism in Literary History" and "Romanticism Reexamined," in *Concepts of Criticism* (New Haven, 1963), pp. 128-221.

[27] Lovejoy, *Essays,* pp. 78-98.

[28] Ibid., pp. 277-295.

which conventional history is made. For Hegel as for Plato, ideas were immortal. So also, one suspects, for Lovejoy: he tended to deal with his unit-ideas as if they were fairly stable and hard, indestructible, like Greek atoms, like Greek atoms endowed with little hooks by which they attached to their fellows in different combinations across time and space. A similar attitude toward methodological units can be detected in the work of two other pioneers, E. R. Curtius and Erwin Panofsky. Curtius' use of *topoi,* or rhetorical commonplaces,[29] and Panofsky's use of "icons"[30]—systematized into "iconology"—to illuminate traditional verbal and visual images recall the platonic Hegel, with his comfortable legacy that there is an irreducible entity of meaning in each unit-idea, each *topos,* each visual symbol. These men were convinced rationalists about their methods, as well: investigation, they suggest, will inevitably demonstrate some pattern of intelligible relationships in the recurrent appearance of the units, no matter how good their disguise or complex their combinations. One can easily fall into tautology here: the evidence that exists can be organized into too beautiful a pattern, often developmental; Mandelbaum's comments on historical discontinuity are important to keep in mind as a corrective to these intellectual dangers.

There is another Hegelian habit of mind very common among intellectual historians, which concerns any idea or all ideas in a given period or milieu, a *Gestalt*-fallacy, one might say. This is the tendency to connect causally parallel manifestations of the same "idea," so common in criticism blessed by the *Zeitgeist.* In an illuminating general article, Stephen Toulmin has presented the major problem for students of intellectual history.[31] He distinguishes between, on the one hand, the atomistic, skeptical, discriminating, unitary study of separate problems, topics, and ideas, as if each were an autonomous, unconnected, integral entity; and, on the other, the synthesizing, connective, paralleling presentation, as if every topic, item, and problem within given limits were "like" every other, or demonstrated common factors. Each position has its radical danger, the first approach leaving us hanging, without a coherent or connective formulation for our ideas; the second (carried on under the wand

[29] Curtius, op. cit.

[30] Erwin Panofsky, *Studies in Iconology* (New York, 1939); *Meaning in the Visual Arts* (Garden City, N.Y., 1955). Hallett Smith, in *Elizabethan Poetry* (Cambridge, Mass., 1952), and Eugene M. Waith, Jr., in *The Herculean Hero in Marlowe, Shakespeare, Chapman, and Dryden* (New York, 1962), apply Panofsky's iconographical and iconological method to works in English renaissance literature with productive results. Rosemond Tuve's *A Reading of George Herbert* (Chicago, 1952) illuminates Herbert's use of imagery by showing the long tradition of Christian iconography upon which it drew.

[31] In *Seventeenth Century Science and the Arts,* pp. 16-17.

of a spirit, after all) dictating its own connective conclusions by its method. If things appear at a certain time and place, according to the *Zeitgeist* theory, they must be related. The skeptic cuts all connectives, the *Zeitgeister* insists upon connecting everything. In literary studies, both atomistic skeptics and *Zeitgeister* abound; "ontological" critics tend to occupy the first category, and "explainers" the second. Ungracious as it seems to criticize so beguiling and influential a book, the abstraction by E. M. W. Tillyard of the idea of social and moral order in sixteenth-century English thought and life, under the title "*the* Elizabethan world picture,"[32] leaves out of account both the multitudinous other meanings of the literature dealt with in his book, as well as the fact that there were other competitive "world pictures," even in Elizabethan times. There is, too, an absence of historical realism in his book as well: one reason for the repeated invocations to order was the evident disorder in which so many men lived their lives, as recorded in legal and administrative documents *ad infinitum.* One runs across similar problems of logic and suitability when struggling with phenomena grouped under such rubrics as "baroque" and "mannerism."[33]

But one must be careful not to denounce *Zeitgeist*-critics and skeptics out of hand: there is much to be gained from both methods. Though I am made uneasy by comparisons, say, on an ideologico-stylistic basis, of El Greco's painting to Shakespeare's sonnet-style,[34] I must admit that some ideas *are* really in the air in some periods. As F. B. Kaye remarked of his monumental study of Mandeville, early in his huge preparation he thought his author highly original, but after reading widely in the literature and subliterature of the late seventeenth and early eighteenth centuries, he came to realize that *The Fable of the Bees* exploited— magnificently, it is true—a stock of literary, intellectual, moral, psychological, and social commonplaces.[35] Without something of Kaye's voluminous evidence to document the assumption, however, it is risky to assign any given idea to "the air": the wings of the time-spirit can be heard behind that hypothesis whenever it is uttered. On the practical level, furthermore, an unfriendly critic can always be trusted to expose the air in

[32] *The Elizabethan World Picture* (London, 1944).

[33] For examples of generalizations of this sort, see Carl J. Friedrich, *The Age of the Baroque, 1610-1660* (New York, 1952); Victor Tapié, *Baroque et classicisme* (Paris, 1957); Arnold Hauser, *Mannerism*, 2 vols. (New York, 1965); for *Zeitgeist*, see George Boas, "Cross Currents in the Italian Renaissance," *Teachers College Record*, LXVII (1966), 239-249.

[34] Wylie Sypher, *Four Stages of Renaissance Style* (Garden City, N.Y., 1955), pp. 100-178.

[35] "Prefatory Note," and "Introduction," to Bernard Mandeville, *The Fable of the Bees* (Oxford, 1924), I, vii-viij; ciij-cxiij.

such hypotheses, as Ronald S. Crane unkindly did in his strict methodological critique of the history-of-ideas interpretations of Gulliver's Fourth Voyage.[36]

Crane's essay, so tight and so solid, is an interesting one to look at in this connection. For all its excellence, Crane's evidence, undeniably "hard," seems a very small peg from which to hang, with all its far-reaching implications, an interpretation of Swift's idea of the nature of man.[37] The single-peg hazard is one of the most common in intellectual history, especially when tackled by literary scholars: for them, it is like finding *the* source to *Hamlet,* or whatever. There are causes for the ubiquitousness of this error, some of them simply in scholars' psychology. One becomes so taken with the experience of one's own discovery that one tends to trot off on that hobby-horse, entirely forgetting that there are other and more efficient means of transport to important centers of the intellectual world. In my work (carried on at widely-separated intervals, in widely-separated places, and, ostensibly at least, on widely-separated topics), I have often been forced, by myself and by kind friends, to give up some beautiful theory which depended on material I happened to unearth. The words are important: that *I* happened to unearth, and that I *happened* to unearth. Though it is demonstrably true that chance favors the prepared mind, and serendipity is rarely arbitrary, one should not bank on the reliability of Pasteur's axiom in relation to one's self. After all, as medieval allegorists and Renaissance mythographers amply demonstrate,[38] anything can be made to connect with anything: the trick is to distinguish the real from the illusory connection. I may object to Sypher's parallel of El Greco's stylistic distortion and Shakespeare's "gored thoughts," but I must produce some rational basis for my reaction; I cannot deny, after all, the similarity he postulates between Bernini's and Crashaw's versions of St. Theresa, and must try to understand my reasons for accepting that likeness and rejecting the first.

There are many applications of intellectual history to literary study, but a few specific samples deserve note. One of these is the study of literature against rhetorical and logical theory: following Whorf's simple insight, that our language shapes our perception,[39] one might well assume that a man's rhetorical and logical training had something to do

---

[36] "The Houyhnhnms, the Yahoos, and the History of Ideas," in *Reason and the Imagination,* ed. J. A. Mazzeo (New York and London, 1962), pp. 231-253.

[37] For more on this topic, see Curt A. Zimansky, "Gulliver, the Yahoos, and the Critics," *College English,* XXVII (October 1965), 45-49.

[38] Systems such as these invariably work, since it is impossible to falsify them.

[39] Benjamin Lee Whorf, *Language, Thought, and Reality* (Cambridge, Mass., 1956).

with the way he expressed his thoughts and emotions. Classical studies, concerned with the *paideia,* have always demanded attention to this problem; in medieval and Renaissance studies, more recently in eighteenth-century studies as well, the subject has had a prominent place.[40] Its success as a *topos* for literary study is confirmed by the ubiquitous reference to two very quirky polemical studies of Renaissance thought and expression, Rosemond Tuve's *Elizabethan and Metaphysical Imagery* (Chicago, 1949), and Walter J. Ong's *Ramus and the Decay of Dialogue* (Cambridge, Mass., 1959). Miss Tuve's assumption that there was a necessary connection between Ramist logic and the argumentative structure of metaphysical poetry came in for some drubbing, though her study was enormously valuable in demonstrating once and for all that the critical canons of Renaissance writers were different in kind from those of new-critical readers. Her work had elements both of undue *Zeitgeisterei* (the "matching" of topical logic with vivid and "logical" poetry) and the single-peg fallacy (Ramist training or exposure accounting for variations in conventional poetic expression). Father Ong's intimidating display of out-of-the-way learning has not yet had its logical critic, to expose its leaps from specific to general—indeed, the book has had some clients who ought to have known better[41]—though it is one of the most flagrant examples of the single-peg hypothesis I know. The "decay of dialogue," with all the social, humane, and divine decadence implied in the phrase, is attributed to the wicked, mechanistic, impersonal, logical system of one Protestant academic. In spite of my strictures on these two fat and impressive books, there is no doubt that in studies of literature before the Romantic revolution, at least, neither logic nor rhetoric has been exhausted as a source for poetics and for literature in any form.

Another subject valuable to the intellectual historian which may prove most useful to the literary student as well is the study of self-conscious groups dedicated to the pursuit of a particular program or the investigation of specific problems. In the late Middle Ages, the literary guilds called chambers of rhetoric offer obvious examples; because the *rhétoriqueurs* formed an international movement, crossing national and linguistic boundaries, and in local areas were characterized by independent ideas and distinguishing practices, so they offer both a large-scale style (analogous to "international Gothic" in the visual arts) and many variations upon it. In later periods, such groups as the men around Ficino at Cosimo's court, or the poets and artists around Lorenzo a little

[40] For example, see Wilbur Samuel Howell, *Logic and Rhetoric in England, 1500-1700* (Princeton, 1956); and Earl R. Wasserman, *The Subtler Language* (Baltimore, 1959).

[41] See Jackson I. Cope's otherwise excellent *Metaphoric Structure of* Paradise Lost (Baltimore, 1962), pp. 27-49.

later, offer important centers for the study of artistic theory and practice; to skip a long period, the nineteenth century was full of such groups of loosely-organized artists and writers—the Metaphysical Society, the Cambridge Apostles, the Pre-Raphaelites, the Nazarenes, the Parnassians, the Impressionists themselves. In the seventeenth century, the men of letters who met at Muiden, Pieter Corneliszoon Hooft's castle outside Amsterdam, were the chief formers of literary taste in the Dutch Golden Age. The model study of such groups, which provides fascinating evidence of the continuity of such collective endeavors, is Frances A. Yates's *The French Academies of the Sixteenth Century* (London, 1947); Miss Yates's interlocking material makes plain how important literary theory was in the general philosophizing of literate life in the French Renaissance.

A specialized subdivision of intellectual history conspicuously fruitful for literary study has been the history of science. A. N. Whitehead's *Science and the Modern World* (New York, 1926) struck historians and literary students alike with its beautiful and suggestive formulations about the passage of science from antiquity to the twentieth century, and other works in the history of science and scientific theory, notably by E. A. Burtt, Thomas S. Kuhn, C. C. Gillispie, and the Halls,[42] are useful in themselves and as background to literary treatments of science. Basil Willey's books are directed to literary students; they deal with the philosophical, scientific, and moral questions preoccupying Englishmen from the seventeenth to the nineteenth century,[43] and are indispensable to students of English literature. The work of Richard Foster Jones, which proceeded directly from his own need to understand seventeenth- and eighteenth-century English literature, was deeply involved in the history of science. His effort to distinguish the English Battle of the Books from the French *querelle des anciens et modernes* led him to an examination of scientific theory and activity in England, with the remarkable result that he was able to document the "modernist" stand of scientists and their influence upon fields other than their own, especially upon

[42] E. A. Burtt, *The Metaphysical Foundations of Modern Physical Science* (London, 1950); Thomas S. Kuhn, *The Copernican Revolution* (Cambridge, Mass., 1957), and *The Structure of Scientific Revolutions* (Chicago, 1962); C. C. Gillispie, *Genesis and Geology* (Cambridge, Mass., 1951), and *The Edge of Objectivity* (Princeton, 1960); A. R. Hall, *The Scientific Revolution 1500-1800* (London, 1962), and *From Galileo to Newton, 1630-1720* (New York and London, 1963); Marie Boas Hall, *The Scientific Renaissance, 1450-1630* (London, New York, 1962).

[43] *The Seventeenth Century Background* (London, 1938); *The Eighteenth Century Background* (London, 1940); *Nineteenth Century Studies* (London, 1949); *More Nineteenth Century Studies* (London, 1946).

literature.[44] Jones's further work illuminated aspects of "simplicity" as a stylistic value in scientific exposition, in religious preaching and writing, and in prose style in general. Marjorie Hope Nicolson's many studies on the relation of science to literature have had an irreversible effect upon studies in the field. Her work ranges from precise studies of the relation of scientific sources to literary works (as in her work on *Gulliver's Travels* and Shadwell's *Virtuoso*), through the effect of scientific instruments on vision and thus upon imagery, all the way to reinterpretations in aesthetics resulting from ideas about the world in their origins scientific.[45] Perhaps her "purest" study of the effect of scientific ideas upon literary works is *Newton Demands the Muse* (Princeton, 1946), an exact examination of the light- and color-imagery of eighteenth-century poets who wrote after the publication of Newton's *Opticks* in 1704. In contrast to the method used by Lovejoy, which began with the "idea" and traced it wherever it led, Miss Nicolson, Willey, and Jones all begin from one or another literary problem and work back into the history of ideas and intellectual history to elucidate literary texts or theories.

Throughout this essay, Clio (a muse, as Trevelyan had to remind us) has been assumed to be the ancilla of her more artistic sisters. Clio has of course a proper dominion of her own, with which students of literature need not be centrally concerned: I would like to recapitulate and to offer some few observations on and instances of the relation of literary to historical study, as well as the relation of history to literature. Plainly, Clio is no mere schizophrenic: she has many personalities, instructs in many different disciplines, and uses many methods of instruction. She is, in short, pluralistic. So much is obvious enough, since Clio's subdivisions clearly overlap one another—social overlaps economic history, both overlap (or underlie) cultural history, cultural and intellectual history are inevitable bedfellows. In dealing with one particular kind of literary problem, involving several interpretations, intellectual history may do considerable service to literary interpretation, by recapturing some of the unspoken assumptions from which an author worked. An example of the uses of intellectual history in accommodating two interpretations, each manifestly "right" and yet evidently irrelevant to each other, may be seen in my experience with Donne's complex Anniversary Poems. Both interpretations come from "intellectual history": Miss Nicolson's reading of the poems as a physico-theological commentary dependent largely upon scientific and philosophical ideas; and Louis L. Martz's reading of

[44] *Ancients and Moderns: A Study of the Background of the "Battle of the Books,"* Washington Univ. Studies (St. Louis, Mo., 1936).

[45] The most convenient introduction to Miss Nicolson's work is *Science and Imagination* (Ithaca, N.Y., 1956); see also *The Breaking of the Circle* (New York, 1960), and *Mountain Gloom and Mountain Glory* (Ithaca, N.Y., 1959).

them against the background of formal religious meditation.[46] Clio can help here, with her pluralism: one can find a way of reading which will subsume both interpretations without doing violence to either if one reads them against contemporary traditions of epistemological speculation. When one reads them thus, the fact that they are a paired *contemptus mundi* and *consolatio philosophiae* also makes sense. We see then that speculative poetry has secular as well as religious sources, and that the poems' preoccupation with both scientific (or worldly) and religious themes is self-explanatory.[47] What is *not* self-explanatory is the magnificent way Donne fitted all the traditions together: but once one can deal with the traditions, then one can tackle the question of his art.

That particular formulation, involving epistemology, brought me upon another problem in the intellectual history of the Renaissance that has proved useful in my own studies of Renaissance literature. Donne's Anniversary Poems, as Professors Bredvold and Ornstein have determinedly demonstrated,[48] belong squarely in both skeptical and stoical traditions. How can this be, since Skepticism and Stoicism are so opposed in doctrine and ethics, as well as in epistemological theory? Examination of the two traditions turned up many interesting points, as well as the overwhelming evidence that these two modes of thought were simultaneously, contrapuntally used by Renaissance thinkers and writers, playing one method off against the other in order not to stick at any particular intellectual point. Erasmus, Montaigne, Henry Cornelius Agrippa, to name some of the most obvious "real" men, were all stoical skeptics, or skeptical stoics; and, to make a fictional man "real" for a moment, so was Hamlet, Prince of Denmark. Some of the structure of the play *Hamlet,* as well as its preoccupation with "knowing," can be illuminated by observing the points at which Hamlet presents himself as stoic and which as skeptic; though it cannot altogether explain the prince's behavior, the alternation of skeptical and stoical roles helps to give some form to the enigmatic alteration of Hamlet's moods. In another place, I argue that the double working of Stoicism and Skepticism is part of the play's theme and helps to explain some problems of structure—though, I

[46] Nicolson, *Breaking of the Circle*; Martz, *The Poetry of Meditation* (New Haven, 1954), pp. 221-248.

[47] See *Paradoxia Epidemica,* Chap. xiii, for an attempt at such accommodation.

[48] Louis I. Bredvold, "The Naturalism of Donne in Relation to Some Renaissance Traditions," *JEGP,* XXII (1923), 474-502; "The Religious Thought of Donne. . . ," Univ. of Michigan Publs. in Language and Literature, I (1925), 193-232; Robert M. Ornstein, "Donne, Montaigne, and Natural Law," *JEGP,* LV (1956), 213-229.

should say at once, to defend this formulation as a total answer to the problems of Hamlet would be to fall victim to the single-peg fallacy.[49]

Though history is so multiple, historical criticism cannot provide all the answers a literary student might need—sometimes, notably in aesthetic matters and matters of assigned value, it cannot even ask the important questions. Nor is one kind of history always appropriate to any given text or writer or genre or theme: in terms of intellectual history, it would be difficult to tackle the poetry of William Carlos Williams (though I have heard it attempted); but it is easy, indeed obvious, to make a case for studying that body of verse against a social background to which it also overtly refers. There is a sense, too, in which Williams' poetry—or any literary work—can be used as a document for the intellectual historian, even though it may not bear much intellectual content; lack of intellectual content is also data for the intellectual historian. Similarly, we cannot really ask biographical and behavioral questions of Sidney's poetry, which may tell us nothing whatever about Sidney's private feelings or the way the historical Sir Philip made love; but it does tell us a good deal about the public place of love and love-poetry in the gilded circle to which Sidney then belonged. William Carlos Williams' poetry, one might venture, reflects twentieth-century American interest in the psychology of perception, as well as in what a medical specialist has called "the integrative action of the nervous system." A student of twentieth-century American social attitudes could derive a great deal of information from Williams' poetry, even though the poetry itself is concerned with political and social events and facts, not with theory. Wallace Stevens, on the other hand, a bookish poet with a strong propensity for metaphysical speculation, lends himself to (indeed, he demands) explication in terms of the intellectual tradition. Most beat poets do not, though obviously they provide documentation to the cold-war world; but a transcendent beat, or super-beat, like Samuel Beckett, can be and has been approached from the strongholds of psychology and philosophy, ancient and modern. Both Descartes and Leibniz have been invoked to help us understand his work. For the intellectual historian, all literature is significant, positively or negatively; for the literary student there is a hierarchy of values in the application to specific pieces of literature of the methods proper to historical study. The literary student can only proceed empirically, to historical examinations that seem implied in the text or texts he works with. In historical disciplines, it is important to ask questions that are somehow relevant to the materials at hand—often

---

[49] In a forthcoming study, I argue the position of Hamlet against the background of Renaissance ideas; in her forthcoming work, Bridget Gellert will locate Hamlet and *Hamlet* within the traditions of melancholy.

more important than to get the "right" answers to those questions. I should say that if the questions are good enough, even wrong answers may turn out to be important too; as an example of this generalization, let me cite a book I regard as extremely valuable, Hiram Haydn's *The Counter-Renaissance* (New York, 1950). Haydn begins by committing a major intellectual and historical sin: he sets up a straw "Renaissance man," a figure of great capacity, energy, and self-sufficiency; against this norm he was able to adduce much evidence pointing to quite different concepts of man in the period—Machiavellian and Calvinistic disesteem for human nature, Montaignian skepticism of human reason, total disillusionment with human morality, as in *King Lear*. What really emerges from Haydn's long demonstration is that high-school textbook generalizations about the "greatness" of "Renaissance man" ought to be altered; that, aside from Pico's topical praise of the dignity of man, there is strikingly little documentation for human divinity in the period. Haydn's real question was the right one: what were the various Renaissance ideas of man? Though his answer was skewed by his polemic, it is enormously helpful and illuminating all the same.

When so good a book demonstrates on its face the difficulties of the method, what is one to do? The moral is, I suppose, to sail on in spite of the hazards, pointing to some intellectual Ithaca—where, like as not, one's nearest and dearest colleague will be at work picking out by night the accomplishments of the day. All we can do is balance the relevant materials and their methods, with all the disadvantages and dangers in them, against each other: to consider the uniqueness of each text, each problem, each subject in comparison with other texts, problems, subjects; after every pronouncement to bethink one's self that one might be wrong. In scholarship there is some hope of achieving accuracy, even "truth," however little we may be able to achieve by ourselves individually. We are all dwarfs standing on giants' shoulders—and sometimes the giants are hunchbacked, too; our shoulders, unbelievable as it may seem to us pygmies, will hold prospectors in their turn.[50] Scholarship, like history, is a collective enterprise, whether we like it or not; our work, right or wrong, will give rise to further work, right or wrong, as long as our particular social institutions shall last. Professional life is self-preservative; to preserve it sweet, we must at least embalm it with the best ingredients and the costliest ointments—which means with scholarly persistence, pains, acumen, judgment, and even intuition.

[50] For a history of this *topos,* see Robert K. Merton, *On the Shoulders of Giants* (New York, 1965).

Literature and Myth

By Northrop Frye

A myth, in its simplest and most normal significance, is a certain kind of story, generally about a god or other divine being. Myths in this sense are associated with primitive cultures or with archaic stages of developed ones, and when we describe certain features of our own time as myths, we tend to imply that they are fixations or survivals. A myth may be studied in regard to its content or in regard to its form. The content of a myth relates it to specific social functions. Seen as content, it becomes at once obvious that myths are not stories told just for fun: they are stories told to explain certain features in the society to which they belong. They explain why rituals are performed; they account for the origin of law, of totems, of clans, of the ascendant social class, of the social structure resulting from earlier revolutions or conquests. They chronicle the dealings of gods with man, or describe how certain natural phenomena came to be as they are. Such myths can hardly be understood, in this context, apart from the cultural pattern of the societies that produced them, and they form the main body of what might be called, and in later religion is called, revelation, the understanding of its traditions, its customs, its situation in the world, which a society accepts as primary data. For although every society produces its own myths, it is rare for a society to realize that its myths are its own creations. Myths are usually thought of as given, as dictated by a deity or descending from a remote antiquity existing *before* history began: *in illo tempore,* in Mircea Eliade's phrase. And, of course, as myths continue to be repeated in traditional form, the fact that they are given rather than invented becomes increasingly true.

Thus there is a curious but persistent connexion between myth and *false* history. That is, what the myth presents is not what happened in the past, but what is said to have happened in the past in order to justify what is in the present. Such myth has the social function of rationalizing the status quo: it explains, not merely why we do the things we do, but why we ought to go on doing them. When a mythology becomes codified in a sacred book, this connexion with false history still shows itself. Sacred books often turn on an alleged historical event, like the giving of the law to Moses, or purport to record the teachings of a charismatic religious leader. But under historical analysis the event usually turns into a myth and the teachings into the body of doctrine which is already held by those who revere the teacher. The Analects of Confucius, according to Arthur Waley, tell us not so much what Confucius said as what Confucians believed, and the Christian Gospels are now generally recognized to be written within the framework of the beliefs of the early Church. It is often assumed that the mythical features of a religion are later accretions on what was originally a historical event, but no sacred book of any of the great religions allows us to separate the historical from the mythical. That is, we cannot with any certainty reconstruct a pre-mythical stage in the establishment of any religion. In some religions, such as Islam or some of the nineteenth-century cults, the sacred book can be seen emerging as part of the historical process, but even there the beliefs are founded on the acceptance of the sacred book as inspired by something outside history. We notice too how often such religions (Mormonism, Anglo-Israelitism) involve a mythical reshaping of history, like the Mosaic contract in the Old Testament.

Myths are thus stories of a peculiar seriousness or importance: the events they recount are believed to have really happened, or at least to explain something of crucial importance to the community. They are mainly stories about the permanent gods of the community who are still worshipped, and so they tend to become permanent stories, attached to others told about the same gods. The power ascribed to the gods, again, gives the stories about them a peculiar significance for and relevance to human destiny. Hence myths expand into a definite canon of stories which we call a mythology. As localities are welded into larger political units, the gods of one locality also tend to become identified with the corresponding gods of another, and this accelerates the growth of a unified mythology. But the more seriously the mythology is taken, the more it acts as a conservative braking force on social change. It presents, in short, a society's view of its own social contract with gods, ancestors, and the order of nature, and later contract theories are rationalized myths of a most significant kind. The importance of myths, studied in relation to their content, is thus mainly sociological, and their study eventually becomes an aspect of social science, assuming that comparative religion, which is one form of such study, is a social science. The relation of myth to *physical* science is of little importance. Perhaps some myths may have satisfied some primitive form of scientific curiosity, but it is not easy to find myths which were primarily designed for this purpose. Myths are stories told in connexion with natural phenomena, rather than stories told as explanations of those phenomena, however allegorical. And to the extent that they are accepted as explanations, as in the Hebrew myth of creation, the rise of science simply annihilates the myth: there is no mutation of the myth into another form, as there is in theories of social contract.

In characterizing the gods of myths, the obvious models are the human beings of the ruling class, who are privileged to be more passionate and capricious than their inferiors. Gods have also some connexion with the order of nature, and the more arbitrary and unpredictable events, such as storms, attract more immediate attention than the orderly circling of the stars in their courses. Hence it is hardly surprising to find gods in myths, even in the myths of a high civilization, presented as cowardly, lustful, or treacherous, as well as taking the high arrogant line with man that masters of indisputable power can afford to take. This causes some conflict when the feeling grows that gods ought to practise what they preach, or have actually been practising it all along and have been libelled by the poets. Hence the attack of Plato on the Homeric mythology, and Plutarch's determination to equate what is true of the gods with what is morally acceptable. But the general conclusion of later Greek philosophy, that all gods were emblems or aspects of a uniform divine or natural order, never coincided with a fixed canon of mythology. The stories told about the gods remained on the "some men say" level. Hebraic religion, on the other hand, did achieve such a canon, as a result of a long and relentless process of editing its traditional myths. The mythological and conceptual aspects of Hebrew religion were unified to such lasting effect that even a century ago Christians were only with great trepidation and soul-searching beginning to admit that the Biblical stories of Adam and Noah were myths. But the conservative and hampering effect of this unified mythology on the development of philosophy and science, even on art and literature, is obvious in Hebrew culture itself, and persisted into the Christian period.

When myths are studied in regard to their form, they are studied primarily as stories, and are to be primarily related, not to their own specific culture, but to other stories of the same shape and kind. If a Greek myth shows a strong similarity in form to an Eskimo one, the similarity is irrelevant to a historian studying the Greeks or to an anthropologist studying the Eskimos: it is not irrelevant to a literary critic. As we shall see more fully later, myths were studied primarily for their content, or supposed content, as long as scholars had only Classical and Biblical myths to study. But the nineteenth-century explosion of knowledge about the myths of other cultures brought about a shift of attention from the content of one specific canon of myths to the forms of many similar ones. The great dividing line is Frazer's *Golden Bough,* which collects myths and rituals of the same general shape from all over the world without regard to the cultural differences involved. This work was intended by Frazer to be a work of anthropology using a "comparative" method much in vogue in the nineteenth century. But it has become increasingly obvious that *The Golden Bough* is not primarily a book on anthropology at all, but, like Frazer's editions of Pausanias, Apollodorus, and the *Fasti,* primarily a work of Classical scholarship using anthropological illustrations and parallels. That is, it is a work of literary criticism, the only field in which his type of "comparative method" is really valid. It is much the same method that is used by scholars who catalogue the themes and motifs of folk tales.

The difference between such terms as myth, folk tale, and legend begins to blur as soon as we think of such things formally, as types of stories. The word legend is perhaps more proto-historical in reference. We have myths of Zeus and Aphrodite; we have legends of beings, like Theseus or Oedipus, thought of as culture-heroes or figures whose descendants can still be pointed to as long as the legend and the culture are connected. Legend, then, is an early and easy-going form of tradition, before there is a general demand for history, conceived as the study of what actually happened. But the boundary line between myth and legend is impossible to draw: the same kinds of stories appear in both. Folk tales, again, are stories similar to, even identical with, myths in their structure. The chief difference seems to be that folk tales lack the particular seriousness that is characteristic of myth: even if they are traditional and believed, they are not central to tradition and belief. But myth, folk tale, and legend form a single corpus of stories: whichever category we concentrate on, the other two adhere to it. In the Old Testament, we recognize myth in the story of Adam, legend in the stories of the patriarchs, folk tale in the story of Samson, and what German critics call *sage* in the story of Elijah. But these are differences of emphasis and context rather than of actual genre. Nowhere is there a clear line between myth, legend, historical reminiscence, history manipulated for didactic purposes, and actual history. It is clear that whatever in the Bible is historically accurate is not there because it is historically accurate, but for reasons that would make inaccurate history (or pure literature, like the Book of Job) equally acceptable.

The total corpus of stories has two characteristics that are important for us. First, it is impossible to trace its origin. Our evidence cannot go back beyond the age of writing, and such story-types vanish into the long ages of oral tradition that must have preceded all written literature. Second, such stories, even when believed to be true, are not obviously credible: that is, they are not plausible. They belong in a world of marvels and mysteries and arbitrary acts, and the obligation to believe them is recognized, from Plato to Sir Thomas Browne and beyond, as an intellectual humiliation, whether the humiliation is resented, as it is by Plato, or gladly accepted as a *sacrificium intellectus,* as it is by Browne. What a man really believes, however, is what his actions show that he believes. By this standard Don Quixote's belief that his windmill was a giant was a genuine belief. But Quixote also remarks to Sancho Panza that the Golden Age would soon return if people would only see things as they are, and not allow themselves to be deluded by enchanters who make giants look like windmills. In other words, a belief which is voluntarily assumed as an intellectual handicap, as something that conflicts with the rest of one's experience, soon modulates from actual belief into an anxiety about belief.

Myths, we said, because of their central and permanent importance in a culture, tend to stick together and form a mythology, whereas folk tales simply travel over the world interchanging their motifs and themes. Folk tales thus have a *nomadic* cultural history, while myths grow up in connexion with a culturally rooted religion. It is not any structural feature in the stories of Phaethon or Endymion that makes them myths, for we could have—and do have—folk tales of the same kind: it is their attachment to a growing body of stories told about Apollo and Artemis, and the further attachment of Apollo and Artemis to the Olympian hierarchy, that makes them myths. Apollo does not appear to begin as a sun-god, but he becomes one, and in doing so he eventually absorbs the Helios of the Phaethon story. The true myth thus becomes an episode in a mythology. And as a culture develops, its mythology, or body of traditional and religious data, tends to become encyclopaedic. At a certain stage of development a mythology produces a theogony, a connected narrative beginning with the origin of the gods and of the departments of nature they personify, such as heaven and earth, the creation and original state of mankind, the inauguration of law and culture, and so on down to what may be called the cultural present. Some theogonies carry on the story to the end of time and the future annihilation of the world, though this is an extension of their normal function, which is to present a version of society's original contract. Besides this, mythology supplies a number of episodic tales illustrating the relations of gods with one another or with man, usually with a cautionary moral; it identifies or interrelates the various gods of local cults; it sanctions the law by giving it a divine origin; it provides a divine ancestry for its kings and heroes. Such a mythological canon does not necessarily exist in one specifically codified form, but it has a real existence none the less. Thus a mythology expands into an account of the origin, situation, and destiny of mankind, or the relevant portion of mankind, an account which is still, in form, a series of stories, but stories with obvious philosophical and moral implications.

As a society develops, its myths become revised, selected, expurgated, or reinterpreted to suit its changing needs. We have noticed that an immense amount of editorial labour obviously intervened between the origins of the myths in the Old Testament and their present form. The more archaic stories are often felt to be in bad theological taste: as Plutarch says, gods represented as doing unworthy things are no gods. Similarly in the Bible: the mistaken impulse of King David to break an ancient taboo and take a census was prompted by an angry Jehovah in the earlier book of Kings, by Satan in the later book of Chronicles. In this way a tradition develops of explaining or rationalizing earlier and more primitive myths. Myths may be interpreted as allegories illustrating moral truths. Hence the device known in Greek culture as *hyponoia,* the attempt, say, to save the faces of both Homer and Aphrodite by explaining the story of Hephaestus' net in the *Odyssey* as an allegory of something profound and respectable. Or mythology as a whole may be interpreted allegorically, as primitive science, as esoteric philosophy, as distorted history. The interpreting of myth, chiefly as moral allegory, was one of the cultural heavy industries of Western Europe between Plutarch and the late Renaissance, and survived as late as Ruskin. The natural direction of *hyponoia,* or the moralizing and allegorizing of myth, is away from the story towards the conception. Thus the story of Narcissus "really means" that pride goes before a fall, or that self-hypnosis is induced by egoism. Story and personality come to be thought of as archaic nuisances or mere disguises for something more serious, intended either to deceive or amuse the superficial. Eventually the story is replaced by the conceptual myth, the abstract ethical or metaphysical doctrine. Even where religious anxieties demand that some myths, at any rate, must still be accepted as true stories, the conceptualizing tendency goes as far as it can.

A second tendency in mythology, already mentioned, is also important for literature: the tendency to identify all the characters, usually gods, who are sufficiently similar for identification to be at all plausible. The most primitive gods appear to be epiphanic or local ones; a large settled civilization develops a definite number of gods, associated with various departments of nature, who absorb a great many of such local divinities by such identification. Sometimes differences in the characters of the local divinities are reflected in some inconsistency in the canonical accounts of the god or hero who absorbs them: the stories of Heracles afford instructive examples. As large civilizations expand into world states, the idea of one God appears, and identification by absorption then becomes total. The wholesale identifying of Greek and Roman gods which has given us Jupiter and Venus as names for Greek deities is a stage in this process. The same tendencies continue after a monotheistic religion has been established: in Christianity the saints play a prominent role in absorbing local gods, and Notre Dame de Chartres is the same person as Notre Dame de Crabtree Mills, Quebec.

It is obvious from what we have said that the corpus of myth, folk tale, legend, and the rest that emerges from the oral tradition, is, in one of its aspects, already literature: it is not something else that develops into literature. It is only by a necessary economy of language that we can speak of *a* myth, *a* folk tale, or *a* legend at all: none of these things really exist except in specific verbal forms, and these verbal forms are literary forms. We notice that the development of literature tends to parallel the social development of the corpus. We might expect to find the growing point of literature in folk tale rather than in myth, so far as these areas can be distinguished. Folk tales are often told purely for entertainment; there is not usually any obligation to believe them; they afford more scope to the story-teller's ingenuity and impulse to vary his material. And of course folk tale, along with legend, is of immense importance in literature. Myths, again, take on a new lease of literary life once their connexion with belief and cult disappears, as Classical mythology did in Christian Europe. It seems curious that collections of myths and stories near to myths should be made for purely literary purposes, as they are in Ovid's *Metamorphoses,* and that poets should be constantly turning to such stories at a time when nobody believed in or worshipped the deities who figure in them, but so it is.

It looks as though there were some inherent connexion between myth and poetry that is closer than the connexion with folk tale and legend. In the first place, the central and permanent significance of myth is reflected in the history of literature as well. As later critics constantly pointed out, the original mythmakers were the poets, and in Greece, where mythology never quite became theology, Homer and Hesiod had a cultural authority that extended beyond literature. In Christian times, we find Dante and Milton turning to different aspects of the mythical structure of Christianity, in spite of the subordination of poetic genius to other cultural demands that the choice of such themes made necessary. When poets recreate myth, they work in a different direction from the conceptual tendencies of the allegorists. The poet's impulse is to retell the story, or invent a new one with the same characters, instead of rationalizing the story. His cultural influence is thus in stressing the concrete, personal, story-telling elements in the myth which the conceptualizers tend to pass over or treat as archaic. Thus Plato was enough of a philosopher to want to censor the poets, and ridicule those who tried to justify them, but enough of a poet to invent his own myths, usually with the familiar names of Zeus and Prometheus. The gods, who are the normal characters of myth, are usually identified with various aspects of nature, and identity makes a relationship metaphorical. Neptune can cause a storm at sea because he is a sea god: in other words he is a metaphor for the sea. This metaphorical link between a natural event and a personality is an obstacle to the allegorist, but essential to the poet. The allegorist tends to try to drop the divine personality and concentrate on the event: the poet tends to see the event only as symbolic of the activity of the personality.

To sum up our argument thus far: myths are a part of the corpus of stories that every society has in its earlier phases of development. They are similar in form to other stories, some of which we distinguish as legends or folk tales, but are regarded as having in their content an element of peculiar and central importance. The question arises: how are we to respond to this importance? One obvious answer is: by believing what the myth says; by attaching its content to the rest of our experience. This is the answer primarily insisted on in the Judaeo-Christian tradition, and for centuries the notion persists that, for example, if the Bible says a great fish swallowed Jonah, there are special rewards for the reader who can swallow both. But even a dogmatic mythology deals with divine beings who can do anything, and who, being so often identified with elements of nature, take little pains to be credible or even moral. Sometimes attempts are made to rationalize a myth on a literal basis: thus either the fish were exempted from the curse of Noah's flood or some special act must have drowned them too. But such efforts soon perish through their inherent fatuity. From here the response to the myth takes one of two directions. Either the myth represents something which is true in spite of the story, or it is a story to be responded to as a story. We may call the first type of response allegorical, the second archetypal. They are not mutually exclusive: they are distinguishable, but they coexist, and help each other to develop. The allegorical response is a semipoetic one: it shifts the basis, as Aristotle says the poet does in comparison with the historian, from what was true, or did happen, to the kind of thing that is true, or does happen. Hence it rescues the dignity of a mythology no longer believed in, like the Classical mythology in the Christian period, as well as providing what Browne calls "an easie and Platonick description" of matters of faith. But it sets up a drift away from the story into the moral or historical truths illustrated by the story. To the allegorist, a myth's nearest relations are with other myths closest to it in subject-matter: the stories of Narcissus and of Phaethon are both *exempla* of pride, different in their fabulous disguise, but identical in their moral truth.

But mythology, regarded as a corpus of stories, united in form to legend and folk tale (and of course to other literary forms, such as hymns, which attach themselves to the myths that are part of a cult), has literary characteristics. The essential link is indicated by the Greek word *mythos,* which means the plot or narrative of a story. Literature inherits a mythology: in this sense the poet finds before him certain stories to which a good deal of traditional weight and authority has already been attached. The distinction between canonical and apocryphal stories reappears in literature; as when European poets inherited a Judaeo-Christian mythology related to what Tillich calls ultimate concern, and a Classical mythology which had lost its connexion with belief and had become purely imaginative and poetic. One would expect poets to concentrate entirely on the latter, as their peculiar province, but in fact, we find that the central position of Christianity in Western culture is reflected in its literature. Now just as the allegorical interpretation of myth is semi-poetic, so the poetic recreation of it is semi-conceptual. The poet tries to make his traditional story imaginatively credible, and he also interprets it incidentally. His primary task, however, is not to interpret but to represent; he transfers an ancient tale from the past to the present, from something inherited to something that confronts the reader immediately; from (if the myth is canonical) the particular event in the past, the truth of which is believed, to the universal event, the significance of which is comprehended.

Individual myths form a mythology; individual works of literature form an imaginative body for which there is (as Aristotle remarked two thousand years ago) no word. If there were such a word, it would be much easier to understand that literature, conceived as such a total imaginative body, is in fact a civilized, expanded, and developed mythology. We saw that one important social function of a mythology is to give a society an imaginative sense of its contract, of its abiding relations with the gods, with the order of nature, and within itself. When a mythology becomes a literature, its social function of providing a society with an imaginative vision of the human situation directly descends from its mythological parent. In this development the typical forms of myth become the conventions and genres of literature, and it is only when convention and genre are recognized to be essential aspects of literary form that the connexion of literature with myth becomes self-evident. The mythical golden age thus becomes the pastoral convention; the mythical accounts of man's fallen and helpless state become the conventions of irony; the mythical sense of the separation between the power of the gods and the pride of man becomes the convention of tragedy; myths of heroic adventures become the conventions of romance.

The relation of literature to mythology may be explicit or implicit. We have explicit relation when Dante and Milton recreate the central Christian myths of redemption or fall, or when Keats and Shelley recreate the myths of Endymion or Prometheus, or when French dramatists from Racine to Cocteau recreate the Greek myths that were already recreated in Greek drama. One reason for the explicit attraction of poets to mythology is technical. Because myths so often deal with divine beings who are identified with aspects of nature or society, the language of myth is metaphorical, and it is the metaphorical freedom that, for instance, the myth of Prometheus gives to Shelley that attracts him to the myth rather than to a contemporary social or political theme, where such mythical conceptions as the return of Atlantis would be absurd. Again, we spoke of the tendency on the part of a mythology to become encyclopaedic, providing a vision of the human situation from myths of beginning (creation, fall, golden age, lost paradise, killing the dragon of chaos, etc.) to myths of end (apocalypse, millennium, Utopia; or else visions of annihilation and Götterdämmerung). Sacred books, notably the Bible, show a tendency to reflect this encyclopaedic form in their structure, and a work of literature, when explicitly mythological, finds an implicit context for its myth in relation to literature as a whole, as a total imaginative body. Thus while the interpreter or commentator on a myth finds the profundity of the myth in its meaning as *allegory,* the poet, in recreating the myth, finds its profundity in its *archetypal framework.*

On the other hand, it often happens that a specific language of mythology petrifies into highbrow slang, as Philomela became a merely facile substitute for the imaginative experience of a nightingale's song in the eighteenth century. Keats's nightingale ode is no less mythical in its treatment of this experience than it would have been if Keats had explicitly alluded to the Ovidian story; the poem is not different in kind from the *Ode to Psyche,* which is explicitly mythical. But the nightingale ode follows the Wordsworthian practice, the theory of which appears to be the principle that archetypes of myth are most vividly experienced when they are not directly named, but when they are rediscovered in ordinary experience. This is one form of the implicit approach to mythology; another form is exemplified by Shakespeare, whose basis of operations is not myth, but legend in tragedy and history and folk tale in comedy. In modern times a great deal of realistic and ironic literature is implicitly mythical in the same way, but may be made explicitly so by a single allusion or sometimes by a title (*Resurrection, Germinal, Sodome et Gomorrhe, Absalom! Absalom!,* etc.). The allusion indicates the author's view of the archetypal context of his work, its place in the total framework that literature reveals to the imagination. The fact that poets think archetypally is often indicated by a reference to myth. When Yeats hopes that his daughter will think opinions are accursed because he once knew a woman who was beautiful and opinionated, a reader may feel that Yeats should have made a statistical survey before making assertions about the correlation between female beauty and female opinions, or that no daughter's opinions were likely to be more absurd than some that Yeats himself held. But Yeats's thought, being poetic thought, is moving up towards the vision of an archetype, to Venus in her aspect as the wife of Vulcan, and to this archetype both his daughter and Maud

Gonne, as well as everything else in that area of his experience, are assimilated.

The moral allegorization of myth depends on a general belief in a permanent body of moral truths which the wisdom of all ages has endeavored to express. As the sense of the relativity of moral and philosophical truth grows, the study of myth tends to become the anthropological and historical placing of the myth in its cultural context which we spoke of at first. The historical student of myth, however, inherits the conception of the myth as a disguise for a real truth. In this new context a great many myths tend to become historical reminiscences, allegories of something that happened earlier. The Biblical flood story is Sumerian in origin, and a layer of mud in Sumerian excavations indicates that a deluge did occur there. Frazer, in his *Folk Lore in the Old Testament,* finds that there are flood stories all over the world (except in Africa, where a story about the sky falling seems to have replaced it) and ascribes them all to local catastrophes of the same type. This, however, seems a kind of unconscious *reductio ad absurdum* of the method, perhaps even an example of the way that Frazer's industry often seems to be part of a curious imaginative obtuseness. Any given myth may have resulted from a local accident, but if it resembles dozens of other myths in form, surely we may suspect a feature in that form which does not oblige us to believe in an indefinite number of local accidents.

I have mentioned this point because it illustrates the difficulty of dealing with similarities of form among myths of different cultures and periods on a purely historical basis. If we keep to the disguise conception of myth, all similarities among myths must result from similarities in the phenomena which they obliquely describe. Hence the student of myth, unless he ignores these similarities and confines himself to the myths of one culture, is strongly tempted to account for them on some general theory of origin. There have been many such theories. Once upon a time there was a school of wise men who concealed all mysteries in fables, and our existing myths are all distortions of these. This version, originally developed to explain the resemblances between Biblical and extra-Biblical myths, keeps turning up in various occult forms, the school of wise men being located in Atlantis or India or ancient Egypt, whence their doctrines and symbols were diffused around the world like the trade winds. Traces of this view still linger in, for instance, Jessie Weston's *From Ritual to Romance.* Once upon a time there was a world-wide mythology of tree-worship, sun-worship, megalithic monuments, and reincarnation: this is the eighteenth-century "Druid" theory, still doing duty in H. G. Wells's *Outline of History.* Once upon a time there was a matriarchal and lunar mythology with a dying god who was the Great Mother's lover, perverted by a later patriarchal and solar myth which made the dying god a sacrifice offered by a father. Thus in Robert Graves, who adopts this version, our present notion of the Judgement of Paris must be the result of a misunderstanding: originally Paris must have been getting the apple from the triple goddess, not giving it. *The Golden Bough* itself, read in the same way, seems to suggest that once upon a time all mankind was organized into tribes with divine leaders who were killed and ceremonially eaten as soon as their strength began to fail. Other schematizations of the origin of myths, reducing them all to sun myths, zodiacal or astrological myths, ancestor or dead-hero myths, and the like, are by-products of the same tendencies.

Now any (or possibly all) of these general theories of origin may eventually be confirmed by archaeology, but in the meantime they are somewhat conjectural. We have so little evidence even from archaeology. Stonehenge appears to be carefully oriented to the sun, but we do not know that its builders had a verbalized mythology. But this kind of prehistoric hypothesis, of a type so remarkably similar to the mythical histories of sacred books, already mentioned, becomes unnecessary if we think of myths as potential literary forms. For the literary critic, at least, the real meaning of a myth is revealed, not by its origin, which we know nothing about, but by its later literary career, as it becomes recreated by the poets. As Ruskin says, in a fine passage of *The Queen of the Air*: "The great question in reading a story is always, not what wild hunter dreamed, or what childish race first dreaded it; but what wise man first perfectly told, and what strong people first perfectly lived by it. And the real meaning of any myth is that which it has at the noblest age of the nations among whom it is current." Thus a mythical story of theme is not a Platonic idea of which all later treatments are approximations, but an informing structural principle of literature, and the more we study the literary developments of a myth the more we learn about the myth. The book in the Bible known as the Song of Songs may have developed from village festival songs centering on a fertility and marriage-myth like that of the Lord and Lady of the May in medieval England. Once in the Bible, it became assimilated to the mythical structure of the Bible and had a flourishing career in mystical poetry as an allegory of God's love for the Church or human soul. The word allegory indicates that the tradition of allegorical interpretation played an important role in this literary development, as it often has done, but it would be uncritical to think of the development as a distortion or corruption of the original myth—so far as there was one.

Normally, however, mythical stories tend to develop by response to a public's growing demand for the plausible or credible, and the waning of its taste for the marvellous. I have elsewhere given the term (borrowed from Freud, though naturally the context is different in him) "displacement" to the process by which mythical stories, about gods who can do anything, become romances about heroes who can do almost anything, or heroines of tantalizing elusiveness or unshakable fidelity, and from there become stories of the foundling Tom Jones, the whorish but unquenchable Moll Flanders, or the virtue-rewarded Pamela. In this development the preservation of the original mythical outline of the story, as the feature that continues to give it shape, suspense, and denouement, is something that it is the concern of the critic to call to our attention.

In literary criticism itself the allegorical tendency reappears in two types of criticism. A work of literature may be studied in relation to its time: that is, it may be studied as a historical allegory. Or it may be studied in relation to the life and experience of the man who wrote it, as a biographical or psychological allegory.

As a historical allegory, the work of literature reflects the social facts of its own age: its historical events, its obsessive ideas, the conflicts and tensions in the social structure. Shelley's treatment of the Prometheus myth is unintelligible unless we relate it to the situation of Europe as Shelley saw it in 1819, after the French Revolution and Napoleon, before the greater revolution that he saw as imminent. We have to think of it also as a product of the cultural *Zeitgeist* that we sum up in the word Romanticism. There are many other elements in the relation of a literary work to its time that the critic is concerned with, and historical criticism gets out of proportion only when it freezes into a dogma, as it tends to do in most if not all Marxist criticism, asserting that what a poem is in relation to the life of its time outside it is in fact what the poem "really means," and that the work of the critic is done when he has established that relation. I have phrased this in such a way as to show that such a critical doctrine is directly descended from the allegorical tradition. Yet the mere fact that Shelley's poem is about Prometheus, and that Shelley in his preface explicitly links his hero with the Prometheus of Aeschylus and the Satan of Milton, indicates that there is another dimension to the myth that is to be sought within literature itself. All literary works have pedigrees of this kind whether they say so or not, even whether the author realizes it or not. Diderot's *Rameau's Nephew,* besides being a work of its time, impresses us also as a portent of the future: we see in it an anticipation of later portrayals of conflicts between an establishment and an anti-hero. But if *Rameau's Nephew* has this literary extension into the future it must have one into the past as well, and if we see it as belonging to the tradition of the Solomon-and-Saturn dialogue, the opposition between socially accepted and socially rejected wisdom, we are, again, seeing it in its archetypal framework or total cultural context.

So far as the work of literature is to be thought of as a conscious and voluntary production of its author, there is little if any difference between its historical and its biographical aspects: the author is simply seen

39

as a man of his time. Since Romanticism we have been increasingly impressed by the involuntary aspects of imaginative work, and by the way, in particular, in which the specifically mythopoeic faculty, the creation of the central metaphorical form of a literary work, seems to be associated with the mental powers which are or seem to be below consciousness. The more thoroughly the unconscious mind has been explored, the more remarkable are the parallels of literature with the dream and other aspects of the struggles of desire and reality in the mind. Certainly since Freud we have been accustomed to see creation as revealing tensions and conflicts within the poet's own psyche as well as in his society. Thus a poem may also be, to some extent, an allegory of the poet's inner life, and there are not lacking those who would claim that what the poet unconsciously reveals of himself in his poem is what that poem "really means." But however remarkable the analogies between the mythopoeic faculty and the unconscious mind, and however true the fact poets do unconsciously reveal and to some extent release their inner tensions in their work, still the mythopoeic faculty can hardly be the same thing as the Freudian repressed unconscious. Unlike the dream, it seeks communication and is aware of an audience, hence it must be something much nearer to consciousness. The poet's craftsmanship may work on a purely conscious level, or it may operate on a level that we vaguely describe as instinctive, intuitive, inspired, or involuntary, when his skill as a writer tells him that something belongs or fits, whether he can explain why or not. And so, just as a poet may consciously relate his work to literary tradition, as Shelley does by his use of the name Prometheus, so he may unconsciously establish similar links in his diction, his imagery, his echoes of work that has influenced him, and the like.

What is called myth criticism in literature, then, is not the study of a certain kind or aspect of literature, much less a patented critical methodology, but the study of the structural principles of literature itself, more particularly its conventions, its genres, and its archetypes or recurring images. As this process goes on, certain external relations of literature come into view, though they have not been much explored as yet, and we can only hint briefly here what they are. In the first place, the identity of mythology and literature indicates that even matters of belief, in religion, have much more to do with vision and with an imaginative response than with the kind of belief that is based on evidence and sense experience. The connection of myth with *assumed* history, already mentioned, does not mean that such mythical structures as the Gospels and the Pentateuch are fraudulent: it means that they have been written in the only form which can address a reader in the present tense, as something confronting him with an imperative rather than revealing a mystery out of the past. Myth, in short, is the only possible language of *concern*, just as science, with its appeal to evidence, accurate measurement, and rational deduction, is the only possible language of detachment. Myth begins in a projected form, in stories about gods who are largely powers of nature and are often indifferent to man, but as a mythology develops it increasingly recovers for its human creators what it originally projected, and finally becomes purely existential, dependent not on assumptions about external reality, whether in time or space, but on imaginative experience. Its truth is not descriptive or evidential, but implicit, contained in the *mythos* or story which is the expression of experience. That is one reason why the real meaning of a myth emerges from its historical development and not from any guess about its original form.

Thus literature is only a part, though a central part, of the total mythopoeic structure of concern which extends into religion, philosophy, political theory, and many aspects of history, the vision a society has of its situation, destiny, and ideals, and of reality in terms of those human factors. It expresses not so much the world that man lives in as the world that he builds. I call it a structure, and sometimes, as in the Middle Ages, it really looks like one, unifying a vast number of imaginative patterns in the different mythopoeic fields just mentioned. Our own age is more aware of the variety and inner disagreements in our visions of concern, yet it is still true that those who have most effectively changed the attitudes of society—Rousseau, Freud, Marx—are those who changed its mythology. This mythology comes to us on every level, from the greatest works of imagination to the steady rain of clichés that come through conversation and mass media. It is particularly in American culture that critics can see the connexion between literary and social mythology, between, say, pastoral conventions in Thoreau or Melville and the same conventions in popular pastoral (e.g., the Western story) or in the pastoral mythology of cliché (the cottage away from it all, the simple log-cabin life corrupted by the big city, etc.). Here we return to the point at which we began, that while the study of myth is an essential activity of literary criticism, it is also essential to the study of the structure of society.

Myth and Myth Criticism: An Introductory Bibliography

This bibliography cannot do more than indicate the general scope and range of myth criticism, and the sort of subject with which it is most likely to be connected: comparative religion, anthropology, psychology, iconography, Biblical typology, allegory, and the like. The arrangement is roughly chronological, and lists mainly secondary sources. It begins with works of Classical and Biblical scholarship, and proceeds to the Middle Ages and the Renaissance, taking particular account of the cosmology, iconography, mythological handbooks, and emblem books in those two periods. The next great mythopoeic age is the Romantic one, beginning in the middle of the eighteenth century and continuing through the nineteenth, when a more scientific approach to comparative mythology began, to Frazer and Freud at the end of the century. There follows a selected list of books since Frazer, most of them strongly influenced by him, a number of works of a type of mythical fiction that would hardly have developed without a similar interest in criticism (it is hardly practicable to list all the parallel tendencies in modern poetry, such as Eliot's *Waste Land* and Dylan Thomas' "Altarwise by owl-light" sequence), and a few examples of works of myth criticism in literature, including more specialized studies of single myth figures. Some attempt is made also to document the remark in the essay about the peculiar aptitude of American (and Canadian) literature for this kind of critical treatment.

At every age myth criticism has been close to highly speculative thinking, in or near the occult area, and as applied to literature it is still in an experimental stage, its scholarly organization not yet completed. Hence, while omission from this bibliography proves nothing whatever about the merits of what may have been omitted only by accident or oversight, there has been a real effort to screen out books of doubtful value. One or two have been listed which do not stand on the same level of scholarship or historical interest as the others, but nothing has been included which would really mislead an experienced reader.

I am greatly indebted to my research associate, Professor Jay Macpherson, for her work on this bibliography.

N. F.

I. General Reference

Cirlot, J. E. *A Dictionary of Symbols.* Tr. [from the Spanish] Jack Sage. London: Routledge & Kegan Paul, 1962. [Bibliography.]

Gruppe, Otto. *Geschichte der klassischen Mythologie und Religionsgeschichte während des Mittelalters im Abendland* . . . Leipzig: Teubner, 1921. [Supplement to Roscher, *Ausführliches Lexikon.*]

Pugin, A. W. *Glossary of Ecclesiastical Ornament and Costume; Compiled from Ancient Authorities and Examples.* 2nd ed. London: Bohn, 1846.

Roscher, W. H. *Ausführliches Lexikon der griechischen und römischen Mythologie.* 6 vols. and 3 supp. Leipzig and Berlin: Teubner, 1884-1937.

Sandys, Sir John Edwin. *A History of Classical Scholarship.* 3 vols. Cambridge: Cambridge Univ. Press, 1903-08.

II. Antiquity

Apollodorus. *The Library.* Tr. Sir James G. Frazer. 2 vols. (Loeb Classical Library.) London: Heinemann, 1921

Buffière, F. *Les Mythes d'Homère et la pensée grecque.* Paris: Les Belles Lettres, 1956.

Carcopino, Jérôme. *Virgile et le mystère de la IVe Eglogue.* Paris: L'Artisan du Livre, 1930.

Collins, Stanley T. *The Interpretation of Vergil with Special Reference to Macrobius.* Oxford: Blackwell, 1909.

Courcelle, Pierre. "Interprétations néo-platonisantes du livre VI de l'Enéide." In *Recherches sur la tradition platonicienne*, pp. 95-136. (Fondation Hardt, Entretiens sur l'antiquité classique, 3.) Geneva: Vandœuvres, 1955.

Cumont, Franz. *Lux perpetua.* Paris: Librairie Orientaliste Paul Geuthner, 1949.

Decharme, Paul. *La Critique des traditions religieuses chez les Grecs, des origines au temps de Plutarque.* Paris: Picard, 1904.

Frutiger, P. *Les Mythes de Platon: Etude philosophique et littéraire.* Paris: Alcan, 1930.

Hersman, Anne Bates. *Studies in Greek Allegorical Interpretation.* Chicago: Blue Sky Press, 1906.

Hirzel, Rudolf. *Plutarch.* (Das Erbe der Alten, 4.) Leipzig, 1912.

Hopfner, Theodor. *Plutarch über Isis und Osiris.* (Monographien des Archiv Orientální, 9.) Prague: Orientalisches Institut, 1941. [Text and commentary.]

Hubaux, Jean, and Maxime Leroy. "Vulgo nascetur amomum." In Université Libre de Bruxelles, *Annuaire de l'Institut de Philologie et d'Histoire Orientales et Slaves* (1932), pp. 505-530. (Mél. Bidez.)

Inge, W. R. *The Philosophy of Plotinus.* Vol. I of 2 vols. New York: Longmans, 1918.

Jeanmaire, Henri. *Le Messianisme de Virgile.* Paris: Vrin, 1930.

Jonas, Hans. *Gnosis und spätantiker Geist.* 2 vols. Göttingen: Vandenhoeck & Ruprecht, 1934-54.

Knight, W. F. Jackson. *Cumaean Gates: A Reference of the Sixth Aeneid to the Initiation Pattern.* Oxford: Blackwell, 1936.

Nitchie, Elizabeth. *Vergil and the English Poets.* New York: Columbia Univ. Press, 1919.

Onians, R. B. *The Origins of European Thought, About the Body, the Mind, the Soul, the World, Time, and Fate.* Cambridge: Cambridge Univ. Press, 1951.

Ovid. *The Fasti.* Ed. and tr. Sir J. G. Frazer. 5 vols. London: Macmillan, 1929.

Pausanias. *Description of Greece.* Tr. with Commentary by Sir J. G. Frazer. 6 vols. London: Macmillan, 1898.

Pépin, Jean. *Mythe et allégorie: Les Origines grecques et les contestations judéo-chrétiennes.* (Philosophie de l'esprit.) Paris: Aubier, 1958.

Porphyry. *De Antro Nympharum.* In *Select Works of Porphyry,* tr. Thomas Taylor. London: T. Rodd, 1823.

Sallustius. *Concerning the Gods and the Universe.* Ed. with Prolegomena and tr. by A. D. Nock, Cambridge: Cambridge Univ. Press, 1926.

Scazzocchio, Lea S. de. *"Poética" y Critica Literaria en Plutarco.* (Investigaciones y estudios, Serie Literatura y Estética, 1.) Montevideo: Universidad de la República, 1957.

Snell, Bruno. *The Discovery of the Mind: The Greek Origins of European Thought.* Tr. [from the German] T. G. Rosenmayer. Cambridge: Harvard Univ. Press, 1953.

Stewart, J. A. *The Myths of Plato.* New York: Macmillan, 1905.

Taylor, A. E. *Platonism and Its Influence.* New York: Longmans, 1943. [Our debt to Greece and Rome.]

Untersteiner, M. *La fisiologia del mito.* (Il pensiero greco, 18.) Milan: Fratelli Bocca, 1946.

Vicaire, Paul. *Platon: Critique littéraire.* (Etudes et commentaires, 34.) Paris: Klincksieck, 1960. [Bibliography.]

Whittaker, Thomas. *Macrobius: or, Philosophy, Science and Letters in the Year 400.* Cambridge: Cambridge Univ. Press, 1923.

—— *The Neo-Platonists: A Study in the History of Hellenism.* 2nd ed. Cambridge: Cambridge Univ. Press, 1928.

III. The Survival of the Gods

Bezold, Friedrich von. *Das Fortleben der antiken Götter im mittelalterlichen Humanismus.* Bonn and Leipzig: Schroeder, 1922.

Liebeschütz, Hans. *Fulgentius metaforalis: Ein Beitrag zur Geschichte der antiken Mythologie im Mittelalter.* (Studien der Bibliothek Warburg, 4.) Leipzig and Berlin: Teubner, 1926.

Seznec, Jean. *The Survival of the Pagan Gods.* Tr. B. F. Sessions. (Bollingen Series, 38.) New York: Pantheon, 1940.

IV. The Bible

Auerbach, Erich. " 'Figura'." Tr. Ralph Manheim, in his *Scenes from the Drama of European Literature: Six Essays,* pp. 11-76. (New York: Meridian, 1959).

Bevan, E. R. *Symbolism and Belief.* London: Allen & Unwin, 1938.

Bréhier, Emile. *Les Idées philosophiques et religieuses de Philon d'Alexandrie.* (Etudes de philosophie médiévale, 8.) Paris: Vrin, 1950. [Bibliography.]

Daniélou, J. *From Shadows to Reality: Studies in the Biblical Typology of the*

Fathers. Tr. Dom Wulstan Hibberd. London: Burns & Oates, 1960. [Bibliography.]

Drummond, James. *Philo Judaeus: or, The Jewish-Alexandrian Philosophy in Development and Completion.* 2 vols. London: Williams & Norgate, 1888.

Farrer, Austin. *A Rebirth of Images: The Making of St. John's Apocalypse.* Westminster: Dacre Pr., 1949.

Goppelt, Leonhard. *Typos: Die typologische Deutung des Alten Testaments im Neuen.* (Beiträge zur Forderung christlicher Theologie, Ser. 2, Vol. XLIII.) Gütersloh: 1939.

Hanson, R. P. C. *Allegory and Event: A Study of the Sources and Significance of Origen's Interpretation of Scripture.* London: SCM Press, 1959.

Hooke, S. H. *The Siege Perilous: Essays in Biblical Anthropology and Kindred Subjects.* London: SCM Press, 1956.

——, ed. *The Labyrinth: Further Studies in the Relation Between Myth and Ritual in the Ancient World.* London: SPCK, 1935.

——, ed. *Myth and Ritual: Essays on the Myth and Ritual of the Hebrews in Relation to the Culture Pattern of the Ancient East.* London: Oxford Univ. Press, 1933.

Kennedy, Harry A. A. *Philo's Contribution to Religion.* London: Hodder & Stoughton, 1919.

Lampe, G. W. H., and K. J. Woollcombe. *Essays on Typology.* London: SCM Press, 1957.

Lubac, Henri de. *Exégèse médiévale: les quatre sens de l'Ecriture.* 4 vols. (Théologie, études, 41, 42, 59.) Paris: Aubier, 1959-64.

Lynch, William F. *Christ and Apollo: The Dimensions of the Literary Imagination.* New York: Sheed & Ward, 1960. [Appendix on "Medieval Exegesis."]

MacCallum, Hugh R. "Milton and Figurative Interpretation of the Bible." *UTQ,* XXI (July 1962), 397-415.

Smalley, Beryl. *The Study of the Bible in the Middle Ages.* 2nd ed. Oxford: Clarendon Press, 1941.

Williams, Arnold. *The Common Expositor: An Account of the Commentaries on Genesis, 1527-1633.* Chapel Hill: Univ. of North Carolina Press, 1948.

Wolfson, H. A. *Philo: Foundations of Religious Philosophy in Judaism, Christianity, and Islam.* 2 vols. Cambridge: Harvard Univ. Press, 1947.

V. Cosmology

Dunbar, Helen Flanders. *Symbolism in Mediaeval Thought, and Its Consummation in the* Divine Comedy. New Haven: Yale Univ. Press, 1929. [Bibliography.]

Lewis, C. S. *The Discarded Image: An Introduction to Mediaeval and Renaissance Literature.* Cambridge: Cambridge Univ. Press, 1964.

Liebeschütz, Hans. *Das allegorische Weltbild der heiligen Hildegard von Bingen.* (Studien der Bibliothek Warburg, 16.) Leipzig and Berlin: Teubner, 1930.

Tillyard, E. M. W. *The Elizabethan World Picture.* London: Chatto & Windus, 1948.

VI. The Middle Ages

Comparetti, D. *Vergil in the Middle Ages*. Tr. E. Benecke. New York: Macmillan, 1910.

Curtius, E. R. *European Literature and the Latin Middle Ages*. Tr. Willard R. Trask. London: Routledge, 1953.

Graf, A. *Roma nella memoria e nelle immaginazioni del Medio Evo*. 2 vols. Turin: Loescher, 1882.

Hopper, V. F. *Mediaeval Number Symbolism: Its Sources, Meaning, and Influence on Thought and Expression*. (Columbia Univ. Studies in English and Comp. Lit., 132.) New York: Columbia Univ. Press, 1938. [Bibliography.]

Hortis, Attilio. *Studi sulle opere latine del Boccaccio, con particolare riguardo alla storia della erudizione nel medio evo e alle letterature straniere*. Trieste: Julius Dase, 1879.

Knight, G. Wilson. *The Christian Renaissance: With Interpretations of Dante, Shakespeare and Goethe*. Toronto: Macmillan, 1933.

Loomis, R. S. *The Grail: From Celtic Myth to Christian Symbol*. New York: Columbia Univ. Press, 1963.

Nolhac, Pierre de. *Pétrarque et l'humanisme*. 2 vols. 2nd ed. Paris: Champion, 1907.

Rand, Edward Kennard. *Ovid and His Influence*. Boston: Marshall Jones, 1925.

Robertson, D. W., Jr. *A Preface to Chaucer: Studies in Mediaeval Perspectives*. Princeton: Princeton Univ. Press, 1963.

——, and B. F. Huppé. *Piers Plowman and Scriptural Tradition*. Princeton: Princeton Univ. Press, 1951.

White, T. H., tr. *The Book of Beasts, Being a Translation from a Latin Bestiary of the Twelfth Century*. New York: Putnam, 1954.

VII. Iconography

Bayley, Harold. *A New Light on the Renaissance, Displayed in Contemporary Emblems*. London: Dent, 1909.

Chew, Samuel C. *The Pilgrimage of Life: An Exploration into the Renaissance Mind*. New Haven: Yale Univ. Press, 1962.

—— *The Virtues Reconciled: An Iconographic Study*. (The Alexander Lectures.) Toronto: Univ. of Toronto Press, 1947.

Freeman, Rosemary. *English Emblem Books*. London: Chatto & Windus, 1948.

Janson, H. W. *Apes and Ape Lore in the Middle Ages and the Renaissance*. (Studies of the Warburg Inst., 20.) London: Warburg Inst., Univ. of London, 1952.

Klibansky, Raymond, with E. Panofsky and F. Saxl. *Saturn and Melancholy: Studies in the History of Natural Philosophy, Religion, and Art*. London: Nelson, 1964.

Mâle, Emile. *L'Art religieux de la fin du moyen âge en France: Étude sur l'iconographie du moyen âge et sur ses sources d'inspiration*. Paris: Colin, 1908.

—— *L'art religieux de la fin du XVIᵉ siècle et du XVIIᵉ siècle: Étude sur l'icono-*

graphie après le Concile de Trente, Italie-France-Espagne-Flandres. 2nd ed., rev. and corr. Paris: Colin, 1951.

—— L'art religieux du XIIIme siècle en France: Étude sur l'iconographie du moyen âge et sur ses sources d'inspiration. Paris: Colin, 1902.

Marle, Raimond van. *Iconographie de l'art profane au moyen âge et à la Renaissance*. 2 vols. (Vol. II, *Allégories et symboles*.) The Hague: Nijhoff, 1931-32.

Panofsky, Dora and Erwin. *Pandora's Box: The Changing Aspects of a Mythical Symbol*. (Bollingen Series, 52.) New York: Pantheon, 1956.

Panofsky, Erwin. *Hercules am Scheideweg und andere antike Bildstoffe in der neueren Kunst*. (Studien der Bibliothek Warburg, 18.) Leipzig and Berlin: Teubner, 1930.

—— *Meaning in the Visual Arts: Papers in and on Art History*. New York: Doubleday Anchor, 1955.

—— *Studies in Iconology: Humanistic Themes in the Art of the Renaissance*. (The Mary Flexner Lectures, Bryn Mawr, 1937.) New York: Oxford Univ. Press, 1939.

——, and F. Saxl. *Dürers "Melancolia I."* (Studien der Bibliothek Warburg, 2.) Leipzig and Berlin: Teubner, 1923.

Praz, Mario. *Studies in Seventeenth-Century Imagery*. 2 vols. (Studies of the Warburg Inst., 3.) London: Warburg Inst., Univ. of London, 1939-47. [Vol. II, *Bibliography*.]

Réau, Louis. *Iconographie de l'art chrétien*. 3 vols. in 6. Paris: Presses Universitaires, 1955-59.

Ruskin, John. *The Bible of Amiens*. London, 1885.

Tervarent, Guy. *Attributs et symboles dans l'art profane, 1450-1600: Dictionnaire d'un langage perdu*. Geneva: E. Droz, 1958.

Wind, Edgar. *Pagan Mysteries in the Renaissance*. New Haven: Yale Univ. Press, 1958. [Bibliography.]

VIII. The Renaissance

Allen, Don Cameron. *The Star-Crossed Renaissance: The Quarrel about Astrology and Its Influence in England*. Durham, N.C.: Duke Univ. Press, 1941.

Bacon, Francis. *De Sapientia Veterum*. London, 1609.

Browne, Sir Thomas. *The Garden of Cyrus*. London, 1658.

Bunyan, John. *The Pilgrim's Progress*. London, 1678. ["The Author's Apology for his Book."]

Eliade, Mircea. *The Forge and the Crucible*. Tr. S. Corrin. New York: Harper, 1962.

Golding, Arthur. *The XV Books entitled Metamorphoses Translated out of Latin into English Meter*. London, 1593. ["To the Reader."]

Harding, Davis P. *Milton and the Renaissance Ovid*. (Univ. of Illinois Studies in Lang. and Lit., 30.) Urbana: Univ. of Illinois Press, 1946.

Harington, Sir John. *Orlando Furioso* (tr.). London, 1591. ["A Brief Apology of Poetry."]

Iversen, E. *The Myth of Egypt and Its Hieroglyphics*. Copenhagen, 1961.

Jung, C. G. *Psychology and Alchemy*. Tr. R. F. C. Hull. (Bollingen Series, 20.) New York: Pantheon, 1953.

Kircher, Athanasius. *Oedipus Aegyptiacus: hoc est, universalis hieroglyphicae veterum doctrinae temporum injuria abolitae instauratio . . .* 3 vols. Rome: Mascardi, 1652-54.

Lodge, Thomas. *A Defence of Poetry, Music, and Stage Plays*. London, 1579.

Nashe, Thomas. *The Anatomy of Absurdity*. London, 1589.

Nichols, John. *The Progresses and Public Processions of Queen Elizabeth*. 2nd ed. London, 1823.

Purchas, Samuel. *Hakluytus Posthumus, or Purchas his Pilgrimes*. 4 vols. (Vol. I, Ch. i, Sects. i-iii.) London, 1625.

Raleigh, Sir Walter. *The History of the World*. (Book I.) London, 1614.

Reynolds, Henry. *Mythomystes, Wherein a Short Survey Is Taken of the Nature and Value of True Poesy and Depth of the Ancients above our Modern Poets*. London, 1630 (?).

Robb, Nesca A. *Neoplatonism of the Italian Renaissance*. London: Allen & Unwin, 1935.

Ruskin, John. *Stones of Venice*. 3 vols. (III, 205-209, on *The Faerie Queene* I.) London: Smith, Elder, 1851-53.

Samuel, Irene. *Plato and Milton*. (Cornell Studies in English, 35.) Ithaca: Cornell Univ. Press, 1947.

Sandys, George. *Ovid's Metamorphoses: Englished, Mythologized, and Represented in Figures*. London, 1640.

Selden, John. *De Diis Syris Syntagmata II*. London, 1617.

Spingarn, J. E. *A History of Literary Criticism in the Renaissance*. New York: Columbia Univ. Press, 1912.

Vaughan, Thomas. *Anthroposophia Theomagica*. London, 1650.

Weinberg, Bernard. *A History of Literary Criticism in the Italian Renaissance*. 2 vols. Chicago: Univ. of Chicago Press, 1961.

Welsford, Enid. *The Court Masque: A Study in the Relationship Between Poetry and the Revels*. Cambridge: Cambridge Univ. Press, 1927.

Wilson, Thomas. *The Art of Rhetoric*. London, 1553.

Yates, Frances A. *Giordano Bruno and the Hermetic Tradition*. London: Routledge, 1964.

IX. Renaissance Handbooks and Their Users

Bourciez, Edouard. *Les Mœurs polies et la littérature de cour sous Henri II*. Paris: Hachette, 1886. [Book 2, "L'Antiquité renaît."]

Bush, Douglas. *Mythology and the Renaissance Tradition in English Poetry*. Minneapolis: Univ. of Minnesota Press, 1932. [Bibliography.]

Gilbert, Allan H. *The Symbolic Persons in the Masques of Ben Jonson*. Durham, N. C.: Duke Univ. Press, 1948.

Gordon, D. J. "The Imagery of Jonson's *The Masque of Blacknesse* and *The*

Masque of Beautie." In Warburg and Courtauld Insts., *England and the Mediterranean Tradition,* pp. 102-121. London: Oxford Univ. Press, 1945.

Laumonier, Paul. *Ronsard, poète lyrique: Étude historique et littéraire.* 3rd ed. Paris: Hachette, 1932. [Bk. II, Ch. i, "Les mythes"; Ch. iii, "Mythologie et allégorie."]

Lemmi, Charles W. *The Classic Deities in Bacon: A Study in Mythological Symbolism.* Baltimore: Johns Hopkins Press, 1933.

Lotspeich, Henry G. *Classical Mythology in the Poetry of Edmund Spenser.* (Princeton Studies in English, 9.) Princeton: Princeton Univ. Press, 1932.

Osgood, Charles G. *The Classical Mythology of Milton's English Poems.* (Yale Studies in English, 8.) New York: Holt, 1900.

Root, R. K. *Classical Mythology in Shakespeare.* (Yale Studies in English, 19.) New York: Holt, 1903.

Sawtelle, A. E. *The Sources of Spenser's Classical Mythology.* Boston: Silver Burdett, 1896.

Schoell, Franck L. *Etudes sur l'humanisme continental en Angleterre à la fin de la Renaissance.* (Bibliothèque de la Revue de Littérature Comparée, 29.) Paris: Champion, 1926.

Starnes, DeWitt T., and E. W. Talbert. *Classical Myth and Legend in Renaissance Dictionaries: A Study of Renaissance Dictionaries in Their Relation to the Classical Learning of Contemporary English Writers.* Chapel Hill: Univ. of North Carolina Press, 1955.

Wheeler, Charles F. *Classical Mythology in the Plays, Masques, and Poems of Ben Jonson.* Princeton: Princeton Univ. Press, 1938.

Whiting, George. *Milton's Literary Milieu.* Chapel Hill: Univ. of North Carolina Press, 1939.

Wilson, Elkin C. *England's Eliza.* Cambridge: Harvard Univ. Press, 1939.

X. Eighteenth Century and Romantic Period.

Bryant, Jacob. *A New System: or, An Analysis of Ancient Mythology Wherein an Attempt Is Made to Divest Tradition of Fable, and to Reduce the Truth to Its Original Purity.* 3 vols. London, 1774-76.

➥Bush, Douglas. *Mythology and the Romantic Tradition in English Poetry.* Cambridge: Harvard Univ. Press, 1937. [Bibliography.]

Creuzer, Friedrich. *Symbolik und Mythologie der alten Völker, besonders der Griechen.* 6 vols. Leipzig and Darmstadt, 1810-23.

Davies, Edward. *Celtic Researches on the Origin, Traditions and Language of the Ancient Britons.* London, 1804.

Dupuis, Charles. *Origine de tous les cultes, ou religion universelle.* 3 vols. Paris, 1795.

Hungerford, E. B. *Shores of Darkness.* New York: Columbia Univ. Press, 1941.

Knight, Richard Payne. *A Discourse on the Worship of Priapus, and Its Connection with the Mystic Theology of the Ancients.* London, 1786.

Manuel, Frank E. *The Eighteenth Century Confronts the Gods.* Cambridge: Harvard Univ. Press, 1959.

Owen, A. L. *The Famous Druids: A Survey of Three Centuries of English Literature on the Druids.* Oxford: Clarendon Press, 1962.

Taylor, Thomas. *The Fable of Cupid and Psyche: With an Introduction Explaining the Meaning of the Fable and Proving That It Alludes to the Descent of the Soul.* London, 1795.

—— tr. *Select Works of Porphyry . . . with an Appendix Explaining the Allegory of the Wanderings of Ulysses.* London, 1823.

Todd, Ruthven. *Tracks in the Snow: Studies in English Science and Art.* London: Grey Walls Press, 1946.

Voltaire, F. M. A. de. *La Philosophie de l'histoire.* Geneva, 1765. [From 1769, incorporated with *Essai sur les Mœurs et l'esprit des nations* as "Introduction."]

XI. Nineteenth Century

Gould, Sabine Baring. *Curious Myths of the Middle Ages.* London: Rivingtons, 1866.

Graf, Arturo. *Miti, leggende e superstizioni del Medio Evo.* Turin: Loescher, 1892.

Hone, William. *Ancient Mysteries Described: Especially the English Miracle Plays, Founded on Apocryphal New Testament Story, Extant among the Unpublished Manuscripts in the British Museum.* London, 1823.

Lang, Andrew. *Myth, Ritual and Religion.* 2 vols. London, 1887.

Lobeck, Christian August. *Aglaophamus, sive de theologiae mysticae graecorum causis, idemque poetarum Orphicorum dispersas reliquias collegit.* 2 vols. Leipzig, 1829.

Nietszche, F. W. *Die Geburt der Tragödie aus dem Geiste der Musik.* Leipzig, 1872.

Rohde, Erwin. *Psyche: Seelencult und Unsterblichkeitsglaube der Griechen.* Freiburg, 1894.

Ruskin, John. *The Queen of the Air: Being a Study of the Greek Myths of Cloud and Storm.* London, 1869.

XII. Frazer and After

Chambers, E. K. *The Mediaeval Stage.* 3 vols. London: Oxford Univ. Press, 1903.

Cook, A. B. *Zeus: A Study in Classical Religion.* 3 vols. Cambridge: Cambridge Univ. Press, 1914-40.

Cornford, F. M. *The Origin of Attic Comedy.* London: E. Arnold, 1914.

Eisler, Robert. *Orpheus—the Fisher: Comparative Studies in Orphic and Early Christian Cult Symbolism.* London: Watkins, 1921.

Frazer, Sir J. G. *Folk-lore in the Old Testament: Studies in Comparative Religion, Legend and Law.* 3 vols. London: Macmillan, 1918.

—— *The Golden Bough: A Study in Comparative Religion.* 3rd ed., rev. and enl. 12 vols. London: Macmillan, 1911.

Frobenius, Leo. *The Childhood of Man: A Popular Account of the Lives, Customs and Thoughts of the Primitive Races,* tr. A. H. Keane. London: Seeley, 1909.

Gaster, Theodor H. *Thespis: Ritual, Myth and Drama in the Ancient Near East.* New York: Schuman, 1950.

Harrison, Jane E. *Prolegomena to the Study of Greek Religion.* 3rd ed. Cambridge: Cambridge Univ. Press, 1922.

—— *Themis: A Study of the Social Origins of Greek Religion.* 2nd ed. Cambridge: Cambridge Univ. Press, 1927.

Kerényi, C., and C. G. Jung. *Essays on a Science of Mythology: The Divine Child and the Mysteries of Eleusis.* New York: Pantheon, 1949.

Levy, G. R. *The Gate of Horn: A Study of the Religious Conceptions of the Stone Age, and Their Influences upon European Thought.* London: Faber, 1948.

—— *The Sword from the Rock: An Investigation into the Origins of Epic Literature and the Development of the Hero.* London: Faber, 1953.

Mackenzie, Donald A. *The Migration of Symbols, and Their Relations to Beliefs and Customs.* London: Kegan Paul, 1926.

Perry, William James. *The Children of the Sun: A Study in the Early History of Civilization.* London: Methuen, 1923.

Phillpotts, Dame Bertha. *The Elder Edda and Ancient Scandinavian Drama.* Cambridge: Cambridge Univ. Press, 1920.

Raglan, F. R. R. S. *The Hero: A Study in Tradition, Myth, and Drama.* London: Methuen, 1936.

Rivers, William H. R. *Conflict and Dream.* London: Kegan Paul, 1923.

Weston, Jessie. *From Ritual to Romance.* London: Macmillan, 1920.

XIII. Modern Fiction Employing Myths

Graves, Robert. *King Jesus.* London: Cassell, 1946.

Jackson, Shirley. *The Lottery: or, The Adventures of James Harris.* New York: Farrar, Straus, 1949.

Lewis, C. S. *That Hideous Strength: A Modern Fairy-Tale for Grown-Ups.* London: John Lane, 1945.

Mitchison, Naomi. *The Corn King and the Spring Queen.* London: Cape, 1931.

Newton, Norman. *The House of Gods.* London: Peter Owen, 1961.

Renault, Mary. *The King Must Die.* London: Longmans, 1958.

Tolkien, J. R. *The Lord of the Rings.* 3 vols. London: G. Allen, 1954-55.

Williams, Charles. *Shadows of Ecstasy.* London: Gollancz, 1933.

XIV. Occultism

Blavatsky, Helena P. *Isis Unveiled: A Master-Key to the Mysteries of Ancient and Modern Science and Theology.* 2nd ed. 2 vols. New York: Bouton, 1877.

—— *The Secret Doctrine: The Synthesis of Science, Religion, and Philosophy.* 2 vols. London: Theosophical Pub. Co., 1888.

Saurat, Denis. *Literature and Occult Tradition: Studies in Philosophical Poetry.* Tr. Dorothy Bolton. London: Bell, 1930.

Waite, A. E. *The Holy Grail, Its Legends and Symbolism: An Explanatory Survey of Their Embodiment in Romance Literature . . .* London: Rider, 1933.

Yeats, W. B. *A Vision*. London: Macmillan, 1961. ["A Reissue with the Author's Final Revisions." Earlier versions 1925, 1937.]

XV. Psychology

Bachelard, Gaston. *L'Air et les songes: Essai sur l'imagination du mouvement*. Paris: Corti, 1943.

—— *L'Eau et les rêves: Essai sur l'imagination de la matière*. Paris: Corti, 1942.

—— *La Psychanalyse du feu*. 4th ed. Paris: Gallimard, 1938.

—— *La Terre et les rêveries du repos*. Paris: Corti, 1948.

—— *La Terre et les rêveries de la volonté*. Paris: Corti, 1948.

Freud, Sigmund. *The Interpretation of Dreams*. Tr. A. A. Brill. London: Allen, 1913.

—— *Totem and Taboo: Resemblances Between the Psychic Lives of Savages and Neurotics*. Tr. A. A. Brill. New York: Moffat, Yard, 1918.

Jung, C. G. *Psychology and Alchemy*. Tr. R. F. C. Hull. (Bollingen Series, 12.) New York: Pantheon, 1953. [Bibliography.]

—— *Symbols of Transformation: An Analysis of the Prelude to a Case of Schizophrenia*. Tr. R. F. C. Hull. (Bollingen Series, 20.) (Original German edition, 1912.) New York: Pantheon, 1956.

Lawrence, D. H. *Fantasia of the Unconscious*. New York: Seltzer, 1922.

—— *Psychoanalysis of the Unconscious*. New York: Seltzer, 1921.

Rank, Otto. *The Myth of the Birth of the Hero: A Psychological Interpretation of Mythology*. Tr. F. Robbins and S. E. Jeliffe. (Original German edition, 1910.) New York: Brunner, 1952.

Silberer, Herbert. *Problems of Mysticism and Its Symbolism*. Tr. S. E. Jeliffe. New York: Moffat, Yard, 1917.

XVI. Single Archetypes and Myth-Figures

Butler, E. M. *The Myth of the Magus*. Cambridge: Cambridge Univ. Press, 1948.

Delcourt, Marie. *Hermaphrodite: Myths and Rites of the Bisexual Figure in Classical Literature*. Tr. Jennifer Nicholson. London: Studio Books, 1961

Hubaux, Jean, and Maxime Leroy. *Le Mythe du Phénix dans les littératures grecque et latine*. (Bibliothèque de la Faculté de philosophie et lettres de l'Université de Liège, 82.) Paris: Droz, 1939.

Kerényi, C. *Prometheus: Archetypal Image of Human Existence*. Tr. Ralph Manheim. (Bollingen Series, 65.) New York: Pantheon, 1963.

Le Comte, Edward S. *Endymion in England: The Literary History of a Greek Myth*. New York: King's Crown Press, 1944.

Palmer, Philip M., and R. P. More. *The Sources of the Faust Tradition, from Simon Magus to Lessing*. New York: Oxford Univ. Press, 1936.

Rougemont, Denis de. *Love in the Western World*. Tr. Montgomery Belgion. New York: Harcourt, Brace, 1940. [Tristan theme.]

Shepard, Odell. *The Lore of the Unicorn*. London: G. Allen, 1930.

Smith, Sir Grafton Elliot. *The Evolution of the Dragon*. London: Longmans, 1919.

Stanford, W. B. *The Ulysses Theme: A Study in the Adaptability of a Traditional Hero*. Oxford: Blackwell, 1954.

Tymms, R. *Doubles in Literary Psychology*. Cambridge: Bowes, 1949.

Weinstein, Leo. *The Metamorphoses of Don Juan*. (Stanford Studies in Lang. and Lit. 18.) Stanford, Calif.: Stanford Univ. Press, 1959.

XVII. Modern Myth-Critics

Bloom, Harold. *Shelley's Mythmaking*. New Haven: Yale Univ. Press, 1959.

Bodkin, Maud. *Archetypal Patterns in Poetry: Psychological Studies of Imagination*. London: Oxford Univ. Press, 1934.

Burke, Kenneth. *Grammar of Motives*. New York: Prentice-Hall, 1945.

—— *Rhetoric of Religion: Studies in Logology*. Boston: Beacon Press, 1961.

Campbell, Joseph. *The Hero with a Thousand Faces*. (Bollingen Series, 17.) New York: Pantheon, 1949.

Eliade, Mircea. *Myth and Reality*. Tr. Willard R. Trask. New York: Harper & Row, 1963.

—— *Patterns in Comparative Religion*. Tr. Rosemary Sheed. New York: Sheed & Ward, 1958.

Fergusson, Francis. *The Idea of a Theater: A Study of Ten Plays: The Art of Drama in Changing Perspective*. Princeton: Princeton Univ. Press, 1949.

Fletcher, Angus. *Allegory, the Theory of a Symbolic Mode*. Ithaca, N.Y.: Cornell Univ. Press, 1964.

Frye, Northrop. *Fearful Symmetry: A Study of William Blake*. Princeton: Princeton Univ. Press, 1947.

Graves, Robert. *The White Goddess: A Historical Grammar of Poetic Myth*. London: Faber, 1948.

Honig, Edwin. *Dark Conceit: The Making of Allegory*. London: Faber, 1959.

MacCaffrey, Isabel G. *Paradise Lost as "Myth."* Cambridge: Harvard Univ. Press, 1959.

Praz, Mario. *The Romantic Agony*. Tr. Angus Davidson. London: Oxford Univ. Press, 1933.

Stauffer, Donald. *The Golden Nightingale: Essays on Some Principles of Poetry in the Lyrics of W. B. Yeats*. New York: Macmillan, 1949.

Still, Colin. *Shakespeare's Mystery Play: A Study of* The Tempest. London: Palmer, 1921.

—— *The Timeless Theme: A Critical Theory Formulated and Applied*. London: Nicholson & Watson, 1936.

Vickery, John B., ed. *Myth and Literature: Contemporary Theory and Practice*. Lincoln: Univ. of Nebraska Press, 1966.

Wheelwright, Philip. *The Burning Fountain: A Study in the Language of Symbolism*. Bloomington: Indiana Univ. Press, 1954.

XVIII. American and Canadian Criticism

Chase, Richard. *Quest for Myth.* Baton Rouge: Louisiana State Univ. Press, 1949.

Fiedler, Leslie. *Love and Death in the American Novel.* New York: Criterion, 1960.

Jones, D. G. "The Sleeping Giant or the Uncreated Conscience of the Race." *Canadian Literature,* No. 26 (Autumn 1965), pp. 3-21.

Levin, Harry. *The Power of Blackness: Hawthorne, Poe, Melville.* New York: Knopf, 1958. [Bibliography.]

Lewis, Richard B. *The American Adam: Innocence, Tragedy and Tradition in the Nineteenth Century.* Chicago: Univ. of Chicago Press, 1955.

Marx, Leo. *The Machine in the Garden: Technology and the Pastoral Ideal in America.* New York: Oxford Univ. Press, 1964.

Matthiessen, F. O. *American Renaissance: Art and Expression in the Age of Emerson and Whitman.* London: Oxford Univ. Press, 1941.

Reaney, James. "The Canadian Poet's Predicament." *UTQ,* xxvi (April 1957), 284-295.

Smith, Henry Nash. *Virgin Land: The American West as Symbol and Myth.* Cambridge: Harvard Univ. Press, 1950.

Wilson, Milton. "Klein's Drowned Poet: Canadian Variations on an Old Theme." *Canadian Literature,* No. 6 (Autumn 1960), pp. 5-17.

Literature and Biography

By Leon Edel

Since biography is a department of literature, it will be proper to examine it not as a separate discipline, but as a form integral to literary study. It is not "extrinsic" to such study as is music, sociology, psychology, or religion. Even those biographies we cannot call works of art, the early crude forms, are still forms of literary narrative, fortuitously assembled chronicles incorporating literary texts, diaries, letters. The new criticism's "genetic" or "biographical" fallacy, if we should agree that such fallacy exists, applies only to the uses of biography in criticism, not necessarily in the wider study of literature, and—as I will try to show—only to certain kinds of biography.

I

In my Alexander Lectures delivered at the University of Toronto in 1956[1] I described three types of literary biography: the chronicle-compendium, the synthesized and summarized narrative (which might be termed the "organic" type), and the literary portrait. The three types are simply different ways of presenting the results of biographical research. The chronicle remains the classical form of biography in English, exemplified by Boswell and his successors. This type consists in the selection and arrangement, usually in strict chronological order, of extensive excerpts from documents, so tissued together as to constitute a continual narrative. Its guiding principle is the "showing" of the materials as if they were on exhibition. By providing sufficient background, explanation, appraisal, this creates the effect of a life seen from the cradle to the

[1] Later published as *Literary Biography* (London, Toronto, and New York), augmented and revised edition, 1959.

grave. The portrait or pictorial life emulates the plasticity and economy of the painter. Background is minimal, we are always in the foreground, character and personality are all-important. Geoffrey Scott's *Portrait of Zélide* is the prototype of this kind of biography in our time. Finally there is the "organic" biography, pioneered in this century by Lytton Strachey and Virginia Woolf: it is less than the chronicle-compendium, and more than the portrait. In this kind of work the biographer melts down his materials and recomposes the figure of the artist; he narrates the story in his own words; he finds a particular form to suit the subject; he may consult modern theories of behavior to better understand personality and character, and he uses quotation only when strictly relevant to his story, in order to enhance artistic effect. His biography is conceived and written as a work of art. It is imaginative in its construction and design; it differs from fiction in that its materials are not imagined.

Each of these types has its own validity; and when the chronicle (which by its nature is the least "structured" of the three) is written by a master, like Boswell, a singular portrait of a life and its times can be created within the massive documentation. But even in Boswell we know there was artful rearrangement, and some day I suspect it will be shown that veracity was sacrificed at times to creation of legend. Common to all types of biography is one continual danger—that of distortion. The chronicle is easily susceptible of this, for selection, arrangement, and juxtaposition of documents can "shape" an argument and even advance a thesis. The portrait makes no pretence of being anything but a personal eye-view of a life. The organic biography runs the gravest risks because it is all summary and synthesis and its quest for form may have its Procrustean side. In a word, there is no such thing as a completely "objective" biography, and any claim to the contrary looks aside from essential truths. We must recognize that a biography embodies within it a continuing quest for objectivity that may or may not culminate in a likeness; the best that can be said, when it has been written, is that it has achieved such a likeness; and our best way of recognizing its qualities lies in determining the reasonableness of appraisal, the judicial balance, the weighing of many alternative answers to often unanswerable questions, and the extent to which intelligent surmise has been used. The biographer cannot remove himself from the story; he is the arranger, the scene shifter, the omniscient author—although he cannot claim complete omniscience. One of his gravest risks is excessive admiration of his subject which may lead him to falsify unpleasant truths of character; another may be an animosity that prompts him to "debunk." The risks of distortion inevitably increase when archives are massive.

If we accept these premises, we must recognize that there is no such thing as a biography which allows the reader to deduce the portrait of the subject for himself. From the moment a reader does not have the total documentation available to him there is bound to be—whether by accident or design—some stacking of the cards; it is as if the reader were invited to take his seat in front of a canvas and were offered a selection of colors to paint his picture. Biographies which pretend to this kind of objectivity are founded on a spurious principle. The biographer, in asking the reader to do his own portrait, in reality abdicates his true role; he knows all the materials, but does not have the confidence to select and use them. Instead he hides behind some of them, as if he were a ventriloquist, and informs the reader that he is allowing the subject to speak for himself. Most readers, in truth, prefer to be told the story rather than to figure it out for themselves. Documents further are always suspect. Many have been fortuitously preserved and they never give us the entire picture; many contain deceptions, intended or unintended; many have been artfully created with an eye to posterity. They require the most careful analysis and explanation; and this task cannot be turned over to the reader. In the hands of amateurs, indolent scholars, individuals with limited understanding of character and personality, the compendium must be regarded with as much suspicion as other types of biography; it usually pretends to be the most truthful because its documents are copious. But it is less a compendium of "facts" than most of its readers suppose.

What all this reflects is considerable confusion about the nature of biography. Literary biography, in particular, has never developed a methodology or a theory; and it needs to be isolated from other kinds of biography because it deals usually with men of the armchair and the study rather than men in the great world of action. It is more often a biography of the imagination and the creative process than the story of an active life; there are exceptions to be sure, like Byron or Hemingway. More often the literary figure simply wrote and talked and meditated. In the past literary biography has been resourceful in research rather than in presentation; but the researches have dwelt on matters often extraneous to the inner creativity. Perhaps this kind of biography has for too long clung to the example of the exceptional Boswell and his exceptional subject. In our time it has to reckon with many new things, not only new approaches to modes of thought and experience, but even new and highly practical methods of research—the tape recorder, Xerox, the collating machine, X-rays, modern library methods; and high on the horizon there looms the computer. All this has greatly increased the problems of the biographer. He has, for instance, more material in his home than he used to have; in the older time he was forced to go to the records office or the research library and copy out relevant passages and summarize his materials. Xerox often brings these to his study; and to work in leisurely fashion, in the midst of such abundance, is an open invitation to prolixity and irrelevance. Biography has only begun to accommodate itself to its new tools.

II

In *Literary Biography* I adumbrated a methodology and it will be useful for the purposes of this essay if I summarize it here:

1. The modern biographer is faced, as I have said, with increasingly massive archives. Research libraries are encouraging writers to save their papers; whole libraries are devoted to the presidents of the United States. New means must be found to cope with such abundance. Boswell's methods no longer apply, since it is obvious that a high degree of selection is now imposed if any biographies are to be written at all. The new biographer must learn to extract the essence of his documents or risk being smothered by them.

2. It might therefore be argued that "organic" biographies will increasingly be written. Not everyone, to be sure, is artistically equipped to write such a biography with the skill of a Strachey or in conformity with the ideas Virginia Woolf advanced in some of her finest essays. Nevertheless some compromise between massive chronicle and greater synthesis should be possible. A study of the methods of Lytton Strachey and those who have followed him is therefore of the greatest importance. Strachey, for the first time in the history of biography, consciously worked as an artist. This is not to say that there had not been artistic biographies before him, but such happy individual accidents were born of arts possessed by the given writer. Strachey's emphasis on character, psychology, form, and brevity—that is, due proportion and the use of narrative skills—provided a distinctively new approach and suggested a unity and style hitherto absent from the majority of biographies. Although Strachey did not write of literary figures, his works are relevant to literary biography because of their artistry. The fact that his work is undermined by personal bias, destructive irony and malice, and a carelessness about historical fact does not invalidate his approach or his methods of presentation. As Lord David Cecil has said, biography since Strachey has become the newest of all the literary forms. While this applies largely to what I have called the "organic" biography, it offers important guidance to compendium-biographers, who may not possess the required narrative arts, but can profit by the ideal of synthesis and selectivity here exemplified.

3. The biographer now has access to psychological disciplines and certain analytic methods which, if properly used, may enable him to say with greater certainty which documents are relevant and which irrelevant. In particular, psychoanalysis offers the literary biographer a new way of reading novels, poems, plays as personal documents revelatory of their authors. The works contain, in their individuality and style, in their verbalizations, fancies, poetic or prose devices, the particular expression of a writer's character, his imagination, his modes of thought; his *persona* is concealed within the disguises he has assumed. All the voices in a

given poem are in the end also a single voice. The individuality of the writer offers the biographer a continuing exercise in analysis of text and a study in thematic apperception.

4. The work of the literary biographer and the work of the literary critic accordingly have much more in common than criticism has hitherto believed. When critics examine a poem they are examining a structure of words irradiated by a personality; and the irradiation is inescapable. It is so much a part of the work that no way has yet been devised for removing it in order to render the work totally impersonal. The critic studies the poem to arrive at a critical evaluation not only of word-structure but to see it as a human document designed for human uses, produced within a tradition and a living culture. The literary biographer does the same, save that in the end he seeks to discover and understand the individual whose imagination created the work. The old-fashioned Boswellian biography focused its attention on the external details of the writer's life, that is the personal habits and idiosyncrasies of the individual—"warts and all." The literary biographer, working with a Stracheyan economy, psychological tools, and the techniques of modern criticism, seeks to discover the imagination at its work. The warts are often irrelevant. "The thing incessantly overlooked," Wallace Stevens once remarked "[is] the presence of the determining personality." Thoreau said this in another way: "Poetry is a piece of very private history, which unostentatiously lets us into the secret of a man's life."

In the foregoing, I am not trying to suggest that a young literary biographer, who has read Kris or Erikson or certain volumes of Freud, is equipped *de chic* to speculate psychoanalytically about biographical-literary materials. The "psychographs" of the primitive period in psychoanalytic exploration, the thesis-biographies written around specific trauma by the early Freudians, the clinical case histories in the psychoanalytical journals have rightly made literary scholars wary. There is no question of "psychoanalyzing" a biographical subject; this is impossible once he is dead; and literary scholars are hardly qualified to psychoanalyze the living. What is involved is the understanding and use, with great discretion, of a sister discipline which can no longer be ignored—any more than we ignore any other discipline germane to the writing of a life. The military biographer must in effect learn his Clausewitz; the biographer of certain painters cannot ignore the methods of a Berenson; and the literary biographer today must make his peace with Freud and with the new ego psychology of Kris, Hartmann, and Lowenstein, as well as the important ideas of Harry Stack Sullivan and other modern theorists. Scholars still speak of the "limitations" of using psychoanalytic methods because of mistakes made four decades ago, and because of the tendency by psychoanalysts, who are fascinated by writers, to use literary lives in a highly clinical way in their work in "applied psychoanalysis." Certain kinds of psychological speculation are today possible and surely these are as permissible as any other kinds of speculation.

III

The relation between psychoanalysis and literary biography may be briefly summarized as follows:[2]

Literary art belongs to the most personal creation of man in the modern world. It draws upon the great mythical reservoir Jung has described and has in its backward reach the world's great anonymous, imaginative store of folk-literature. In our civilization, for many hundreds of years, we have come to attach the story-telling art in all its forms to the creating individual; we know it as his use of words to express feelings and experiences which have belonged to him but which he universalizes for us. The work in the end may be judged impersonal although it is not anonymous, and certainly we need not expect an author to supply his biography with it. But the same work is in a certain sense a kind of supreme biography of the artist and a projection of his *persona* in many disguises. It is in his work that the artist asserts himself; and it is in his work that he writes his name, records his voice, forges his personal style—his and no one else's—so that we identify it unmistakably. The descriptive adjectives, Shakespearean, Miltonic, Pateresque, Hawthornesque, testify to this.

If we examine the works of a poet or novelist (if possible in the sequence in which they were written), we can always discover an inner pattern. Due caution must be taken to read the pattern *out of* and not *into* the work. I speak inevitably of the writer of genius and not of the hack, that is, of the artist who produces out of personal necessity and not out of the expediencies of employment and the assignments of journalism. Psychoanalysis assumes that creative writers do their work out of profound inner dictates and in response to the ways in which their emotions and their views of the world have been formed. With all the world to choose from, they invariably select subjects closest to their inner feelings; and when they choose subjects seemingly alien to them, they invariably alter them to correspond to their personal condition, even though what emerges may seem, to the uninitiated, remote and unrelated. This is a fundamental belief of the modern study of behavior; and we can state it as a literary axiom. The subject selected by an artist more often than not reveals some emotion the writer had to express, some state of feeling,

---

[2] I am using here a discussion to be found in more extended form in the chapter on criticism in *Literary Biography*; also in my Library of Congress lecture "Willa Cather: The Paradox of Success" (1959). See also my essay on "The Biographer and Psychoanalysis" (1961).

some view of life, some inner conflict or state of disequilibrium in his being, which sought resolution in the form of art. In this sense it might be said that writers—and writers of fiction in particular—are always engaged in creating parables about themselves.

In seeking the innermost statement of poem or novel or play we are merely doing what has been obvious for a long time: we are asserting that a poem is the poet's and that the novel is the novelist's. No one but Proust could have written his work; and Swinburne's poetry is unlike any other in the English language. It is perhaps in the light of this that Stephen Spender recently wrote an essay urging critics to restore the poet to his poem. The poet belongs there because the poem is tissued out of his emotions and memories, memories of experience as well as of reading, stories lived and stories told. In stating this we reject the old notion that a story simply "flies" into a novelist's mind, or a poem into a poet's; that creation is a fortuitous circumstance, a happy inspiration. The inspiration is there, but it rises from within, no matter what outer circumstances may have prompted it. In using the psychoanalytic approach, literary biography thus focuses on the choices open to the artist and tries to determine from all the material in the text the relevance of these choices. What an artist chooses to say is as important as the ways in which he ultimately says it: the ways themselves constitute further choices of his imagination: form and style are autobiographical as well.

IV

The most serious objections made by critics to the use of psychoanalytic methods in literary biography are that the poem, the play, the novel, when created by a transfiguring imagination, does not record life but re-imagines it. One therefore does violence, it is argued, in trying to read literary texts as if they were autobiographical. These objections are reasonable when the works are read as if they literally reproduced life experience. But psychoanalysis is probing a more subterranean kind of experience: it reads the works not for their surface content but for what they may reveal of the writer's characteristic way of putting together a story, the situations he contrives, the solutions he offers, the kind of fantasy he "dreams." The surface experience in <u>Hemingway</u>, for example, is fairly obvious and dovetails with what we know about his career. But the problem of the literary biographer is to discern the swaggering masculinity that is the common denominator of Hemingway's writings, the fundamental attitude towards women implied in each work, the deeper meaning of a kind of story-telling which so consciously sought physical and sensory experience. Every writer's work is susceptible to this kind of analysis and this kind of questioning—(I cannot pretend to have exhausted the questions to be asked about Hemingway)—and the sum total of such probing would embody the fundamental truths of the writer's imaginative life. Indeed we arrive at a paradox: the greatest truths about his life are buried in a writer's work.

Willa Cather's story "Paul's Case" tells us more about her feelings during her life in Pittsburgh than her letters. In the letters she puts on a bold face to cover her inner despair. But the tale, together with evidence in other stories, suggests that she was profoundly unhappy with her boarding-house life and the drudgery of newspaper work. When she saw her friends, she gave them the impression of a great sense of release from the provincial life of Nebraska. The traditional biographer would have taken her letters and the reminiscences of those who knew her at face value; the new biographer is prompted to question this testimony because of what the work reveals. Miss Cather's personal malaise at this time is also suggested in the course her life took: she abandoned journalism and took up teaching; she extricated herself from boarding-house life by taking up residence in the home of a patroness of the arts; and in this way ultimately found conditions for work more congenial than the difficult existence which had caused her so much despair. A close reading of "Paul's Case" reveals evidence of such despair not available in the documents of Miss Cather's daily life.

Eugene O'Neill offers a more striking illustration. No one familiar with his early play, *Desire Under the Elms,* would have seen in it any particular autobiographical statement. It is a sordid play of a grasping New England farmer's conflict with his sons, his late marriage to a young woman, and the quasi-incestuous love affair of the youngest son with his stepmother, the birth of their child and its murder by the mother in a moment of fierce hate and guilt. But when, many years later, O'Neill's autobiographical play, *Long Day's Journey into Night,* was produced, it was possible to see how the disguises of art had masked much of O'Neill's experience—his deepest feelings—in *Desire Under the Elms.* The portrait of the farmer and his sons suggests the O'Neill family in *Long Day's Journey.* In both plays sons are in bitter feud with their fathers; and in the autobiography-play there is a bond of empathy between the young Eugene-character and his mother, as there is in *Desire* in the overt passion between the youngest son and the stepmother. In psychological terms it can be seen that what was only implicit in the autobiography—the deep attachment of the son for the mother—had been fully expressed in the earlier "unconscious autobiography" of *Desire.*[3]

More significantly we discover one autobiographical fact of importance in the work of O'Neill's imagination not contained in the candid autobiographical play. As the dramatist's second wife remarks in her memoirs: "Who, having seen *Long Day's Journey into Night* would ever

---

[3] See Philip Weissman, M.D., *Creativity in the Theatre* (1965), pp. 113-145.

realize that Edmund [Eugene], the youngest son, had been married and divorced, and was the father of a child nearly three years old, on that August evening in 1912," when the play takes place. Thus the incest, the child, O'Neill's complex attitude toward marriage and fatherhood are available in the play which is not consciously autobiographical, and are unavailable in the conscious autobiography. I suspect that many autobiographies are less "autobiographical" and candid than they pretend. They project a preferred self-image and often unconsciously (though sometimes deliberately) alter or omit parts of experience which we can discover reflected with great accuracy in the imagined creations. A work of art may thus be found to contain truths—and direct facts—which a biographer can hardly ignore.

Another fundamental question raised by criticism is that of the role in a writer's life of the ideas, traditions, conventions, to which he is heir. It is argued that there exists in every creative life a context of ideas and a *Zeitgeist* which are a part of the history of the writer. Should not his biography reckon with these? and are they not part of his conscious existence rather than the unconscious which psychoanalysis seeks to probe? The answer, fairly obviously, is that writers cannot avoid the spirit of their time or the traditions of their form. The new biography, however, asks for more than a mere recording of the writer's current intellectual or artistic background: it seeks to determine how—and in what manner—the available world has been transfigured; which ideas, conventions, traditions the writer has accepted and which rejected. In literary biography a writer's relationship to his time can be discovered in the sequence of his works. We not only are enabled to see growth and decline, but the ways in which the writer constantly reshapes his world. Great artists are not slaves of tradition or convention, they "use" them and modify them, often in the subtlest ways. A "sequential analysis" offers us the themes and variations of artistic fantasy. Critics who deal with isolated works and treat them as *de facto* structures of words forget that each work is a fragment of a large tapestry. This is particularly true with writers such as Yeats or James who lived and created continually, passing through many phases and transformations of their work—a reflection of transformations in their personalities. They reversed the usual conditions of creativity, creating their finest works in the periods of their physical decline. Their growth was irregular, their development unpredictable, and the continual weaving and reweaving of their thematic experience can only be understood in the light of the closest study of their evolution, decline, and renewed growth. No literary biography of either of these writers, and of others like them, is possible if the works are treated in isolation; no generalizations are possible about any given phase which are not often contradicted by other phases. Even though the single work may be regarded as sovereign, the works are members of a commonwealth, and they are subtly linked by the creative intelligence which fathered them even while functioning within traditions and conventions.

V

In the interest of clarity I will at this point summarize my argument: literature and biography are intimately related. The study of the one involves—directly and indirectly—the study of the other. The new biography seeks the characteristic modes of thought, perception, emotion in the writer—what might be called his whole operative imagination. His writings embody these in a manner more truthful than in the conscious statements he makes about himself. Indeed his entire use of conscious experience, of convention, tradition, personal relationships, behavior is illuminated by poem or tale or drama. Criticism offers one kind of analysis of these writings; modern studies in behavior and human motivation offer another. Psychoanalysis can be of assistance to both the biographer and the critic in working with the same materials. When I use the term psychoanalysis, I refer not to the therapeutic methods invented by Freud, but his insights into man's way of constructing his dreams and using symbols. The common ground of the literary discipline and that of psychoanalysis is man's capacity to create and use symbols. To examine the literary symbol, using either discipline, is to be involved in the primary stuff of creation.

All art, it follows, is personal and impersonal at the same time. We can most truthfully study literature when we link the poem to the poet, even as psychoanalysis never interprets a dream without the memories and associations of the dreamer. Criticism runs the risk of losing itself in conjecture and in empty formalism unless it verifies its own findings by consulting the poem's context. It must remember that the greatest artists have never divorced their creations from their operative imagination: Coleridge was fascinated by his mind's recesses; the autobiographies of Yeats and James are a veritable gloss to their writings; and T. S. Eliot, for all of his advocacy of the "impersonal," constantly probes his own experience in a vein of charming reminiscence in his critical writings. "A book," said Proust in challenging the biographical methods of Sainte-Beuve, "is the product of a different self from the one we manifest in our habits, in society, in our vices." Henry James was saying the same thing when he remarked that the literary artist "is present in every page of every book from which he sought so assiduously to eliminate himself." Eliot's formulation of the poem as the "objective correlative" of the poet's hidden emotions and ideas is in effect still another expression of the same thought. We might multiply examples, from Goethe's inquiry into "poetry and truth" to the Rousseau of his *Confessions*; few artists have failed to recognize the delicate bonds that unite their creations to their deepest feelings. For this reason, literary biography which deals exclusively with the externals of the artist's life, however interesting, is incomplete. The biography which looks also to the writings for its truths is more useful to literary study.

When it does this it supplies also important correctives to critical speculation. It provides checks against undue subjectivity on the part of the critic; it enables him to move, as did the creator, between the house of life and the house of art with greater sureness and authority. I wonder whether critics are aware of the extent to which biographical knowledge has enabled us, for instance, to take the true measure of so complex a figure as the author of *Ulysses*. The first critical reaction to Joyce was that he was a novelist of extraordinary imagination. Biographical evidence tended at a later stage to demonstrate the contrary, and to penetrate as well the elaborate legend with which Joyce and his acolytes surrounded his work. It demonstrated that Joyce did not have the particular kind of imagination by which novelists create and people an entire world —men like Scott, Dickens, Thackeray, Balzac, Tolstoy. Joyce hewed so closely to Dublin's realities that one-for-one equivalents are constantly found between his experience and what he set down in *Dubliners* and *Ulysses*. He himself called *A Portrait of the Artist as a Young Man* an autobiographical novel. There is an astonishing literalness in Joyce which exegesis by literary historians has disclosed. It showed also that Joyce's great power lay elsewhere than in the domain of fiction: he had a verbal and mythical imagination, akin to the poet's; and we have come to recognize that this is his truest claim to greatness and that *Finnegans Wake* is its fullest expression.

Sometimes criticism is so prolific, and so ingeniously speculative, that it swamps, by surfeit, the original work. A student encountering Henry James's "The Turn of the Screw" for the first time is confronted by so much critical opinion and such a tissue of guesswork as to be wholly bewildered. Theories about this enigmatic work have grown more and more elaborate; the governess is noble, the governess is mad; little Miles is wicked, little Miles is innocent; and some critics have even ventured to argue that at the end of the story Miles does not die, but lives to be the narrator of the story many years later. To have everything explained in a hundred different ways is in reality to have nothing explained. To eliminate the guesswork and the speculation from the valid and sensitive interpretations, we must apply the tests of literary biography and literary history. Anyone who is steeped in James can properly analyze James's comments on the story; he can also juxtapose James's theories about ghost stories; he can set this story into the important sequence of tales to which it belongs; he can see that the "recognition" scene, over which there has been so much argument, is tangential to any discussion of the governess' state of mind; and he can place this within James's theories of "point of view." But we can go further still. We can attempt to see what in James's character and personality was devious and indirect, and how he was led to the indirections of his art in "The Turn of the Screw." There is much in his life which can explain the intellectual structure of this tale and its uncanny subtleties. No mass of exegesis of a story in our time reveals to such an extent the irresponsibilities of criticism; and nothing could set these to right more easily than the established knowledge, abundantly documented, of the literary biographer.

Critical judgment, in other words, must accord with all that we know of a writer's temperament and the literary ambiance in which it functioned. As well discuss the leaf of a tree, having torn it from its twig, without saying that it is a leaf, and that it belongs to a particular tree. Criticism which insists on doing the minute and parochial thing gives us a microscopic study of the leaf without reference to anything else; it is a very small part of the literary study. And one of the saddest aspects of our modern emphasis on criticism is that we are now inundated with personal readings of texts which can be only as valuable as the reader. Biographical and historical evidence are the foundations upon which criticism can truly function. Without them we are in realms of gratuitous speculation and ultimately of critical anarchy.

The materials of biography and history must be used with great discipline. We should be as certain of our facts as we are of our text. Nothing else can have as great a value or authority in literary study as the text within its context. And in a time when there are more books than any one scholar can read, the process of critical selection and discrimination weighs upon us as a heavy and continual burden. All of Edmund Wilson's judgments as a critic are in constant relation to all the evidence available to him. That is why his literary criticism is among the most instructive of our time.

VI

Understood in this way the new biography comes closer to being intrinsic to literary study than the old biography; it is less irrelevant, and a great part of it is based on the common ground of critical and textual inquiry practiced by criticism itself. Certainly Cleanth Brooks was speaking entirely of the old concept of biography when he described it as an "appendage" to criticism with the implication that it has no organic relationship to it. Biography (and bibliography which is a part of the biographical record) provides the dates and sequences of publication, gives us possession of relevant contexts, occasionally illuminates obscurities in poem or novel, clearly defines the relationship between the life materials and the autobiographical elements in the text, where such a relationship may be required. It helps also to reveal the symbolic world of the writer and, by seeking for their inner context, can lessen the dangers of reckless interpretation or extension of the symbols to the faraway, impersonal ⎦ boundaries of myth and folklore.

There remains one question of the highest significance concerning literary biography. This is the criticism—repeatedly made—that it is "reductive," that it tends (no matter how subtle and probing it may be) to simplify the work and to rob the writer of all his mystery—of the aura of greatness which attaches to him, since we know him only through his imagination; that biography in other words reveals him to be a creature of flesh and blood.

One remembers how shy and unliterary the Faulkner of the drawing room was; one reads of Hawthorne's trouble in relating to his fellows; one recalls Joyce's difficulties in social situations. Or, reaching back to an earlier time, we recall the stories of how healthy and humdrum Browning was in London's great houses. Henry James wrote a story about him to suggest that there were two Brownings, the poet who stayed home and wrote his poetry, and the mortal *alter ego,* the healthy diner-out who talked about the weather and a thousand common things.

These objections are important. There is no doubt that literary biography, in revealing the writer within the work, dissipates certain mysteries—and mystery always adds a touch of wonder to our experience. So long as Robert Louis Stevenson was in Samoa, far from civilization, he was a figure to conjure with; and his works only added further mystery. But when he died and his letters and life were published, the legend disappeared. To say this is merely to say that all inquiry robs man of some of his mysteries. As critical inquiry unveils the mysteries of a text, so historical and biographical inquiries provide answers to other mysteries; in the process some of the magic is rubbed off. But knowledge and insight are gained.

Literary biography has to take this into account, nevertheless; and we have a recent example which suggests to us that it is possible for the biographer, in dissipating mysteries, to offer us in their place a picture of achievement and triumph which might compensate in some measure for what has been lost.

Whatever shortcomings Lord David Cecil's biography of Max Beerbohm may have, no one seems to have paid attention to the structure and form the biographer invented for his difficult materials. The form, in the end, may have been too large for the slight dapper figure, as W. H. Auden has argued; but its contours show an artistic hand, and if error there is, the portrait is still the work of a master-biographer. Indeed it is the art he has used which saves David Cecil's story, brings Max to life— as it happens, most unpleasantly for those who have cherished a very special place in their affections for him. I suspect those who have disliked the book did so because they ended by not liking Max—whom they had liked so much before. The nasty, aggressive side of Max's nature was suddenly revealed in all its juvenility. This is certainly embarrassing. The full portrait, however, happens to be biographical truth, and Lord David Cecil has indeed been, as Desmond MacCarthy said of biographers, an artist under oath.

Yet in a certain way, I suppose, it might be argued that the biography shows us Max's shortcomings without sufficiently making explicit how they were converted into his triumphs. The wonderful thing about Max Beerbohm was that possessing all those petty little traits, remaining as he did in his inner life an arrested little boy, he nevertheless developed a side which reached full maturity: that is, he found a way of meeting the world, and a style for everything he did, by which his petty aggressions and unpleasantness were harnessed and subdued, expressed with such charm and feeling and delicacy that usually Max's subjects themselves joined in the fun he was poking at them and recognized the high art of his caricatures. Max, the little boy incorporated in the fussily dressed adult, is almost intolerable; Max triumphant over the little boy in him, giving the world the gaieties of his wit and the felicities of his prose, is the true subject of the biography, for here he created his truest myth; here he transcends the forces that would have rendered him mediocre and mortal. We must judge biographies as different as Ellmann's Joyce and Painter's Proust by the same token: do we have a Joyce triumphant over his obsessions and compulsions, his pedantry and his literalness, the Joyce of the high verbal imagination, who plucked time out of eternity and whose myth-creating vision recognized the life cycles and the many-hued symbol of the dream? Are we to have the poor sad sickly Proust, the allergy-ridden little man with his psychosexual wounds, or the Proust who created out of suffering and discipline the beauties of his past and made the sensitivities of his illness the sensitivities of his art? If the biographer gives us a picture of a warped and damaged man instead of the artist within, he indeed performs an act which may be called "reductive." But if he shows the heroism of the artist overcoming the assaults of his existence and triumphing over the drives that would destroy the best in himself—so common in the pathology of art—then we have a true literary biography, the only one worth writing, indeed the only one which genuinely lives up to its name. Such a biography achieves its primary purpose of being a work of literary art; and works of literary art—need I add?—are the foundation stones of literary study.

Bibliographical Note

While there have been many volumes written about biography, the subject of "literary" biography—that is of the writing of the lives of writers—has not been isolated, and so far as I know my Alexander Lectures, *Literary Biography* (Toronto, 1957; New York, 1959), represented the first such attempt. It is to be noted that as late as 1948 Wellek and Warren in *Theory of Literature* were pointing out that general biographical theory had not distinguished between the lives of literary artists and the lives of other figures. "In the view of a biographer," they wrote, "the poet is simply another man whose . . . life can be reconstructed and can be evaluated." They added that "no methodological distinction" exists for literary biography.

A valuable history of literary biography has since been published by Richard D. Altick, *Lives and Letters* (New York: Knopf, 1965). Two authoritative historical works on early English biography were written by the late Donald O. Stauffer: *English Biography before 1700* (Cambridge, Mass., 1930) and *The Art of Biography in 18th Century England*, 2 vols. (Princeton, N.J., 1941). Edgar Johnson's survey, *One Mighty Torrent,* originally published in New York in 1937 and republished in 1955, includes autobiography, memoirs, diaries, and letters. Autobiography has been studied by Wayne Shumaker in *English Autobiography: Its Emergence, Materials and Form* (Berkeley, Calif., 1954).

Lytton Strachey's preface to *Eminent Victorians* (London, 1918) contains an admirable and much-quoted statement on biography. One might consider it as an informal manifesto for modern biography. His miscellaneous essays and book reviews also contain many suggestive ideas on the biographical art.

Virginia Woolf's essays on biography were grouped together in *Granite and Rainbow* (New York, 1958), a posthumous volume edited by Leonard Woolf. This contains 14 papers on the subject; but her discussion of the art is to be found in other of her writings and in her experiments in biographical forms, including the fantasy *Orlando* (1928) and her *jeu d'esprit*—the life of Elizabeth Barrett Browning's dog *Flush* (1933). Her only conventional biography was that of her friend Roger Fry (1940). An account of the writing of this work is contained in Leon Edel, "Biography: The Question of Form," published in *Friendship's Garland* (essays in tribute to Mario Praz) (Rome, 1966), II, 343-360.

A valuable survey of biography in general is to be found in Harold Nicolson, *The Development of English Biography*, Hogarth Lectures, No. 4 (London, 1927). André Maurois's *Aspects de la biographie* (Paris, 1928) contains the six Clark Lectures he delivered at Cambridge University during May 1928.

An extensive bibliography on the subject is contained in John A. Garraty, *The Nature of Biography* (New York, 1957), in his "Essay on Sources," pp. 261-

289. Finally there exists an admirable anthology of biographers' writings about biography compiled by James L. Clifford, *Biography as an Art* (Oxford, 1962).

Overlooked by most biographers is Sigmund Freud's significant statement on biography contained in his address of acceptance of the Goethe medal conferred upon him by Frankfurt in 1930. This can be read in the standard edition of Freud's works, in the English translation, published by the Hogarth Press, XXI (London, 1961), 208-212.

Literature and Psychology

By Frederick C. Crews

I must begin by explaining a drastic simplification of my topic.[1] Despite the fact that psychoanalysis has weaker empirical credentials than the experimental schools that prevail in American universities,[2] "psychology" will here be contracted to mean psychoanalysis. There are several reasons for this, beyond a wish to avoid the spirit of meandering tourism. Psychoanalysis is the only psychology to have seriously altered our way of reading literature, and this alteration is little understood by the affected parties. To dwell at length on the possible literary implications of physiological psychology, of perception and cognition psychology, or of learning theory would be to say more than the psychologists themselves have been able to say. Even Gestalt psychology, which does promise enlightenment about the perception of artistic form, has told us virtually nothing about literature.[3] We must give our attention here to those who have claimed it.

[1] I am grateful for the useful comments of Professors Norman N. Holland, Simon O. Lesser, and Leonard F. Manheim. Work on this chapter was greatly facilitated by a Humanities Research Fellowship from the University of California, an ACLS Study Fellowship, and a Fellowship of the Center for Advanced Study in the Behavioral Sciences, Stanford, California. All benefactors are hereby thanked.

[2] For a schematic analysis of the present status of psychoanalysis, see Gardner Murphy, "The Current Impact of Freud on American Psychology," *Freud and the Twentieth Century,* ed. Benjamin Nelson (New York, 1957), pp. 102-122.

[3] This fact may be attributable to the lack of allowance for dynamic factors in Gestalt psychology, coupled with an exclusion of thematic considerations, a tendency to elevate "good Gestalt" (whole form) into a criterion of excellence,

Frederick C. Crews

The historical prominence of psychoanalysis in literary studies is readily understandable. Literature is written from and about motives, and psychoanalysis is the only thoroughgoing theory of motives that mankind has devised. The moment we perceive that works of art can express emotional conflict, or that they contain latent themes, or that their effect on us is largely subliminal, we have entered the realm of interest that is uniquely occupied by Freudianism and its offshoots. The psychoanalyst offers us, with a presumption we are likely to resent, a view of the writer's innermost preoccupations, a technique for exposing those preoccupations behind the defenses erected against them, and a dynamic explanation of how the literary work is received and judged. It is not merely that literature illustrates psychoanalytic ideas, as it does the ideas of other systems, but that the psychoanalyst alone undertakes to find motives for every rendered detail.

Needless to say, literary people have been anxious to debate the validity of such awesome claims. Much of the debate, however, has been acrimonious and irrelevant, thanks partly to the embarrassing subject matter of psychoanalysis and partly to professional rivalry. The traditional critic sees the analyst as an uninvited guest whose muddy boots will smudge the figure in the carpet; the analyst pities the critic his inhibitions and offers him sexual enlightenment free of charge. And both of them frequently speak of psychoanalysis as if it were contained in the personality and tastes of its founder, who still evokes obedience or hostility nearly three decades after his death. If we are to do any better here, it might be well to review the nature of Freud's interest in literature and make a sharp distinction between this interest and the independent possibilities of psychoanalysis in the hands of a literary critic.

We may say that literary people have taken offense at both the special presumptions and the special successes of Freud. Profoundly influenced though he was by Sophocles, Shakespeare, Dostoevsky, and Ibsen, Freud had little patience with what we like to call the integrity of

---

and an incapacity to deal with the cumulative and reflective sense of form involved in reading. But see Herbert J. Muller, *Science and Criticism: The Humanistic Tradition in Contemporary Thought* (New Haven, 1943), pp. 157-167; H. E. Rees, *A Psychology of Artistic Creation as Evidenced in Autobiographical Statements of Artists* (New York, 1942); Werner Wolff, *The Expression of Personality: Experimental Depth Psychology* (New York, 1943); and E. H. Gombrich, *Art and Illusion: A Study in the Psychology of Pictorial Representation* (New York, 1960). For a psychoanalytic critique of Gestalt art theory see Anton Ehrenzweig, *The Psycho-Analysis of Artistic Vision and Hearing* (London, 1953). Recent evidence that "active perception" psychology may illuminate literary form is offered by Morse Peckham in *Man's Rage for Chaos; Biology, Behavior, and the Arts* (Philadelphia, 1965).

the work of art. The work, in Philip Rieff's explanation, "is something to see through; it is presumably best explained by something other than— even contradicting—itself. Every work of art is to Freud a museum piece of the unconscious, an occasion to contemplate the unconscious frozen into one of its possible gestures."[4]

Thus Freud was interested not in art but in the latent meaning of art, and then only for illustrative purposes. Like dreams, myths, and fairy tales, works of art supplied useful evidence of the primordial and monotonous fantasies of mankind, and of the processes of condensation, displacement, and symbolism through which those fantasies are both expressed and disguised. Such an emphasis is insulting to the artist, who *thought* he knew what he meant to say, and to the moral or formal critic, who prefers to dwell on what Freud regards as peripheral "manifest content" and "secondary elaboration." And the insult is compounded by its success. We may assume that if Freud had been wholly mistaken in his notion of buried themes, he would long since have ceased to provoke defenders of literary tradition into outbursts against "reductionism," "pan-sexualism," and "psychoanalyzing the dead."

Freud's challenge to the creator and the lover of literature is not contained merely in his undermining of surface effects and stated intentions. The artist, Freud tells us, has "an introverted disposition and has not far to go to become neurotic. He is one who is urged on by instinctual needs which are too clamorous; he longs to attain to honour, power, riches, fame, and the love of women; but he lacks the means of achieving these gratifications. So . . . he turns away from reality and transfers all his interest, and all his libido too, on to the creation of his wishes in the life of phantasy, from which the way might readily lead to neurosis."[5] If, as an heir of the Romantic movement, Freud sometimes credited art with visionary truth, as a bourgeois, a scientist, and a utilitarian he suspected it of unreality and evasion.[6]

Thus the literary critic is not altogether wrong in seeing Freud as a disrespectful intruder. Yet to move from perceiving this to denying the relevance of dynamic psychology to criticism is, to say the least, a hasty step. We are free to use Freud's interpretive techniques without endors-

[4] *Freud: The Mind of the Moralist* (New York, 1959), p. 121.

[5] *A General Introduction to Psychoanalysis,* tr. Joan Riviere (New York, 1960), p. 384.

[6] For Freud's Romanticism see Rieff, pp. 204-219, 345 f., and Ernest Jones, *The Life and Work of Sigmund Freud,* 3 vols. (New York, 1953-57), I, 28-30. For his reflection of both artistic and bourgeois ideals see Lionel Trilling, "Art and Neurosis," *The Liberal Imagination: Essays on Literature and Society* (Garden City, N.Y., 1953), pp. 159-178, and Norman N. Holland, *Psychoanalysis and Shakespeare* (New York, Toronto, London, 1966), pp. 9-44.

ing his competitive and ambivalent remarks about artists. Post-Freudian psychoanalysis, furthermore, offers theoretical grounds for taking the consciously "adaptive" aspect of literature more seriously than Freud did, and Freud's own views lead us beyond the static "museum piece" criticism he usually practiced. Tempting as it is to dispose of a complex and disturbing subject by means of *ad hominem* ridicule, such a method of argument is unworthy of scholars.

Everything hinges on whether psychoanalysis gives a true or sufficiently inclusive account of mental processes—a question that obviously cannot be settled here. Certainly it would be futile to cajole the reader who has decided that his own common sense is psychology enough. Yet most literary students, I feel, are of two minds about psychoanalysis; they may be impressed by its wide acceptance but reluctant to undertake an arduous and confusing course of reading. To justify this reluctance they vaguely entertain some of the many persisting grievances against psychoanalysis and psychoanalytic criticism. In order to put the matter on more rational grounds I propose to review the most common of these grievances and ask whether they do in fact warrant the theoretical neglect of a field which has already influenced our critical practice— often, to be sure, in a surreptitious or ignorantly popularized way. Before turning to literary applications I shall deal with prevalent objections to psychoanalysis as a body of knowledge:

1. *Being unverified and unverifiable by experiment, psychoanalysis cannot be called a science at all. It is simply a technique of therapy, or a system of metaphors.*

It is in the nature of all experiments that variables be kept to a minimum and that the path of inference from effect to cause be fairly direct. Any theory of complex and dynamic mental acts, and especially one that includes an idea of unconscious "overdetermination," must therefore remain largely unverified by experiment. Yet it is questionable whether this is a telling point against psychoanalysis. The psychological school which most insists on laboratory verification, namely Behaviorism, has necessarily confined most of its researches to animals and to relatively simple problems of stimulus and response. The gain in verifiability is achieved at the cost of never approaching the complexity of uniquely human motives.

In any case it is incorrect to say that psychoanalysis remains wholly unverified. Certain of its aspects *have* been tested by experiment, and have withstood as much scrutiny as experiment could cast on them.[7] De-

[7] See E. Pumpian-Mindlin, ed., *Psychoanalysis as Science: The Dixon Lectures on the Scientific Status of Psychoanalysis* (Stanford, 1952). Recent years have seen a certain *rapprochement* between those psychoanalysts who are sensitive

spite some overpublicized defections, furthermore, the confirmation and refinement of Freud's discoveries have been proceeding in a fairly orderly way for many years; the essential concepts of psychoanalysis have been adequate to characterize the findings of innumerable independent workers. Corroboration of unconscious themes and processes is also offered by an abundance of materials external to the analytic experience: jokes and errors, primitive institutions and ritual, myths, and of course literature itself. For an unverified science psychoanalysis has had a remarkably profound effect on such apparently unrelated disciplines as anthropology, sociology, and educational theory. While the literary scholar is righteously declaring himself free of Freudian influence, his wife may be absorbing it in homeopathic doses from Dr. Spock.

The charge that psychoanalysis is metaphorical is true but easily misinterpreted. Such concepts as id, ego, and superego are not meant to describe physiological entities but spheres of interest that must be postulated to account for the observed fact that mental acts express compromised intentions.[8] Curiously enough, the most questionable part of psychoanalysis in the eyes of many post-Freudians is its least metaphorical, most biological side, namely the theory of instinctual psychic energy.[9] The strength of psychoanalysis may be said to lie in the precision of its metaphors—by which I mean their capacity for economically describing a vast range of evidence for which no other descriptive terms have been found. Where those metaphors need further refinement, as in the unwieldy overlapping of "topographic" and "structural" systems, the task will not be to adopt a more physical vocabulary but to achieve a parsimony of inferred concepts.[10]

2. *The layman has no basis for choosing among the many schismatic sects of psychoanalysis, and so should ignore them until they settle their differences.*

---

to empirical criticism and those academic psychologists who are weary of the stimulus-response rat race. One promising meeting-ground is the building of conceptual models that combine mental processes which have been experimentally verified in piecemeal form. See especially Gerald S. Blum, *A Model of the Mind: Explored by Hypnotically Controlled Experiments and Examined for its Psychodynamic Implications* (New York and London, 1961), and Silvan S. Tomkins and Samuel Messick, eds., *Computer Simulation of Personality: Frontier of Psychological Theory* (New York and London, 1963).

[8] For a defense of the role of metaphors in science see Abraham Kaplan, *The Conduct of Inquiry: Methodology for Behavioral Science* (San Francisco, 1964).

[9] I am referring not only to Freud's late, much-criticized reduction of all instincts to Eros and Death, but also to his hydraulic account of quantities of libido. One group of adaptational psychologists, for example, holds that "It is

This would be sound advice if there were any likelihood that individual psychoanalysts, ambitious of glory, would stop founding new ideologies on isolated portions of theory. The student who cannot wait forever to decide what to think about human motivation must try as best he can to discriminate between such popular ideologies and genuinely empirical critiques of psychoanalysis (like those cited in footnotes 7, 9, and 10). If, for example, a rival system has had no medical consequences and has become a program of secular salvation rather than of therapy; if it has abandoned or attenuated the idea of dynamic conflict in favor of a monolithic and omnipresent explanation (trauma of birth, inferiority complex, collective unconscious, etc.); if it depends upon the support of religious and literary pieties and moral commonplaces divorced from clinical evidence—then, I think, suspicion is demanded. The literary student seems peculiarly vulnerable to pseudo-scientific improvements of psychoanalysis which dispense with sexual nastiness and glorify creativity. "Of the artist's relations to the psychologist," Edward Glover has written, "it can be said with some justice that their cordiality is in inverse ratio to their depth."[11]

This is not to say that one may fall back on Freudian orthodoxy as if it were revealed truth. Like all systems originating in a feeling for the indescribable, psychoanalysis has seen its metaphors reified, its hypotheses hardened into dogma, and its particular area of interest mistaken for total existence. Freud himself was not always above these tendencies, and few of his followers have shared his grasp of the difference between psychological reality and the conceptual framework needed for discussing that reality. Furthermore, on the positive side, present-day psychoanalysis has passed beyond Freud's almost exclusive emphasis on instinctual demands and infantile traumas to consider adaptive functions at all stages of development. The result remains "Freudian"—nearly all the principles of ego psychology are derived from hints in Freud's later writ-

---

irrelevant to our clinical understanding to posit an energy whose existence can never be demonstrated for behavior which is meaningful only in terms of motivation, psychologic mechanism, and ultimate action"—that is, in the other terms of psychoanalysis. See Abram Kardiner, Aaron Karush, and Lionel Ovessey, "A Methodological Study of Freudian Theory," *Journal of Nervous and Mental Disease,* cxxix (July-October 1959), 11-19, 133-143, 207-221, 341-356. Other cogent attacks on Freudian neurophysiology, delivered from a standpoint of sympathy toward the behavioral observations of psychoanalysis, may be found in Norman S. Greenfield and William C. Lewis, eds., *Psychoanalysis and Current Biological Thought* (Madison and Milwaukee, Wis., 1965).

[10] Significant critiques of the higher-level abstractions of psychoanalysis may be found in Heinz Hartmann, Ernst Kris, and Rudolph M. Loewenstein, "Comments on the Formation of Psychic Structure," *The Psychoanalytic Study of the Child,* II (1946), 11-37; Kenneth Mark Colby, *Energy and Structure in Psycho-*

ings—but not in the reductive sense that has most frequently alienated non-Freudians. By reference to the so-called "conflict-free sphere of the ego," analysts now take better account of normal mental processes. Mastery of conflict is now as prominent as submission to conflict—a fact of moment for students of artistic creativity.

When this shift is considered along with Freud's own reformulations from decade to decade, the layman will feel properly discouraged from using any single text as his guide to psychoanalysis. If he intends to involve himself in the subject at all he had better be resigned to plodding through a certain amount of dreary polemics. Fortunately, however, clear explanations of the progress and quarrels of psychoanalysis are readily available and may be used to supplement a reading of one of Freud's sets of introductory lectures, which remain the most engaging means of initiation.[12]

I turn now to objections to the effect of psychoanalytic ideas and methods on literary criticism:

3. *The psychoanalytic view of the writer as a neurotic is presumptuous and condescending. Psychoanalysis is unequipped to describe the way writers really work.*

Even Freud was careful never to say that the artist is directly neurotic, and he admitted—perhaps hastily, many now feel—that psychoanalysis "can do nothing towards elucidating the nature of the artistic gift, nor can it explain the means by which the artist works—artistic technique."[13] Certainly Freud's disproportionate emphasis on unconscious factors had a pernicious effect on the first ventures into psychoanalytic criticism. Ludicrous diagnoses of writers' mental diseases, uninfluenced by historical or biographical knowledge or by literary taste, continue to appear regularly in the pages of clinical journals. Yet these

---

analysis (New York, 1955); David Rapaport, *The Structure of Psychoanalytic Theory* (New York, 1960); Peter Madison, *Freud's Concept of Repression and Defense* (Minneapolis, Minn., 1961); and Merton M. Gill, *Topography and Systems in Psychoanalytic Theory* (New York, 1963). Regrettably, the preponderance of clinical and theoretical writing shows that such clarifications have been unheeded.

[11] *Freud or Jung* (London, 1950), p. 165.

[12] See Freud, *A General Introduction to Psychoanalysis* (New York, 1920), *New Introductory Lectures on Psycho-Analysis* (New York, 1933), and *An Outline of Psychoanalysis* (London, 1939). The first work takes fullest account of the skeptical reader's doubts, but lacks reference to Freud's important concept of the superego. Charles Brenner's *An Elementary Textbook of Psychoanalysis* (New York, 1955) repairs this and other omissions. However far the student continues his reading, he should not overlook Freud's early masterpiece, *The Interpretation of Dreams* (1900; James Strachey's translation of 1953 is now a paperback, New York, 1965). Useful surveys of the movement's bewildering history are Ruth L.

efforts are more than bad criticism, they are bad psychology as well. It cannot be too strongly affirmed that psychoanalytic theory, especially in recent years, finds no necessary connection—at the most a useful analogy—between artistic production and the production of neurotic symptoms.

This analogy rests on the supposition that both art and neurosis originate in conflict and may be conceived as ways of managing it. But whereas the neurotic's solution is the helplessly regressive and primitive one of allowing repressed ideas to break into a disguised expression which is satisfying neither to the neurotic himself nor to others, the artist has the power to sublimate and neutralize conflict, to give it logical and social coherence through conscious elaboration, and to reach and communicate a sense of catharsis. The chief insistence on creative strength—on the artist's innate capacity for sublimation, his ability to handle dangerous psychic materials successfully—has come from within the psychoanalytic movement, not from outraged traditionalists. In truth, the theory that the artist is an especially morbid type antedates psychoanalysis and serves the very un-Freudian purpose of exaggerating the non-artist's freedom from conflict. It is thus a form of philistinism—one to which bad psychoanalysts have been susceptible but which is contrary to the whole spirit of the movement. "Of all mental systems," Lionel Trilling has justly written, "the Freudian psychology is the one which makes poetry indigenous to the very constitution of the mind. Indeed, the mind, as Freud sees it, is in the greater part of its tendency exactly a poetry-making organ."[14]

In a psychoanalytic view the artist is exceptionally able to make imaginative use of capacities which are present in everyone, but which are largely unavailable to expression in the non-creative man and are bound to self-destructive strife in the neurotic. The artist may, of course,

---

Munroe, *Schools of Psychoanalytic Thought: An Exposition, Critique, and Attempt at Integration* (New York, 1955), and J. A. C. Brown, *Freud and the Post-Freudians* (London, 1961). Edward Glover's *Freud or Jung* (London, 1950), while hardly impartial, is indispensable for an understanding of the logical incompatibility of two systems which literary people sometimes tolerantly blend. A rigorous but non-clinical critique of the Freudian revisionists is to be found in Herbert Marcuse, *Eros and Civilization: A Philosophical Inquiry into Freud* (New York, 1962), pp. 217-251. Among the numerous books about Freud himself, Philip Rieff's *Freud: The Mind of the Moralist* (New York, 1959) is perhaps the most helpful in placing psychoanalysis in the context of the intellectual and scientific history and the ethical assumptions from which it emerged. See also Ernest Jones's biography, cited above, n. 6.

[13] *An Autobiographical Study* (London, 1948), p. 119.

[14] "Freud and Literature," *The Liberal Imagination*, p. 60.

be impelled by a certain degree of neurotic conflict to submit himself to unconscious dictates; this corresponds to the undeniable observation that great numbers of artists *are* neurotic. But neurosis alone cannot produce art and is inimical to the preconscious elaboration and the sublimation that make art possible. Insofar as he is neurotic, therefore, the artist is deficient in the functions that distinguish art from symptom-formation.[15]

This is not to say, of course, that we are free after all to treat artistic creation and the aesthetic experience as special events in which the laws of mental dynamics are suspended. Many literary scholars are eager to believe those psychologists who, like C. G. Jung and his followers, sweep the element of personal conflict out of view and thus prepare the way for a mystic reverence for artistic truth.[16] But the literary work which is completely free from its biographical determinants is not to be found, and in many of the greatest works—the prime example is *Hamlet* —unresolved emotion and latent contradiction are irreducibly involved in the aesthetic effect. To appreciate why there are gaps in the surface we must be prepared to inspect what lies beneath them.

An aesthetic theory which ignores the possibility that latent and manifest content, unconscious and conscious purpose may be imperfectly harmonized is, to my mind, more reductive than a theory in which art represents a complex, "overdetermined" adjustment of varying psychic interests. One must decide whether to see art as a mental activity or as a direct apprehension of truth and beauty. The former attitude is less exalted, but it leaves the critic freer to trace the actual shape of a work, including its possible double meanings or confusions and its shifts of intensity and mood. The final word on the tiresome debate about art and neurosis should be that art need not express neurotic traits, but may very well do so in any individual case; the critic must wait and see.[17]

[15] See Glover, pp. 185 f.; Louis Fraiberg, "Psychology and the Writer: The Creative Process," *Literature and Psychology*, v (November 1955), 72-77, and "New Views of Art and the Creative Process in Psychoanalytic Ego Psychology," *Literature and Psychology*, xi (Spring 1961), 45-55; Ernst Kris, *Psychoanalytic Explorations in Art* (London, 1953), pp. 13-63; and Lawrence S. Kubie, *Neurotic Distortion of the Creative Process* (Lawrence, Kan., 1958), passim.

[16] See, e.g., Erich Neumann, *Art and the Creative Unconscious* (London, 1959). Neumann's attack on the "personalistic" approach enables him to argue that art communicates "numinous" archetypal powers which "are eternal, and . . . touch upon the eternal existence of man and the world" (p. 129). This is not psychology but Neo-Platonism—a fact that becomes especially clear when Neumann praises Beethoven for "a break-through into the realm of essence" (p. 103). For a defense of the Jungian position, however, see Morris Philipson, *Outline of a Jungian Aesthetics* (Evanston, Ill., 1963). The outstanding Jungian contribution to

4. Psychoanalytic criticism neglects literary form, reduces all writers to an undifferentiated substratum of sexual obsession, and discards a writer's stated intention for a supposed unconscious one.

If this is taken as a description of much psychoanalytic criticism to date, rather than a statement of inherent limitations in the psychoanalytic attitude, then I must agree that it is accurate. Unfortunately, most literary people do not recognize this distinction; the "Freudian reductionist" is used as a scarecrow to protect the scholar's private harvest of literary history or factual detail or didactic moralism. It is true, of course, that a critical method which seizes upon a few unconscious themes and pronounces them the whole meaning of the work is grossly levelling; it is also true that Freud's technique of dream interpretation lends a certain inadvertent sanction to this approach. But the differences between dream and literature have long been recognized, as have the differences of purpose between the psychoanalyst, who is interested only in the mind that produced the dream or poem, and the critic, who must respect the object itself—including the elements in it which the analyst would regard merely as subterfuge. To say that psychoanalytic criticism *cannot* do justice to literary complexity is to suppose, as the worst psychoanalytic critics do, that an interest in psychological evidence can have no other purpose than to explain away manifest emphasis.

In shifting toward ego psychology, psychoanalytic theory has become better adapted to a study of the higher mental processes that enter into artistic creation, and to recognition of a communicative as well as a self-expressive function. It was a psychoanalyst, Ernst Kris, who insisted that the "reality" from which a literary creation proceeds is not only the reality of the author's drives and fantasies, but also the structure of his artistic problem and the historical state of his genre.[18] Indeed, nothing (other than inadequate acquaintance with tradition) prevents the psychoanalytic critic from considering exactly the same factors that concern the literary, the social, and the intellectual historian. As psychoanalysis has approached a point of reconciliation with social psychology, so too have psychoanalytic critics begun to turn their attention to broader mat-

---

criticism (its references to Freud are merely courteous, not eclectic) is Maud Bodkin, *Archetypal Patterns in Poetry: Psychological Studies of Imagination* (London, 1934). See also Jolande Jacobi, *Complex / Archetype / Symbol,* tr. Ralph Manheim (New York, 1959).

[17] See, however, William Phillips' judicious caution against using terms like "neurotic" and "healthy" to characterize works of art. *Art and Psychoanalysis,* ed. William Phillips (Cleveland and New York, 1963), "Introduction: Art and Neurosis," pp. xii-xxiv. This paperback anthology is the best of several available collections of psychoanalytic criticism.

[18] *Psychoanalytic Explorations in Art,* p. 15.

ters than the unconscious fixations of a few unhappy writers. There have been numerous recent attempts to define the psychological quality of entire genres and movements, and even to take a psychological view of forces operating through history.[19] Nor has the psychology of form and style remained unexamined. Kenneth Burke—himself a Freudian of a maverick sort—once defined form as "an arousing and fulfillment of desires."[20] The idea has been pursued by several investigators, perhaps most successfully by Simon O. Lesser.[21] Form is being increasingly recognized not only as an aid to perception but as a vehicle of pleasure, including the pleasure of reducing the anxieties that other aspects of the work bring into play.

As for the author's stated intention, the subtlest modern critics have rightly placed little value on it—but not always for good reasons. The most celebrated dogma of the New Criticism has been that statements made before or after the literary fact must be considered less reliable than statements inferred from the text. All too often, however, this sound principle allows the critic to overstate the work's unity of effect or to drain off its passion and leave behind only a fragile tissue of symbols. By invoking the Intentional Fallacy the critic may fail to consider divisions of intention that are intrinsic to the work's structure and effect. I submit that we are entitled to consider *both* overt purpose and the perhaps contradictory purpose (or purposes) that may emerge from imagery or the shape of a plot. Psychoanalytic criticism has customarily occupied itself with the latter sort alone, but here too the historical reasons for this bias have lost their strength. In principle at least, the theory of overdetermination should enable us to feel more at home with literary tensions and contradictions than the critic who is searching only for leading ideas or unitary "meaning."

[19] Representative examples of the recent interest in the psychology of genres and movements are F. L. Lucas, *Literature and Psychology* (London, 1951), Ernst Kris, *Psychoanalytic Explorations in Art* (London, 1953), Simon O. Lesser, *Fiction and the Unconscious* (Boston, 1957), William Wasserstrom, *Sex and Sentiment in the Genteel Tradition* (Minneapolis, Minn., 1959), Leslie A. Fiedler, *Love and Death in the American Novel* (New York, 1960, 1966), Irving Malin, *New American Gothic* (Carbondale, Ill., 1962), and Angus Fletcher, *Allegory: The Theory of a Symbolic Mode* (Ithaca, N. Y., 1964). For psychoanalytic approaches to history itself see Erik H. Erikson, *Young Man Luther: A Study in Psychoanalysis and History* (New York, 1958), Norman O. Brown, *Life Against Death: The Psychoanalytical Meaning of History* (Middletown, Conn., 1959), and Bruce Mazlish, ed., *Psychoanalysis and History* (Englewood Cliffs, New Jersey, 1963). Erikson's work in particular is an eloquent refutation of the opinion that psychoanalytic premises necessarily make for a reductive view of events (including literary events) which demand interpretation on several levels.

5. *It is impossible to psychoanalyze dead writers, and anachronistic to apply Freudian rules to writers who lived before Freud.*

Freud himself maintained the former truism, though he egregiously violated it in his study of Leonardo. There is a difference, however, between guessing at the infantile sources of trauma in an absent figure and identifying general psychological themes in a literary document. Freud's brilliant essay on Dostoevsky provides a model of the latter, more legitimate, kind of investigation.[22] To be sure, Freud draws on biographical materials and his own clinical knowledge to arrive at a speculation about the source of Dostoevsky's dominant theme; but our apprehension of Dostoevsky's literary qualities is richer for the speculation. An analysis of imagery or a repeated theme, when handled with discretion, can supply for the critic part of what the practicing analyst might gather more reliably from the patient's associations. It is a risky business, as countless pratfalls by psychoanalytic critics remind us. Most recent Freudians have acknowledged the dangers of biographical inference and have turned their attention to the structure of the literary work at hand, or to the varying responses it elicits from the reader.[23]

One may also detect a new caution about ascribing a psychological prehistory to literary characters—the most ridiculed of all Freudian practices. Much early psychoanalytic criticism, especially the efforts by physicians who were only dabbling in literature, perpetuated the quaint Victorian error of treating *homo fictus* as a completely knowable person. There is a qualitative gap between Mrs. Clarke's *Girlhood of Shakespeare's Heroines* and Ernest Jones's *Hamlet and Oedipus* (London, 1949), but they are connected by an embarrassing thread of tradition. Still, Jones is more faithful to the genuine puzzle of *Hamlet* than are the circumspect followers of E. E. Stoll, who solve essentially psychological problems by recourse to theatrical convention. What psychoanalytic criticism needs, in my opinion, is not an injunction against seeing arrested development in literary heroes, but a vocabulary for describing a work's implied psychological pattern without mistaking that pattern for the

---

[20] *Counter-Statement* (Los Altos, Calif., 1953), p. 124. For a more rigorously psychoanalytic exposition of the same idea, see Appendix I of the second edition of Frederick J. Hoffman's *Freudianism and the Literary Mind* (Baton Rouge, La., 1957).

[21] *Fiction and the Unconscious* (New York, 1962), pp. 121-187.

[22] See *Leonardo da Vinci and a Memory of His Childhood,* tr. James Strachey (New York, 1964), and "Dostoevsky and Parricide," *Collected Papers,* 5 vols. (New York, 1959), v, 222-242.

[23] For a defense of this new attitude see Norman N. Holland, *Psychoanalysis and Shakespeare* (New York, 1966), pp. 293-349.

hero's case-history. Hamlet may not have an Oedipus complex, but *Hamlet* does.

The charge of anachronism is easy to refute. It implies that at a certain moment in time Freud made human nature Freudian. To say that pre-Freudian men cannot illustrate psychoanalytic principles is simply to say that psychoanalysis is wrong—a position which ought to be argued without recourse to the sophistry of anachronism. Academic logic has never been shakier than in recent efforts to prove that the psychological insight of certain writers may be completely explained by the mental theories current in their day. The reader must be dull of soul who can be persuaded that Shakespeare is contained in Timothy Bright, or that Hawthorne and Melville were disciples of the sunny moralist Thomas C. Upham. Perhaps we need to be reminded of Freud's own discovery that the essential features of his system were anticipated by poets and novelists—or, more simply, perhaps we should have some faith in the literary imagination.

6. *Psychoanalytic criticism identifies unconscious content with literary value.*

Like other objections we have reviewed, this one is historically but not theoretically warranted. The psychoanalytic movement has carried with it a fringe of zealots—we may include in this category such otherwise diverse persons as the Surrealist painters, D. H. Lawrence, Wilhelm Reich, and Norman O. Brown—who have preached a total escape from repression. This is not the goal of psychoanalysis, nor is it the *summum bonum* of Freudian criticism. Freud's aim was not to celebrate and release the unconscious but to bring its destructive tendency under rational control. While treasuring the evidence of unconscious processes in literature, he did not imagine that mere seizure by unconscious forces made a good writer or a good work.[24] On the contrary, he complained of Dostoevsky that "his insight was entirely restricted to the workings of the abnormal psyche," and he showed how this narrowness warped Dostoevsky's representation of love.[25] Psychoanalytic critics have naturally been tempted to place aesthetic value on what they have brought to light, and more often than not it has been some compulsive pattern. But psychoanalytic theory clearly states that art depends on the ability to manage and shape unconscious materials, not on those materials alone.[26]

[24] See, however, his indulgent *Delusion and Dream: An Interpretation in the Light of Psychoanalysis of* Gradiva, a Novel, *by Wilhelm Jensen*, tr. Helen M. Downey (New York, 1917).

[25] See the letter quoted by Theodor Reik, *From Thirty Years with Freud* (New York and Toronto, 1940), p. 175.

[26] We may also take note of the position opposite to Lawrence's, namely that

7. *Psychoanalytic criticism is jargon-ridden.*

Here too we may grant the charge but deny that it will inevitably apply to subsequent efforts. For several reasons the temptation to write in technical jargon has been greater for psychoanalytic critics than for most others. They have been subject both to a pride in sounding scientific and to a despair of placating the inevitable academic reviewers who will decry all technical language not drawn from the humanistic sewing-circle.[27] One detects a Thersites-like pleasure in the analysts' declaration that the heart of some beloved classic is rotten with polysyllabic fixations which the reader will not be able to find in his college dictionary. Such tendencies can of course be kept in check.

At the same time, it seems to me doubtful that psychoanalytic criticism can ever be, as one of its distinguished advocates would like, "rendered completely acceptable to the non-psychologically oriented scholars."[28] Beyond a certain point the disguise of one's premises amounts to abandonment of them. How, for example, can one substitute the term "conscience" for "superego" without blurring the irrationality—even the savagery—with which self-punishment is often inflicted in literary plots? How can one substitute "self" for "ego" without losing the often necessary sense of conflicting interests *within* a character's "self"? True jargon is technical language used imprecisely or unnecessarily. The real danger is not that the critic will have to resort to clinical terms (thereby offending those who would have rejected his argument anyway), but that he will allow his focus to stray from the literary work to the psychological system (thereby using the system as a club rather than a tool).

I would not want this essay to be taken as a plea for recruits to a militantly Freudian criticism. While psychoanalytic ideas have permeated our intellectual life, attempts at relating psychoanalysis to literature in

---

art is valuable insofar as it approaches total control over the unconscious. See, e.g., Franz Alexander's essay, "The Psychoanalyst Looks at Contemporary Art," *Art and Psychoanalysis,* ed. William Phillips (Cleveland and New York, 1963), pp. 346-365. Alexander defends his discomfort in the presence of modern art by equating abstraction with infantilism, and he wishfully predicts, "After the scientific mastery of the unconscious, its artistic mastery will follow" (p. 364). Here we may say that the therapeutic aim of psychoanalysis *has* been retained by the critic, and with a very banal result.

[27] For a penetrating discussion of this prejudice and the whole matter of psychoanalytic terminology in criticism, see Lesser, *Fiction and the Unconscious,* pp. 294-308.

[28] Leon Edel, "Notes on the Use of Psychological Tools in Literary Scholarship," *Literature and Psychology: Reprint of Leading Articles and Bibliographies from Volumes I and II* (September 1953), p. 8.

a programmatic way have been handicapped by the need for cumbersome explanations of theory and for rapid passage from one example to the next.[29] Our most respected critics—I think offhand of I. A. Richards, Edmund Wilson, W. H. Auden, William Empson, Kenneth Burke, Alfred Kazin, Lionel Trilling—have neither ignored Freudianism nor made it a battle-cry; they have absorbed it into their literary sense, along with other complementary approaches. I would urge, however, that such eclecticism be distinguished from indifference to theory. Something more than intellectual fashion is involved in the choice of psychological premises; the critic who disavows any taint of Freudianism usually ends by concocting his own psychology, a home-brew of conscious "experience" and moral prejudice. What Allen Tate once said of philosophy must therefore be said of psychological theory as well: by pretending not to use it in literary studies we are using it badly.[30]

[29] See Frederick Clarke Prescott, *The Poetic Mind* (New York, 1922), Otto Rank, *Art and Artist: Creative Urge and Personality Development* (New York, 1932), Hanns Sachs, *The Creative Unconscious: Studies in the Psychoanalysis of Art* (Cambridge, Mass., 1942, 1951), Roy P. Basler, *Sex, Symbolism, and Psychology in Literature* (New Brunswick, N. J., 1948), Arthur Wormhoudt, *The Demon Lover: A Psychoanalytical Approach to Literature* (New York, 1949), Edmund Bergler, *The Writer and Psychoanalysis* (Garden City, N. Y., 1950), Daniel E. Schneider, *The Psychoanalyst and the Artist* (New York, 1950), and Philip Weissman, *Creativity in the Theater: A Psychoanalytic Study* (New York and London, 1965). For the effect of psychoanalysis on creative writers themselves, see Frederick J. Hoffman, *Freudianism and the Literary Mind* (Baton Rouge, La., 1945, 1957). Other psychological studies of literature may be located in Norman Kiell, *Psychoanalysis, Psychology, and Literature: A Bibliography* (Madison, Wis., 1963), and in the bibliographies and book reviews in the journal *Literature and Psychology*. See also Louis Fraiberg, *Psychoanalysis and American Literary Criticism* (Detroit, 1960)

[30] See *On the Limits of Poetry: Selected Essays: 1928-1948* (New York, 1948), p. 53.

Literature and Sociology

By Leo Lowenthal

I

To explore the relationships between sociology and literary scholarship involves dealing with two sociological complexes. There is, on the one hand, the sociology of literature, which brings sociological categories to bear on the elucidation of specific problems of the literary arts, such as genres, periods, the artist, styles, literary fashions. A somewhat different approach is to ponder the possible usefulness of sociological knowledge for the literary scholar, whether or not it is explicitly concerned with literature or any of the other arts.

Almost no significant attempt has been made on the part of the literary expert to consider the body of sociological knowledge per se as a useful tool, and I hasten to add that the picture is equally blurred when we ask ourselves about the degree to which sociologists have made use of the work of their colleagues concerned with belles lettres. This blackout is particularly characteristic of the American scene where we find ignorance not infrequently leading to distrust and stereotypes as to what the humanistic scholars may have to say about the work of their colleagues in the social sciences and vice versa. The humanists have a tendency to conceive of social scientists and particularly sociologists as people who primarily play with computers and dream up quasi-scientific schemes with which to manipulate individuals or groups, if not whole nations; and the social scientists in turn seem to presume that except for exercises in philology and linguistics, the humanists, particularly those devoting themselves to literature, are hardly worthy of the name of serious scholars and should rather be classified as nesting in a never-never land between philosophy and poetry.[1]

---

[1] To cite one example of each of the antagonists: Joseph Wood Krutch had this to say about social scientists: "The social scientist grows arrogant because

Leo Lowenthal

The situation is somewhat different in Europe, particularly in France and Germany, due to the origins of sociology in history and philosophy, or, to use the by now well-known term, due to the prevailing orientation of sociology in terms of the *Geisteswissenschaften*. Eminent scholars such as Wilhelm Dilthey and Georg Simmel come readily to mind; both are founding fathers of European sociology as well as authors of major literary analyses. A great deal of German literary scholarship has been profoundly influenced by such concepts as understanding or empathy or life processes, just to name a few which are closely tied to the German sociological tradition of the first two decades of this century.

Thus, within the confines of French and German intellectual life, the application of sociological investigation for the study of literature, as well as the sociological analysis of literature proper, has always been significant pursuits. In particular, the term sociology of literature has been well established on the Continent for many decades, while it still is rarely used in the United States. Probably one of the contributory reasons for the institutionalization of sociological perspectives of literature in Europe has been the enormous influence of Marx and Marxian scholars who, from the very beginning of this intellectual movement, have paid considerable attention to the interpretation of literature from the standpoint of class analysis.

Yet I do not wish to imply that a productive encounter of the humanistic and the social sciences in general and of literary scholarship and sociology in particular are hopeless propositions on the American scene. On the contrary, there are signs on the horizon which look rather promising. For one, within the span of the last generation a significant number of sociologists have become engaged in studying literary products for the mass market. The whole field of mass culture, with its emphasis on the analysis of popular printed and broadcasting media, not to forget the

of the success of his statistical predictions in dealing with something far more complicated than either the toss of a coin or the behavior of a gaseous molecule. He ought to be, but usually is not, far more aware than the physicist of the whole dubious nature of even physical 'laws.' What he is trying to do is to watch the behavior of human beings as the physicist watches that of atoms and molecules. He tries, or thinks he tries, to detach himself as far as possible; to treat what he knows about himself as though it were as irrelevant as self-knowledge used to be assumed to be for the natural scientist; and he tries to put himself at a sufficient distance so that nothing but the movements of the aggregate can be seen. But he ought not hope to prove what many physicists now admit is not only unprovable but false."—Joseph Wood Krutch, *The Measure of Man: Freedom, Human Values, Survival and The Modern Temper* (Indianapolis, Ind.: Bobbs-Merrill, 1954). And the sociologist James H. Barnett on the humanists: "Discussion of contemporary studies will be limited primarily to those which seek movies, constitutes in fact a study of a literary subculture. Over the years, these studies have become increasingly refined, having started with the measurement of effects of these mass products on a variety of audiences, now moving toward the analysis of the meaning and function of these phenomena for society and culture in general. It is true that these sociological endeavors have been undertaken primarily by specialists who are not particularly sensitized to serious literature, a circumstance which has deflected the interests of literary scholars in these researches on modern mass culture. Yet even here we see some weakening of the barriers, and the last ten years have seen a number of conferences and publications in which social scientists and humanists have joined forces to explore their common grounds and basic differences. One example is the book, *Culture for the Millions? Mass Media in Modern Society,* edited by Norman Jacobs (Van Nostrand, 1959), and based on a conference on the mass media and the arts to which sociologists such as Paul F. Lazarsfeld and Edward Shils and humanists such as Randall Jarrell and James Johnson Sweeney contributed. Two other examples are the well-known readers, *Mass Culture: The Popular Arts in America,* edited by Bernard Rosenberg and David M. White (Free Press, 1957), and *Mass Leisure,* edited by Eric Larrabee and Rolf Meyerson (Free Press, 1958). Also in this tradition are the debates on the implications of David Riesman's work, participated in by social scientists and humanists alike. (See, e.g., *Culture and Social Character: The Work of David Riesman,* edited by Seymour Lipset and Leo Lowenthal, Free Press, 1961.)

These are at least symptoms of a tentative communication, though I would venture to say that most of the scholars committed to either of the two fields are still worlds apart. Perhaps C. P. Snow's well-worn phrase of the two cultures could be more significantly applied to the gulf which separates the humanistic from the social sciences than to the dividing line between the natural sciences and the rest of us. An excellent programmatic statement on the difficulties accounting for the current estrangement between the social sciences and the humanities as well as some possible solutions is Gertrude Jaeger and Philip Selznick, "A Normative Theory of Culture" (*American Sociological Review,* October 1964). They state that "The time has come for forthright consideration of a rapprochement between the humanist and social science concepts of

---

to study art from the *scientific, rather than the humanistic,* viewpoint. This will necessitate omitting comment on such well-known works as Edmund Wilson's *Axel's Castle* and Erich Auerbach's *Mimesis."* [Emphasis supplied.]—James H. Barnett, "The Sociology of Art," in *Sociology Today: Problems and Prospects,* ed. by Robert K. Merton, Leonard Broom, and Leonard S. Cottrell, Jr. (New York: Harper Torchbooks, 1965).

culture," and that is indeed what they set out to do. Their conception of culture is one of "expressive symbolism, and any social product, including language, contributes to culture insofar as it sustains symbolic experience" (p. 653). For the time being, however, such sociological observations are exceptional.

II

Given my own background and inclinations, I feel rather comfortable in the world of the social scientist and of the humanist alike, and it is not my intention to recommend any radical innovations. I believe, however, that some of the concerns of the modern sociologist may be of some interest to the literary scholar. Such concerns are particularly relevant for the study of contemporary literature where yardsticks are hard to establish because we ourselves are deeply involved in the scene for which the literary artist bears witness. There are, indeed, both areas of concern and certain basic concepts in sociology which may help the literary scholar to refine the instruments of objective assessment. As a matter of fact, such concepts as anomie and alienation, the conflict of generations, the role of urbanization, technology, bureaucracy, and the notion of mass society have imperceptibly moved back and forth between sociology and the humanities. Although it is obviously impractical for the specialized literary scholar to attain comprehensive knowledge in sociology and related fields, there are points of contact that are both well-established and useful. I therefore would like to suggest some bibliographical sources which might provide sufficient acquaintance with sociological theory and research to stimulate the imagination of the literary scholar—particularly if his work is devoted to the contemporary scene.

Turning first to the problem of *alienation and anomie*—a vast field indeed, reflected by many protagonists of modern drama and fiction and many motifs of modern poetry—I would recommend as a first introduction to sociological theory in this area a recently published study by Ephraim Mizruchi, *Success and Opportunity* (Free Press, 1964). A rich source for further readings on the various implications of alienation in modern society is a reader published under the title *Mass Society in Crisis: Social Problems and Social Pathology,* edited by Bernard Rosenberg, Israel Gerver, and F. William Howton (Macmillan, 1964).[2] While this collection, as the subtitle intimates, is primarily organized in terms of social problems and social institutions, there is another volume available which may even be closer to the heart of the literary scholar since it centers specifically around the individual: *Identity and Anxiety: Survival*

---

[2] While I am not exactly an enthusiastic admirer of the format of a reader, I think it is a very legitimate source of orientation for the non-specialist.

of the Person in Mass Society, edited by Maurice R. Stein, Arthur J. Vidich, and David Manning White (Free Press, 1960). This publication is, by the way, another example of the rapprochement between the social sciences and the humanities; while social science contributors outnumber the humanists, the latter are nevertheless significantly represented by names such as C. M. Bowra, Martin Buber, and Karl Jaspers. The book has also a subsection dealing with "Personal Styles and the Arts."

To learn how a sensitive sociologist synthesizes theoretical perspective and empirical research, attention may be drawn to the book by Robert Blauner, *Alienation and Freedom: The Factory Worker and His Industry* (University of Chicago Press, 1964). There is also a volume which is designed to integrate the concerns of sociology and literature, namely the two-volume reader called *Alienation: The Cultural Climate of Our Time* (Braziller, 1964), edited and with introduction by the well-known sociologist Gerald Sykes. Although this work contains many literary excerpts which pertain to various aspects of alienation, it reminds us as much of work yet to be done as of that being achieved, since it comprises rather precious collections of bits and pieces of literary work without much interpretation. Finally, I would like to recommend to the literary scholar a small book by Edward A. Tiryakian, *Sociologism and Existentialism* (Spectrum, 1962), in which he offers an excellent comparison of existentialist and sociological orientations in modern intellectual life.

One of the main issues of the contemporary novel is the fate of modern man in *the changing ecological scene.* The village has long been submerged in the American landscape, and the small town is giving way to the metropolitan octopus. The social problems involved have not escaped the sociological scholar, and many of the studies on conformity, of which William H. Whyte's *Organization Man* is the most popular example, focus on this area. A good deal of the sociological literature on urbanization is rather technical and often closely tied to studies in demography and population, making for tough going for the non-specialist. I would, however, put in a word of strong recommendation for two extremely literate sociological publications which deal with modern life styles in our period of ecological transition. I am referring to Morris R. Stein, *The Eclipse of Community: An Interpretation of American Cities* (Harper Torchbooks, 1964), and Arthur J. Vidich and Joseph Bensman, *Small Town in Mass Society: Class, Power and Religion in a Rural Community* (Anchor Books, 1958). Another sociological author who has increasingly published very readable material on styles of life in urban society is Herbert J. Gans. A good introduction is his article, "Urbanism and Suburbanism as Ways of Living: A Re-evaluation of Definitions," republished in a book of readings, *Human Behavior and Social Processes:*

An Interactionist Approach, edited by Arnold M. Rose (Houghton Mifflin, 1962). This reader, by the way, provides a good survey of the relevance of social psychology for the sociologist, and should be of more than passing interest to the literary scholar, for the central socio-psychological category is symbolism. Recently Mr. Gans has published a very interesting study, *The Urban Villagers* (Free Press, 1962), exploring the social, psychological, and cultural consequences of urban renewal which, while providing technically advanced housing, at the same time threaten family and minority group cohesion. This study is rich in its analysis of the uprooted individual in metropolitan culture, a theme which we find in many variations in modern literary narratives.

Closely connected with the entrenchment of metropolitan civilization is the issue of *bureaucracy*—certainly one of the central topics depicted in modern literature. A book profitably to be studied by the humanistic scholar has been published by two younger sociologists who have, not by chance, a sophisticated understanding of artistic qualities and aesthetic concerns; I am referring to the work by Joseph Bensman and Bernard Rosenberg, *Mass, Class, and Bureaucracy: The Evolution of Contemporary Society* (Prentice-Hall, 1963). A more complete survey of sociological thinking on bureaucracy in modern society is easily available in an excellent book, the *Reader in Bureaucracy,* edited by Robert K. Merton, Ailsa P. Gray, Barbara Hockey, and Hanan C. Selvin (Free Press, 1952). It lists in its bibliography "some literary portraits of bureaucracy."

What I have tried to suggest thus far are sociological readings dealing with basic problems of modern civilization—mass society and mass culture, alienation and anomie, urbanization and bureaucratization. Obviously many titles throughout the nineteenth and twentieth centuries could be subsumed under one or several of these areas of social analysis: individuals portrayed in these works experience the vicissitudes of their lives—conflicts, compromises, acts of despair, or what have you—in their exposure to powerful social trends and institutions analyzed in sociological literature. Certainly, the sociologist does not deal with all these phenomena as though they were lacking ambiguity. It may, nevertheless, be suggested that the literary critic might acquire some additional articulateness in doing his work by familiarizing himself with the mode of thought of the social scientist.

But before we cease borrowing from one field for the enrichment of another, I should say one final word about sociological contributions to what is the life nerve of the literary work, i.e., people. There seem to be two clusters of people in the modern world who are of equal concern to the literary creator and to the sociologist. They are the primary alienated subcultures: intellectuals and youth. Increasingly, *the intellectual* and more specifically the artist and the writer, and even the professor, have become favorite topics of the contemporary novel.[3] Curiously enough, there is a scarcity of studies of the intellectual world, though some well-known research on the academic community has been published over the last ten years. I might cite Theodore Caplow and Reese J. McGee, *The Academic Marketplace* (Basic Books, 1958) and Paul F. Lazarsfeld and Wagner Thielens, *The Academic Mind* (Free Press, 1958). A useful reader on the intellectual in modern society is *The Intellectuals: A Controversial Portrait,* edited and with an introduction and overviews by George B. de Huszar (Free Press, 1960). Two others should be required reading for the literary scholar in this area of the intellectual in modern society, one dealing with the role of the intellectuals in the '50's in the United States by Daniel Bell, *The End of Ideology* (Free Press, 1960), and a more recent work which gives a good comprehensive history of the background and emergence of the modern intellectual, with strong emphasis on the artist, *Men of Ideas: A Sociologist's View,* by Lewis R. Coser (Free Press, 1965).

Turning now to the subculture of the *youth,* unfortunately mainly explored within the framework of juvenile delinquency, there are several publications which have signal significance for the critic of modern literature. There is, first of all, the special issue of the *Annals of the American Academy of Political and Social Science* (November 1961) called "Teen Age Culture." The book by T. R. Fyvel, *The Troublemakers: Rebellious Youth in an Affluent Society* (Schocken, 1962), has the great advantage of being a comparative study presenting material from Western and Eastern Europe as well as England and the United States. Finally (and this is by far the best book on the subject and a very readable one indeed), the study by David Matza, *Delinquency and Drift* (Wiley, 1964).

I do not assume any particular interest of the literary scholar in specialized sociological methodology (nor would I recommend it). There is one methodological complex, however, which is close to the heart of the literary critic (though under different names), namely, *content analysis.* The student of literature may very well smile indulgently when he learns that content analysis is sociological jargon for research into the overt and implied subject matter of a communication, and may very well refer to himself in a jocular mood as a bourgeois gentilhomme who didn't know before that he had spoken prose all his life. Yet the by now rather sophisticated methods of quantitative codification of subject matter may be a worthwhile tool for the elucidation of certain details of lit-

---

[3] I differ here from Victor Brombert, *The Intellectual Hero: Studies in the French Novel, 1880-1955* (Phoenix Books, 1964), who believes that the intellectual as a hero is rather typical for the French and extremely anti-typical for the American novel (see pp. 12 ff.).

erary matters, as long as the critic does not neglect the analysis of the structure and the work as a whole, or succumb to an over-involvement in the technical detail. My colleagues in the literary field may rest assured that sociologists are in no way agreed on a merely quantitative approach to content analysis; while Bernard Berelson's *Content Analysis* (Free Press, 1952) adheres strictly to the "hard" quantification method, others, including the author of this essay, have stressed the need for critical, qualitative, and value-oriented research. A very instructive statement on this sociological controversy, of obvious interest to the literary scholar, is contained in the article by George Gerbner, "On Content Analysis and Critical Research in Mass Communication" (in *People, Society, and Mass Communications,* edited by Lewis Anthony Dexter and David Manning White, Free Press, 1964, pp. 476 ff.).

III

The sociological interpretation of literature—artistic or popular—is not a favorite son of organized social science. By the same token, almost everybody with a fair access to reading and writing feels qualified to offer his own historical, aesthetic, and sociological generalizations on any given literary work. Incidentally, the academic disciplines which have been traditionally charged with the history and analysis of literature have been caught unprepared or unconcerned by the impact of mass literature, the best seller, the popular magazine, the comics, and the like, and they have maintained an attitude of indifference to the lower depths of imagination in print. A field has thus been left open to challenge the sociologist.

Historically the concept of literature as a product of social forces explainable in part by the special value system and the prevailing social and political features of a given society goes back a long way. For the early eighteenth century, Giambattista Vico comes to mind, and around the turn of the century Madame de Staël, at least in retrospect, put sociology on the map as an instrument of literary interpretation by titling her well-known essay *De la littérature considérée dans ses rapports avec les institutions sociales.* More significant are the various formulations which Charles de Bonald, in many of his treatises (which are unfortunately not available in English translation), gave to the thesis that literature is the expression, if not the yardstick, of a society—a thesis which later on John Ruskin shared with the great French philosopher of the counter-revolution. The sociological orientation, though not under this name, gains momentum in Hippolyte Taine's *History of English Literature.* As Harry Levin puts it: "It was left for Hippolyte Taine . . . to formulate a sociological approach."[4] Levin, by the way, gives an excellent survey of such pre- and extra-sociological approaches

---

[4] Harry Levin, *The Gates of Horn* (New York: Oxford University Press, 1963), p. 8.

all through the nineteenth and the beginning of the twentieth centuries, including figures such as Stendhal and Balzac as well as Georg Brandes and our own V. L. Parrington. Yet this pre-history of a sociological perspective, fascinating as it would be as a chapter of intellectual history, would contribute only marginally to the endeavors of the modern sociological and literary critic.

I envisage four major tasks confronting the contemporary sociologist of literature.[5]

1. *Literature and the Social System.* The problems envisaged under this heading are twofold. The primary task is to place literature in a functional frame within each society, and within the various strata of that society. In certain primitive societies and a few highly developed ones, literature is not clearly differentiated as an independent entity apart from ceremonials of cult and religion. It is, rather, an outlet of these institutions as, for example, tribal chants, early Greek tragedy, or the medieval passion play. In the modern world, on the other hand, literature leads a clearly separate existence from other cultural activities, with many functional differentiations. It may become the escapist refuge of politically frustrated groups, as in early romanticism, or of social frustration on a mass scale, as in the current phenomenon of literary mass entertainment. Then again, literature may function as an ideological instrument in the proper sense of that word, by exalting a specific system of domination and contributing to its educational goals, as was the case with the Spanish and French dramatists in the era of absolutism.

A secondary aspect, perhaps less fertile in terms of research materials, but no less rewarding in social perspectives, lies in the study of literary forms. The epic as well as lyric poetry, the drama, and the novel, have affinities of their own to a particular social destiny. The solitude of the individual or the feeling of collective security, social optimism or despair, psychological self-reflection or adherence to an objective scale of values are among the conceptualizations that lend themselves to a re-examination of literary forms in terms of social institutions.

2. *The Position of the Writer in Society.* The creative writer is the intellectual per se for whom objective source materials are merely an arbitrary arsenal which he uses, if at all, according to his particular aesthetic aims. He thus represents the prototype of intellectual behavior, and the lively discussion among sociologists about the role of the intelligentsia could perhaps be extended to a more concrete level if it were supported by a historically documented analysis of both the self-portraits and the functions of one of the oldest groups among the intellectual professions.

It must suffice here to enumerate a few points of departure and to

[5] For extended discussion, see Leo Lowenthal, *Literature, Popular Culture, and Society* (Englewood Cliffs, N. J.: Spectrum, 1961), pp. 141-161, passim.

mention—under the heading of self-portraits—the prophetic, the mission-ary, the entertaining, the strictly handicraft and the professional, political or money-making conceptions of literary producers. On the objective level we shall have to inquire into the sources of prestige and income, the pressure of institutionalized agencies of social control, visible or anonymous, the influence of technology and the market mechanisms, all bearing on the stimulation and dissemination of artistic writing, and the social, economic, and cultural situation within which writers find them-selves at various historical stages. The relationships of the princely courts, the academies and salons, the book clubs and the movie industry to the literary craft exemplify the relevant topics for systematic discus-sion. Then there are problems which span the subjective and objective aspects, such as whether, under conditions of modern book and maga-zine production, the writer is still an independent entrepreneur or in fact an employee of his publisher and advertiser.

3. *Society and Social Problems as Literary Materials.* Here we enter the traditional area of sociological research in literature. There are innumerable books and papers on the treatment of the state or society or the economy or other articulate social phenomena by any number of writers in any number of countries and languages. These repositories of factual information, though written for the most part by literary people and therefore somewhat haphazard in matters of social theory, cannot be dismissed lightly. They evaluate literature as secondary source material for historical analysis and become all the more valuable the scarcer the primary sources for any specific period. Furthermore, they contribute to our knowledge of the kind of perception which a particular social group —the writers—has of specific social phenomena, and they belong there-fore to propaedeutic studies of a history and sociology of social con-sciousness.

Nevertheless, a sociologist with literary interest and analytical expe-rience in the field of belles lettres must not be satisfied merely to inter-pret literary materials which are sociological by definition; his task is also to study the social implications of literary themes and motives which are remote from public affairs. The treatment which a creative writer gives to nature or to love, to gestures and moods, to situations of gregar-iousness or solitude, the weight given to reflections, descriptions, or con-versations, are all phenomena which on first sight may seem sterile from a sociological point of view but which are in fact primary sources for a study of the permeation of the most private and intimate spheres of indi-vidual life by the social climate. For times that have passed, literature often becomes the only available source of information about private modes and mores. It is the task of the sociologist of literature to relate the experience of the imaginary characters to the historical climate from which they stem and, thus, to make literary hermeneutics a part of the sociology of knowledge. He has, so to say, to transform the private equation of themes and stylistic means into social equations.[6]

4. *Social Determinants of Success.* By and large the legitimate business which the sociologist of literature may have in the field of communications research consists in formulating hypotheses for research on "what reading does to people." But he cannot simply pass the task on to his colleague, the empirical data researcher, after having done his historical, biographical, and analytic work. There are certain factors of social relevance which, though very decisive for the measurement of effects, will have to undergo sociological exploration on the level of theory and documentary study.

There is, first of all, the problem of finding out what we know about the influence of all-embracing social constellations on writing and the reading public. Are times of war or peace, of economic boom or depression more or less conducive to literary production? Are specific types of the literary level, literary form, and subject matter more or less preponderant? What about the outlet of distribution, the publishing house, the circulation figures, the competition between books and magazines in these various periods? What do we know about readership figures in public and university libraries, in the Army and the hospitals—again broken down according to changing social conditions? What do we know, qualitatively and quantitatively, about the ratio between literature distributed and consumed and other media of mass communication?

A second auxiliary source of theory lies in the area of social controls. What do we know about the influence of formal controls of production and reading? We must deal with the worldwide phenomenon of the use of tax money for public libraries, with the European practice of governmental subsidies for theaters, and with the American experience of supporting creative writers out of public funds during the New Deal administration or by appointing them at universities, as we do increasingly today. We have to study the impact of selective and cherished symbols of public rewards, from the Nobel Prize for literature to the contests arranged by publishing houses, from the Pulitzer Prize to the honors bestowed by local or regional communities on successful authors whose cradles were fortunately situated in particular localities. We should study "manipulated controls": publishers' advertising campaigns, the expectations of profit tied up with book clubs and film production, the far-flung market of magazine serializations, the reprint houses, and so on. We must not forget the area of censorship, of institutionalized restrictions from the Index of the Catholic Church to local ordinances prohibiting the sale of certain books and periodicals, and self-censorship in the teaching

---

[6] This is the guiding thesis in my book, *Literature and the Image of Man: Studies of the European Drama and Novel, 1600-1900* (Boston: Beacon, 1957).

of literature. And, finally, we would have to analyze and systematize what we know about the impact of informal controls, of book reviews and broadcasts, of popular write-ups about authors, of opinion leadership, of literary gossip and private conversations.

A third, and certainly not the least, social determinant of success is connected with technological change and its economic and social consequences. The phenomenal development of the publishing business, putting out literary products on all levels in the low price field, is surpassed only by the still more spectacular modes of production in other media of mass communication. Thus, it would be worth studying whether the financial returns received by writers in the last few decades can be attributed in large measure to improved technical facilities, including the author's working instruments, and whether this change in technique has changed the social status of writers as a group. Relatively little is known about the cumulative effects of one medium on another. Do more people read more books because they see more pictures or listen to more broadcasts, or is it the other way around? Or is there no such interdependence? Is there a relationship between the high degree of accessibility of printed material and the methods by which educational institutions on all grade levels avail themselves of this material?

The following bibliographical survey starts with the modern tradition of the evaluation of literature by the professional sociologist. It then turns to the considerable amount of work done in the Marxian tradition and, within this context, adds a special word on the fashionable wedding of Marxism and existentialism. After these more general approaches, consideration is given to studies focussing on popular literature as an indicator of social and socio-psychological trends. While all the foregoing materials are very close to sociological specialization (though some of the contributors have different disciplinary credentials), we next turn toward a most significant category, i.e., publications which try to bridge the gap between a strictly sociological and a strictly literary interpretation. It is within this category that the most promising contributions to a unified perspective of culture and society can be found. One aspect of bridge building is furnished by writings which conceive of literature as a manifestation of social history, and it is to this broad view that our next section is devoted. In addition to reviewing the more comprehensive studies, this section touches upon concerns such as the profession of the literary artist and the social nature of his public. We cite finally a few books and offer a few comments on programmatic statements about the interdependence of literature and society, with primary emphasis on contributions made by literary scholars.

1. *The Modern Sociological Tradition*

(1) Albrecht, Milton C. "The Relationship of Literature and Society." *American Journal of Sociology*, Vol. LIX, No. 5 (March 1954), pp. 425-436.

(2) —— "Does Literature Reflect Common Values?" *American Sociological Review*, Vol. XXI, No. 6 (December 1956)

(3) Barnett, James H. *Divorce and the American Divorce Novel, 1858-1937.* Philadelphia, 1939.

(4) —— "The Sociology of Art." In *Sociology Today: Problems and Prospects.* Ed. Robert K. Merton, Leonard Broom, and Leonard S. Cottrell, Jr. Harper Torchbooks, 1965.

(5) Bloch, Herbert A. "Towards the Development of a Sociology of Literary and Art-Forms." *American Sociological Review*, Vol. VIII, No. 3 (1943), pp. 313-320.

(6) Duncan, Hugh Dalziel. *Language and Literature in Society.* Chicago: Univ. of Chicago Press, 1953.

(7) Gordon, Milton M. "*Kitty Foyle* and the Concept of Class as Culture." *The American Journal of Sociology*, Vol. LIII, No. 3 (Nov. 1947), pp. 210-217.

(8) Inglis, Ruth A. "An Objective Approach to the Relationship between Fiction and Society." *American Sociological Review*, Vol. III, No. 4 (1938), pp. 526-533.

(9) Lerner, Max, and Edwin Mims, Jr. "Literature." In *Encyclopedia of the Social Sciences*, Vol. IX, pp. 523-541. New York: Macmillan, 1933.

(10) Mukerjee, Radhakamal. "The Meaning and Evolution of Art in Society." *American Sociological Review*, Vol. X, No. 4 (1945), pp. 496-502.

(11) Sorokin, Pitirim. "Fluctuations of Ideation, Idealistic, and Sensate Forms of Art." Part II of *Social and Cultural Dynamics.* Boston: Porter Sargent, 1957.

(12) Tomars, Adolph S. *Introduction to the Sociology of Art.* Mexico City: 1940.

(13) Gerth, H. H., and C. Wright Mills, eds. *From Max Weber: Essays in Sociology.* New York: Oxford Univ. Press, 1958.

(14) Wilson, Robert N. *Man Made Plain: The Poet in Contemporary Society.* Howard Allen, 1958.

Looking through the professional American journals one is impressed by the scarcity of work done in the sociology of literature. Not counting book reviews, the contribution of American sociologists, at least as reflected in periodicals, is pretty much exhausted with (1), (2), (5), (7), (8), and (9). As the titles betray, most of this material is rather programmatic and sketchy and probably will not be too rewarding for the literary critic. Milton Albrecht's essay (1) deserves some attention because it contains an intelligent, though by needs abbreviated, discussion of scholarly literature. The only full-length book in the area is (6), but Duncan's discussion lacks clarity and significance because of a precious neo-Kenneth Burkian approach without, however, the brilliance of the master. The main value of this book is a very extensive bibliography—about 100 pages of titles published before 1953. The old essay in the *Encyclopedia of the Social Sciences* (9) is still readable and stimulating though somewhat schematic in its treatment of social history. Sorokin's theory (11) represents a kind of sociological metaphysics full of sparks but lacking in solid scientific foundation. A good insight into the utter neglect of literature and the arts in general in our sociological circles is (4); the publication as a whole is supposed to be a codification of what the "problems and prospects" are in contemporary society, but Mr. Barnett's essay is limited to about seventeen pages with all the arts, including music, thrown in. The most stimulating and, for the literary scholar, the most useful title in this group is (14). Wilson, who is well trained in sociology and psychology, has made a personal study of leading American poets and their social roots; his treatment of the origins, careers, and orientations of eminent poets is a model for students of the sociology of modern literature.

In passing I want to point out how different the scene is in Europe. The leading German sociological journal, the *Kölner Zeitschrift für Soziologie und Sozialpsychologie,* fairly regularly publishes full-length articles and surveys in reviews. For instance, Vol. XVII, 1965, No. 1, contains an essay on Tocqueville's sociology of literature. In addition, the famous periodical of the Belgian Institut de Sociologie, *Revue de l'Institut de Sociologie,* published a few years ago a special issue of close to 250 pages on problems in the sociology of the novel. A third example of European contributions is the small volume by Robert Escarpit, *Sociologie de la littérature* (Presses Universitaires de France, 1958). The author, a humanist scholar, explicitly aims at making a contribution to sociology. While the organization of the book is indeed sociological in nature, centering around the categories of production, distribution, and consumption, it is, by and large, not a very successful enterprise. A good deal of the weakness is due to a somewhat naive idea about sociological methods. Escarpit abounds in what he imagines to be statistical analyses and reasonings. The book is burdened by tables and curves, but, for the most part, they are either hard to decipher or are scholarly pleasantries, as, for example, the comparison of peak periods of production in the life span of poets, dramatists, and novelists.

2. *The Marxian Tradition*

(15) Marx, Karl, and Friedrich Engels. *Literature and Art: Selections from Their Writings.* New York: International Publishers, 1947.

(16) Mehring, Franz. *Zur Literaturgeschichte von Calderon bis Heine.* Berlin: Soziologische Verlagsanstalt, 1929.

(17) —— *Zur Literaturgeschichte von Hebbel bis Gorki.* Berlin: Soziologische Verlagsanstalt, 1929.

(18) Plekhanov, George V. *Art and Society.* Tr. from Russian. New York: Critics Group, 1937.

(19) Trotsky, Leon. *Literature and Revolution.* Ann Arbor: University of Michigan Press, 1960.

(20) *Dialectics: A Marxist Literary Journal.* New York: Critics Group, 1937 ff.

(21) Lifshitz, Mikhail. *The Philosophy of Art of Karl Marx.* Tr. from Russian. New York: Critics Group, 1938.

(22) Flores, Angel, ed. *Literature and Marxism: A Controversy by Soviet Critics.* New York: Critics Group, 1938.

(23) Engels, Friedrich, et al. *Henrik Ibsen: A Marxist Analysis.* Angel Flores, ed. New York: Critics Group, 1937.

(24) Smirnov, A. A. *Shakespeare: A Marxist Interpretation.* Tr. from Russian. New York: Critics Group, 1937.

(25) Strachey, John. *Literature and Dialectical Materialism.* New York: Covici Friede Publishers, 1934.

(26) Caudwell, Christopher. *Illusion and Reality.* New York: International Publishers, 1947

(27) Farrell, James T. *Literature and Morality.* New York: Vanguard Press, 1946.

(28) —— *A Note on Literary Criticism.* New York: Vanguard Press, 1936.

(29) Finkelstein, Sidney. *Art and Society.* New York: International Publishers, 1947.

(30) Fox, Ralph. *The Novel and The People.* London: Lawrence and Wishart, 1937.

(31) Henderson, Philip. *Literature and a Changing Civilization.* London: John Lane, 1935.

(32) Hicks, Granville. *Figures of Transition.* New York: Macmillan, 1939.

(33) Lukács, Georg. *The Historical Novel.* Boston: Beacon Press, 1963.

(34) Goldmann, Lucien. *The Hidden God.* Tr. Philip Thody. London: Routledge & Kegan Paul, 1964.

(35) Sartre, Jean-Paul. *Search for a Method.* Tr. Hazel E. Barnes. New York: Alfred A. Knopf, 1963.

(36) *Revue de l'Institut de Sociologie,* II (1963). [Special issue: "Problèmes d'une sociologie du roman."]

(37) Levin, Harry. "Toward a Sociology of the Novel." *JHI,* XXVI (1965), 148-154.

As the preceding sample of twenty-three publications shows, Marx and the various scholars of Marxism have consistently been fascinated with literature as source material for a specific social theory. An analysis of these materials could in itself form the background of a one hundred years' study of intellectual and political history. In any case, it reflects trends, within Marxism as well as within the Communist movement. The contributions of Marx (and to some extent of Engels) are the least schematic and doctrinaire. (See 15.) The philosophical roots of Marx are clearly visible in his high sensitivity to aesthetic qualities and his very often successful attempt to reconcile a profound admiration for the great masters such as Shakespeare and Balzac with his basic concepts of the pattern of world history. Unfortunately he never wrote a major piece on literature, and we are limited to occasional and fragmentary statements. Franz Mehring, the German historian of Marx and the German Social Democratic Party, contributed over the years many articles on literature to leading German Socialist magazines (16 and 17), most of which have not been translated into English. His work is rather traditional in its primarily biographical approach, interspersed with the schemata of class struggle and class ideology. A more succinct theoretical rationale in terms of the theory of historical materialism was contributed by Plekhanov (18), and Trotsky tried to apply Plekhanov's prescriptions to an analysis of the early writers of the Russian Revolution (19). The 'thirties witnessed a whole vogue of Marxist interpretations very much in the style of the Popular Front ideology, with a definite Communist Party slant, and the various pamphlets (see 20 through 24) covering the whole spectrum from Shakespeare to Thomas Mann make for somewhat painful reading today. The theoretical spokesmen during this period were Caudwell (26), Fox (30), Henderson (31), and John Strachey (25) in England, and James Farrell (27, 28) and Granville Hicks (32) in this country. These Marxist spokesmen in Anglo-Saxon letters are still in part quite interesting because they were fairly well grounded in their particular philosophical persuasion as well as—and particularly so in the case of Caudwell and Hicks—highly sensitized to aesthetic qualities.

By far the most significant figure is Georg Lukács, and only a very small fraction of his *œuvre*, which in addition to many books and essays on literature extends to the history of philosophy, aesthetics, and sociology, has been made accessible to the English reader. (See 33 as one of the few exceptions.) Lukács, who originally came from the neoromantic tradition and whose beautiful small book written in 1918, *Theory of the Novel*, is accessible only in an obscure English translation, must draw the attention of any sophisticated literary critic with any concern for social history and the possible contributions of the dialectic method. A recent interpretation of his work (implicitly or explicitly) may be found in some of the writings of Jean-Paul Sartre (35) and Lucien Goldmann (34), who try to synthesize a politicized concept of existentialism with orthodox Marxian analysis. Goldmann's book on French seventeenth-century literature, primarily on Pascal and Racine, is an excellent study, though his present existentialist pronunciamentos primarily contained in (36) have been severely criticized, and justifiably so, by Harry Levin (37).

3. *The Sociology of Popular Literature*

(38) Altick, Richard D. *The English Common Reader.* Chicago: Univ. of Chicago Press, 1957.

(39) Berelson, Bernard, and Patricia J. Salter. "Majority and Minority Americans: An Analysis of Magazine Fiction." *Public Opinion Quarterly* (1948), pp. 168-190.

(40) Dalziel, Margaret. *Popular Fiction 100 Years Ago.* London: Cohen and West, 1957.

(40a) *Dædalus.* Winter 1963. [Special issue entitled *The American Reading Public.*]

(41) Hart, James D. *The Popular Book.* Berkeley: Univ. of California Press, 1961.

(42) Hoggart, Richard. *The Uses of Literacy.* London: Chatto and Windus, 1957.

(43) Jacobs, Norman, ed. *Culture for the Millions? Mass Media in Modern Society.* Princeton, N. J.: Van Nostrand Co., 1961.

(44) Lowenthal, Leo. *Literature, Popular Culture, and Society.* Englewood Cliffs, N.J.: Spectrum, 1961.

(45) MacDonald, Dwight. "A Theory of Mass Culture." *Diogenes,* No. 3 (Summer 1953).

(46) Martel, Martin U., and George J. McCall. "Reality-Orientation and the Pleasure Principle: A Study of American Mass-Periodical Fiction (1890-1955)." In *People, Society and Mass Communications.* Ed. Lewis Anthony Dexter and David Manning White. Glencoe, Ill.: Free Press, 1964.

(47) Mott, Frank Luther. *Golden Multitudes.* New York: Macmillan, 1947.

(48) Orwell, George. *Dickens, Dali & Others.* New York: Reynal & Hitchcock, 1946.

(49) Smith, Henry Nash. *Virgin Land: The American West As Symbol and Myth.* New York: Vintage Books, 1957.

(50) Webb, R. K. *The British Working Class Reader.* London: George Allen & Unwin, Ltd., 1955.

(50a) Wilensky, Harold L. "Mass Society and Mass Culture: Interdependence or Independence." *American Sociological Review,* Vol. xxix, No. 2 (April 1964), pp. 173-197.

(51) Winick, Charles. "Teen-agers, Satire, and *Mad.*" In *People, Society and Mass Communications.* Ed. Lewis Anthony Dexter and David Manning White. Glencoe, Ill.: Free Press, 1964.

This is, of course, the area where most of sociological work proper has been done; studies of the content material of the broadcasting media, the motion pictures, and the comics abound, but I suppose that the literary critic will be primarily interested in sociologically oriented studies of popular books. Curiously enough, the majority of important contributions have been made by literary scholars rather than by social scientists. I refer specifically to the work of Altick (38), Hoggart (42), and Smith (49), and in addition to James Hart (41), Webb (50), as well as Mott (47) and Orwell (48). Dwight MacDonald and the author of this essay have tried to trace the social history of the relationship between great artistic literature and popular literature since the Renaissance. (See 44 and 45.) An up-to-date survey on the present state of the treatment of artistic literature and mass literature is contained in the symposium edited by Norman Jacobs (43), which will also give the reader a feeling for the controversy raging on the social functions and usefulness of the mass media. (See also 40a.)

4. *Bridging the Gap*

(52) Auerbach, Erich. *Mimesis: The Representation of Reality in Western Literature.* Garden City, N. Y.: Anchor Books, 1957.

(53) Bennis, Warren G., ed. "Aesthetic Probings of Contemporary Man." *The Journal of Social Issues* (Special Issue), xx (Jan. 1964).

(54) Bloch, Donald S., ed. *The Arts and the Behavioral Sciences.* (A Bulletin of the Multidisciplinary Research Group, Arts Center, Boston University.) Vol. I, No. 2 (November 1959), No. 3 (January 1960), No. 4 (February 1960).

(55) Brombert, Victor. *The Intellectual Hero.* Chicago: Univ. of Chicago Press, 1964.

(56) Daiches, David. *The Novel and the Modern World.* Chicago, 1930.

(57) —— *Poetry and the Modern World.* Chicago, 1940.

(58) Grana, Cesar. *Bohemian Versus Bourgeois.* New York: Basic Books, 1964.

(59) Guérard, Albert. *The Life and Death of an Ideal.* New York: George Braziller, 1956.

(60) Howe, Irving. *Politics and the Novel.* New York: Meridian Books, 1962.

(61) Hughes, H. Stuart. *Consciousness and Society.* New York: Alfred A. Knopf, 1958.

(62) Lowenthal, Leo. *Literature and the Image of Man.* 2nd ed. Boston: Beacon, 1963.

(63) Levin, Harry. *The Gates of Horn: A Study of Five French Realists.* New York: Oxford Univ. Press, 1963.

(64) Stephen, Leslie. *English Literature and Society in the Eighteenth Century.* New York: Barnes and Noble, 1962.

(65) Thomson, George. *Aeschylus and Athens: A Study in the Social Origins of the Drama.* London, 1941

(66) Trilling, Lionel. *The Liberal Imagination.* New York: Viking Press, 1950.

(67) Watt, Ian. *The Rise of the Novel.* Berkeley: Univ. of California Press, 1957.

(68) Wilson, Edmund. *Axel's Castle: A Study in the Imaginative Literature of 1870-1930.* New York: Charles Scribner's Sons, 1959.

(69) Wilson, Robert N., ed. *The Arts in Society.* Englewood Cliffs, N. J.: Prentice-Hall, 1964.

The titles (52) through (69) are an indication of the promising rapprochement of social scientists and humanists. All these books are informed by attempts to evaluate the reflections of social and individual reality in literary works and to view the artist as the formulator of prevailing values and conflicts. Particular attention should perhaps be paid to Auerbach (52) and his ingenious application of a minute *explication de texte* for social analysis, and to Grana's successful interpretation of the French men of letters of the nineteenth century as the clearest manifestation of the alienation of the intellectual in modern bourgeois society (58)—an enterprise augmented by the monumental studies of the French realists by Harry Levin (63).

It is within this specific category of bridge building that we find a veritable interdisciplinary symposium, as it were, of literary scholars such as Auerbach, Trilling (66), Ian Watt (67), Levin, and Irving Howe (60), to name just a few, of historians such as Leslie Stephen (64) around the turn of the century, and Stuart Hughes (61) in our time, and of sociologists such as Grana and the author of this essay (see 62). If I had to make a decision, I would say that the most successful attempt to synthesize the literary and sociological approach is represented by Ian Watt's analysis of the English literary scene of the eighteenth century; he has demonstrated that an interdisciplinary orientation among the social sciences and the humanities need not be mere lip service. He has set the "rise of the novel" as a new literary genre in the social context of eighteenth-century England, with emphasis on the predominant middle-class features of the period.

The best introduction to the present state of cooperation of humanists and social scientists as far as they are interested in literature and in the arts in general is represented by the collection of essays edited by Robert Wilson (see 69).

5. Literature and Social History

(70) Aydelotte, William O. "The England of Marx and Mill as Reflected in Fiction." In *The Tasks of Economic History* (Supp. VIII, 1948, *Journal of Economic History*), pp. 42-58.

(71) Bramsted, Ernest K. *Aristocracy and the Middle-Classes in Germany.* Chicago: Univ. of Chicago Press, 1964.

(72) Knights, L. C. *Drama and Society in the Age of Jonson.* London: Chatto and Windus, 1937.

(73) Hauser, Arnold. *The Social History of Art.* Vol. I. Tr., in collaboration with author, Stanley Godman. New York: Knopf, 1951.

(74) —— *The Social History of Art*. Vol. II. Tr., in collaboration with author, Stanley Godman. New York: Knopf, 1951.

(75) Kennedy, William F. "Humanist Versus Economist: The Economic Thought of Samuel Taylor Coleridge." *Univ. of California Pubs. in Economics*, XVII (1958).

(76) —— "Economic Ideas in Contemporary Literature—The Novels of Thomas Wolfe." *The Southern Economic Journal*, Vol. XX, No. 1 (July 1953), pp. 35-50.

(77) Williams, Raymond. *Culture and Society, 1780-1950*. New York: Columbia Univ. Press, 1958.

(78) —— *The Long Revolution*. London: Chatto & Windus, 1961

(79) Wright, Louis B. *Middle-Class Culture in Elizabethan England*. Chapel Hill: Univ. of North Carolina Press, 1935.

My original strictures with regard to the usefulness of sociological work for the literary scholar need a correction. While I still would maintain that sociology can be particularly useful in the analysis of contemporary literature, I have to add now and to state almost dogmatically that no good literary history can be written without a thorough knowledge of social history. Since, unfortunately, the American sociologist is not strongly oriented toward historical analysis, the literary critic may have to look elsewhere in social science literature to remain within the mainstream of meaningful interpretation. While Arnold Hauser's work is to some degree a failure because of its encyclopedic pretensions, it represents nevertheless, in my opinion, a wealth of stimulating aphorisms, if you will, on social history as it impinges upon literature and the arts (73-74). His work is a variation of the Marxist theme but in a very unorthodox fashion. Successful attempts to bring social history to bear on literary criticism are the works by Knights (72) and Louis B. Wright (79). The publications of Raymond Williams (77 and 78), rich as they are in their data, suffer somewhat under the inclination of the author to argue with history in the name of the English Labor Party. Yet they are of considerable interest for the professional sociologist, and I should assume that Williams' broad concept of culture makes his studies on nineteenth-century England valuable for the literary critic as well.

6. The Sociology of the Writer and his Public

(80) Altick, Richard D. "The Sociology of Authorship." *Bulletin of the New York Public Library*, LXVI (June 1962), 389-404.

(81) Collins, A. S. *Authorship in the Days of Johnson*. New York, 1927.

(82) —— *The Profession of Letters (1780-1832)*. New York, 1928.

(83) Guérard, Albert. *Literature and Society*. Boston: Lothrop, Lee and Shepard, 1935.

(84) Harbage, Alfred. *As They Liked It: An Essay on Shakespeare and Morality.* New York: Macmillan, 1947.

(85) Holzknecht, Karl J. *Literary Patronage in the Middle Ages.* Philadelphia, 1923.

(86) Leavis, Q. D. *Fiction and the Reading Public.* London, 1932.

(87) Miller, Edwin Haviland. *The Professional Writer in Elizabethan England: A Study of Non-dramatic Literature.* Cambridge: Harvard Univ. Press, 1959.

(88) Saunders, J. W. *The Profession of English Letters.* London: Routledge and Kegan Paul, 1964.

(89) Schücking, Levin L. *The Sociology of Literary Taste.* New York: Oxford, 1945.

(90) Sheavyn, Phoebe. *The Literary Profession in the Elizabethan Age.* Manchester, 1909

Here we deal again with a group of studies where the social scientist has more to learn from the humanists than vice versa. Particularly in this country, historical studies on the sociology of the intellectual as well as studies on the publics of the artist are not very numerous. A recent exception is the book by Lewis Coser, *Men of Ideas* (Free Press, 1965), to which I have referred in the first section of this essay. But otherwise we are primarily indebted to Altick (80), Miller (87), and Saunders (88) for the expositions of the social position and function of the writer—an area to which, by the way, Ian Watt has also significantly contributed. (See 67.) Of particular interest for the sociologist is Miller's analysis of the relationship of the Elizabethan writers to the developing publishing houses as well as to the system of patronage.

In the field of the sociology of the reading publics the standard publication is of course the essay by the German Anglicist Schücking (89), by now somewhat dated, as are the contributions of Guérard (83). And every English scholar is familiar with the work on Shakespeare's public by Harbage (84) and the modern reading public by Mrs. Leavis (86).

7. Programmatic Statements

(91) Daiches, David. *Literature and Society.* London, 1938.

(92) Read, Herbert. *Art and Society.* New York: Pantheon Books, 1945.

(93) Watt, Ian. "Literature and Society." In *The Arts in Society* (see 69), pp. 229-314.

Finally, there are more programmatic statements on the relationship of literature and society. In addition to the classical book by Guérard under this title (see 83), we refer again to the brilliant statement of

Harry Levin, "Literature as an Institution" (see 63), to Herbert Read's work, whose programmatic statements, however, are primarily directed to the fine arts (see 92), to the survey-like thesis of Daiches (91), and to Ian Watt's stimulating article "Literature and Society" (93).

Auguste Comte – coined term *societas* + *logos*

Emile Durkheim – Sorbonne
(1858 – 1917)
  "Rules of Soc. Method"
              anomie
              (social isolation)
        see Dominick LaCapra. E. D. Sociologist & Philosopher
                  (Cornell, 1973), 315 pp.

Literature and Religion

By J. Hillis Miller

The relations of religion and literature involve methodological problems which may be specified easily enough. To specify them, however, is not to solve them. They constitute one version of that tension between extremes which characterizes all interpretation of literature. One set of these problems has to do with the relation between the critic and the work criticized. Another has to do with the relation between the work and the personal, cultural, or spiritual reality it expresses. I shall discuss the problems in that order.

I

Most students of literature today would agree that the aim of their discipline is elucidation of the intrinsic meanings of poems, plays, and novels. They want to know exactly what a sonnet by Shakespeare, an ode by Keats, or a novel by Trollope *means*. Poetic language, they tend to assume, is self-contained or self-referential. Whatever meanings a poem has are there on the page, shining forth from the words and their relations.

But though the words of a poem may contain its meaning, they do not do this in the way a cigarette package contains its cigarettes, or even in the way a tree contains its sap, a flower its aroma. A poem is not just black marks on the page or sonorous vibrations in the air. It comes into existence as a poem only in the mind and feelings of its reader or auditor. Though its meanings are intrinsic, they are intrinsic to an experience which includes the reader as well as the black marks, the listener as well as the sounds. A poem, unlike a scientific formula or a mathematical proof, cannot even be understood if the reader is too detached from it and regards it with too critical an eye. It exists partly as the emotions inhering in it, and these come into being only when it is read with sympathy. The reader or listener, however, is not a neutral machine for bringing verbal meanings into existence. He has a personality and a history of his own. The inherence of the reader in the poem leads to one of the difficulties involved in the relation of religion and literature.

It is natural for the reader of literature to have religious convictions, however vague or contradictory these may be. Even indifference to religious questions or rejection of them is of course a religious position. On the other hand, many works of literature have religious themes, whether overtly, as in the case of *The Divine Comedy,* the poems of St. John of the Cross, or *Murder in the Cathedral,* or more indirectly, as in the case of the poems of Hölderlin, Keats, or Arnold. The problem arises when a critic, with his own religious convictions, confronts the religious subject matter of a work of literature. Critics have usually chosen one of three characteristic ways of dealing with this problem. Each may lead to its own form of distortion. The critic may tend to assimilate writers to his own religious belief. He may be led to reject writers because they do not agree with his religious views. He may tend to trivialize literature by taking an objective or neutral view towards its religious themes.

Certainly a critic should be granted the right to his religious opinions. The mature man is the committed man, and where is it more important to be committed than in the area of religion? But even though religious faith is not incompatible with the view that God's house has many mansions, nevertheless in practice there is often conflict between the strength of a religious commitment and the historical relativism which the study of literature seems to demand and confirm. An evident fact about literature is the diversity of beliefs which have characterized poets of various times and places, and the knowledge of the way "world views" have varied throughout history is as much a part of present-day assumptions about literature as are the notions of intrinsic meaning and organic form. At one time and place people saw the world in one way and at another time and place in another way, and these endlessly changing views of things are incompatible. Homer, Dante, Shakespeare, Blake, and Wallace Stevens cannot all be equally right about the nature of things. Since this is the case, the first responsibility of the critic, it appears, is to abnegate his own views so that he may re-create with objective sympathy the way things seemed to Homer, Shakespeare, or Stevens. Literary study must be pluralist or relativist because its object is so. The literary critic must be a shape-shifter, a twentieth-century descendent of Keats's poet of negative capability. Having no nature of his own, he must be able to take on the nature of whatever poet he studies, wearing for a time the mask of Shelley, Marlowe, or Chaucer.

And yet to ask the man who holds religious views of his own to give these up when he studies literature is to ask him to become a divided man, keeping two important areas of his life separate. It is not easy, however, to open the frontiers between these areas.

If the critic tries to reconcile his religious belief and his love of literature he may be led to say that the works he reads agree with the insights of his faith, though when viewed with different eyes they do not appear to do so. After all, such a critic says, the world is really as my faith tells me it is, and even those writers who do not know this will testify unwittingly to the truth. Greek and pagan myths, it was once thought, are really distorted versions of Christian revelation. This view, or some modification of it, is still occasionally held. Medieval and Renaissance commentators were able to make Virgil into something like a great Christian poet. In our own day critics both Catholic and Protestant have sometimes argued that the works of a writer like Kafka or Camus are centrally Christian in meaning or at least may be assimilated into a Christian view of things. Another version of this is the anachronism of reading a writer like Coleridge or Shakespeare as a great "existentialist" poet. Such readings may import the categories of a modern religious or quasi-religious philosophy into works of literature to which they are alien. Jean-Paul Sartre, in his book on Baudelaire and in other studies, and Martin Heidegger, in his essays on Hölderlin, have found support for their views in interpretations of earlier works of art or literature, though their studies have been criticized for representing that form of distortion I am discussing.[1] But if Sartre and Heidegger are right about human existence there seems no reason why their insights should not be confirmed by anticipation in earlier poems or paintings. To hold this, however, is implicitly to contradict the notion that there is an intrinsic particularity in the world view of each age or individual, a particularity which may not with impunity be blurred by trans-historical schemes of interpretation.

Even the best of the overtly Christian critics, Jacques Maritain, Allen Tate, or Thomas Gilby among the Catholics, Amos Wilder, Nathan Scott, or W. H. Auden among the Protestants,[2] though they may

[1] See Jean-Paul Sartre, *Baudelaire* (Paris, 1947), and Martin Heidegger, *Erläuterungen zu Hölderlins Dichtung* (Frankfurt am Main, 1951).

[2] See Jacques Maritain, *Art and Scholasticism*, trans. J. F. Scanlan (London: Sheed & Ward, 1930); *Frontières de la poésie et autres essais* (Paris, 1935); with Raïssa Maritain, *Situation de la poésie* (Paris: Bruges, 1938); *Creative Intuition in Art and Poetry* (New York: Pantheon, 1953); Allen Tate, *Reason in Madness* (New York: Putnam, 1941); *On the Limits of Poetry* (New York: Swallow Press, William Morrow & Co., 1948); *The Man of Letters in the Modern World* (New York: Meridian, 1955); *Collected Essays* (Denver, Colo.: Alan Swallow, 1959); Thomas Gilby, *Poetic Experience: An Introduction to Thomist Aesthetic* (London: Sheed & Ward, 1934); Amos Wilder, *The Spiritual Aspects of the New Poetry* (New York, London: Harper & Bros., 1940); *Modern Poetry and the Christian Spirit* (New York: Scribner, 1952); *Theology and Modern Literature* (Cambridge, Mass.: Harvard Univ. Press, 1958); W. H. Auden, *The Enchafèd*

respect the individuality of non-Christian works, tend to make criticism a dialogue between their own religious views and the world views of the writers they discuss. They ask in effect: "Of what use is Camus, or Kafka, or Melville to a man who believes as I do?" and their studies often have compound titles which suggest this confrontation: *Modern Literature and the Religious Frontier, The Christian and the World of Unbelief, Christianity and Existentialism, The Tragic Vision and the Christian Faith.*[3]

It is easy so see why it is that the relations of religion and literature are now of special concern. In a time when the power of organized religion has weakened, people have turned, as Matthew Arnold said they would, to poetry as a stay and prop, even as a means of salvation. Many people who are authentically religious in the sense that they seek a supernatural meaning for their lives have made for themselves a religion compounded of a bit of their own inherited faith, a bit of existentialism, a bit of Maritain, a bit of Kafka, a bit of Zen Buddhism, a bit of Rilke, a bit of Ananda K. Coomaraswamy, and so on.

Arnold, however, was wrong, and T. S. Eliot was right. Literature is not a means of salvation. It is the Virgil which can take the pilgrim only so far. Beyond that point only Beatrice can lead the pilgrim farther.[4] Nevertheless, to take a man even so far is in a way a religious service. It may seem unpredictable but scarcely absurd that Paul Claudel should have been converted to Catholicism in part at least by his reading of Rimbaud.[5] Kafka's writings, for example, do have religious themes, as do Rimbaud's, and a critic needs much theological acumen to understand them. It is natural that scholars trained in theology should concern themselves with Kafka's work, or with Shakespeare's, or even with Camus's. Yet such a scholar, if he wishes to remain a literary critic and not become something else, must resist the temptation to grind his own axe.

Flood (New York: Random House, 1950); *The Dyer's Hand and Other Essays* (New York: Random House, 1962); Nathan A. Scott, Jr., *Rehearsals of Discomposure: Alienation and Reconciliation in Modern Literature* (New York: Columbia Univ., King's Crown Press, 1952); *Modern Literature and the Religious Frontier* (New York: Harper & Bros., 1958); *The Broken Center: Studies in the Theological Horizons of Modern Literature* (New Haven and London: Yale Univ. Press, 1966).

[3] For *Modern Literature and the Religious Frontier* see n. 2; *The Christian and the World of Unbelief* (New York: Abingdon Press, 1957) is by Libuse Lukas Miller; *Christianity and Existentialism* is a collection of essays edited by C. Michaelson; *The Tragic Vision and the Christian Faith* (New York: Association Press, 1957) is a collection of essays edited by Nathan A. Scott.

[4] See T. S. Eliot, *On Poetry and Poets* (New York: Farrar, Straus and Cudahy, 1957), p. 94.

[5] See Arthur Rimbaud, *Œuvres,* préface de Paul Claudel (Paris, 1912).

Nor are critics without explicit religious commitment exempt from this danger. Even a great critic like R. P. Blackmur could, because of his distaste for what seemed to him the weirdly heterodox metaphysics of Yeats's poems, sometimes argue that since the poems are so beautiful the bad metaphysics cannot be an intrinsic part of their meaning,[6] and some of the early criticism of Gerard Manley Hopkins' work is marred by the assumption that Hopkins' Catholicism must be more or less irrelevant to his poems.[7]

Another case in point is the work of the brilliant French critic Maurice Blanchot. Blanchot is fascinated by a certain conception of the relation between literary creation and a devouring darkness which, for him, underlies language and the human mind. He has written dozens of essays on widely different authors, many of them most impressive in the depth of their penetration. Nevertheless a curious process of assimilation operates in these essays. Whatever Mr. B. reads turns into Mr. B. Though he may begin with objective discussion, his own obsessive ideas are an engulfing whirlpool which sweeps Kafka, Beckett, Joubert, Musil, Rilke, and the rest into an irresistible swirling of language, dissipates their individual contours, and absorbs them into itself, so that each essay can end with another statement of those notions which are, in Blanchot's criticism, repeated again and again in almost the same form. The essays are in their movement a perfect imitation of the conception of literature which they presuppose, but the reader is left wondering whether he should call Blanchot's work literary criticism or give it some other name.[8] Only the wisest and best of men can avoid distorting the writers he studies in the direction of his own beliefs, and this tendency is all the more powerful the more firmly he holds those beliefs.

Suppose, then, we imagine a critic who recognizes this danger and who wishes nevertheless to remain a whole man. He will take a work of literature seriously enough to put in question the truth of its picture of

---

[6] A single sentence cannot do justice to the subtlety of Blackmur's essays on Yeats and to the energy with which he grapples with the problem of belief in Yeats. See, however, p. 97 in "The Later Poetry of W. B. Yeats," *Language as Gesture* (New York: Harcourt, Brace, 1952), where he proposes the following "remedy" for our inability to accept Yeats's "magical mode of thinking": "to accept Yeats's magic literally as a machinery of meaning, to search out the prose parallels and reconstruct the symbols he uses on their own terms in order to come on the emotional reality, if it is there, actually in the poems—when the machinery may be dispensed with."

[7] See, for one example of this, Vivian de Sola Pinto, *Crisis in English Poetry, 1880-1940* (London: Hutchinson's University Library, 1952), p. 72.

[8] See Maurice Blanchot, *La Part du feu* (Paris, 1949); *Lautréamont et Sade* (Paris, 1949); *L'Espace littéraire* (Paris, 1955); *Le Livre à venir* (Paris, 1959).

things, and will have the courage to reject those works which seem to him morally or religiously mistaken. What use can a poem have, however beautiful it may be, if it pictures the world falsely? If such a critic finds Wagner salacious, Milton the holder of an inhuman theology, or Yeats's metaphysics absurd, he will not think these elements extrinsic to their art.[9]

T. S. Eliot was a man of such courage. He expounds in "Tradition and the Individual Talent" a view of history which sees the literature of Europe from Homer to the present as forming a harmonious whole. If this is the case, then the addition of an authentic new work will alter the meanings of all the works back to *The Iliad,* and the meaning of the new work will lie in its relation to the others, its conformity to them.[10] But what of the work which does not conform? In a sense such a work will not exist at all, as, in Christian theology, evil has only a negative existence. The consequences for analysis and judgment of this view of literature are expressed in *After Strange Gods,* Eliot's most intransigent polemic.[11] Hardy, Lawrence, and Yeats receive the harshest criticism. Because they thought for themselves, or dared, as Yeats said of himself, to make a new religion "of poetic tradition, of a fardel of stories,"[12] they are heretics all. They dwell outside the closed community of European letters and must be condemned for whoring after strange gods. This condemnation follows logically enough from Eliot's religious commitment, and yet his paragraphs on Yeats, Hardy, and Lawrence (as F. R. Leavis has argued for the latter[13]) are hardly satisfactory as criticism, hardly give the reader much sense of the richness and complexity of the work of these writers. Eliot here comes close to substituting censorship for criticism.

The work of Albert Béguin offers another striking example of this.

[9] See William Empson, *Milton's God* (London: Chatto & Windus, 1961), and Yvor Winters, *The Poetry of W. B. Yeats* (Denver, Colo.: Alan Swallow, 1960). The books of Basil Willey and H. N. Fairchild attempt to combine historical objectivity with judgment based on religious commitment, but in the work of these scholars, particularly in Fairchild's, the religious conviction sometimes enters into the historical description and makes what began as unbiased research turn into polemical judgment. Fairchild's last three volumes, for example, are often an argument against the evil effects of romanticism and science on English poetry. See Basil Willey, *The Seventeenth Century Background* (London: Chatto & Windus, 1934); *The Eighteenth Century Background* (London: Chatto & Windus, 1940); *Nineteenth Century Studies* (London: Chatto & Windus, 1949); *More Nineteenth Century Studies* (London: Chatto & Windus, 1956); Hoxie Neale Fairchild, *Religious Trends in English Poetry,* Vol. i: 1700-1740, *Protestantism and the Cult of Sentiment* (1939); Vol. ii: 1740-1780, *Religious Sentimentalism in the Age of Johnson* (1942); Vol. iii: 1780-1830, *Romantic Faith* (1949); Vol.

His early book, *L'Ame romantique et le rêve,* is one of the masterpieces of twentieth-century criticism. With great learning, subtlety, and penetration, and above all with an unparalleled power of sympathetic understanding, Béguin re-creates the spiritual itineraries of the major German and French romantic writers. As the years passed, however, his capacity for sympathetic identification gradually narrowed. In the end his full sympathy and approval could go out only to a small group of writers, those representing a certain kind of modern Catholic spirituality: Dostoevski, Georges Bernanos, Léon Bloy, Charles Péguy. Even Pascal, who might be expected to fit Béguin's definition of authentic writing, did not escape his growing tendency to exclusions. Certain pages in one of Béguin's last books, the "Par lui-même" volume on Pascal, describe Pascal as alien to the deepest spiritual experience of today. A remorseless logic seems to have led this great critic to narrow more and more the circle of admissible writers.[14]

Suppose then that the critic decides to keep his own views out of his work. Literary study is objective and public, the establishment of the facts about literary history, part of that vast collective body of research which makes up the teamwork of modern scholarship. A man's religious views are his private business and need have nothing to do with his public life as a scholar. Even if literary analysis is to be thought of as the reliving from within of the world view of an author and its creation anew in the words of the critic, still this need have nothing to do with the critic's religious life. He must efface himself before the experience of literature, seek nothing for himself, give his mind and feelings to understanding the work at hand and to helping others to understand it through his analysis.

The problem of the relation between the religiously committed critic and the work of criticism seems to have been solved at one stroke. If

---

iv: 1830-1880, *Christianity and Romanticism in the Victorian Era* (1957); Vol. v: 1880-1920, *Gods of a Changing Poetry* (1962) (all published in New York by Columbia Univ. Press).

[10] See T. S. Eliot, *Selected Essays: 1917-1932* (New York: Harcourt, Brace, 1947), pp. 4-11.

[11] New York: Harcourt, Brace, 1934.

[12] *The Autobiography of William Butler Yeats* (New York: Macmillan, 1953), p. 70.

[13] See *D. H. Lawrence, Novelist* (London: Chatto & Windus, 1955).

[14] See *L'Ame romantique et le rêve,* 2 vols. (Marseille, 1937), nouvelle édition (Paris, 1939); *La Prière de Péguy* (Neuchâtel, 1944); *Léon Bloy: Mystique de la douleur* (Paris, 1948); *Poésie de la présence* (Paris, 1957); *Bernanos par lui-même* (Paris, 1954); *Pascal par lui-même* (Paris, 1952). For Béguin's reservations about Pascal, see "Pascal sans histoire," in *Pascal par lui-même,* pp. 59-111.

this solution is followed rigorously, however, it may turn literary criticism into a trivial pastime. The secret possibility of this triviality undermines the attitude of historicism, as it is present in Nietzsche's thought or in Ortega y Gasset's, or is developed in the criticism of Wilhelm Dilthey, Bernhard Groethuysen, and others, or is present in another form in the work of A. O. Lovejoy and other students of the so-called history of ideas.[15]

Historical relativism has close connections, as Nietzsche's work shows, with that modern form of nihilism which sees all cultural attitudes, all the masquerades that time resumes, as hollow because based on nothing outside man himself. Nietzsche tells man to experiment tirelessly with new life-forms, new world views. This experimentation is a way man can affirm his freedom from any supernatural law and assert his sovereign will to power over the world. What Nietzsche called the "death of God" is the presupposition of his historicism. Dilthey's aim of an exhaustive re-creation of all the types of life-forms leads to admirable works of criticism, but these may leave the reader in the end asking, "Wherefore? If all these forms of life are relative, what value do they have, and why should I bother to relive them?" Dilthey was not unaware of this implication of his work. The conflict between historical relativism and man's need for a universally valid knowledge seemed to him the essential problem raised by historicism.[16] This problem, he felt, could be solved only by pushing the historical sense to its limit. Man can go beyond history only through history. But where would a man be if he were beyond history? To have exhausted all cultural forms, in W. B. Yeats's view at least, is to be face to face with what he calls in "Meru" the "desolation of reality." The vision of all personages of history as relative to their times and places is likely to lead to the world-weariness of Paul Valéry in "La Crise de l'esprit," or to the rage for destruction of Yeats in "Nineteen Hundred and Nineteen."

The negative energy present in a rigorous historicism is especially

[15] See W. Dilthey, *Gesammelte Schriften,* 12 vols. (Leipzig & Berlin, 1923-36); Bernhard Groethuysen, *Die Enstehung der bürgerlichen Welt- und Lebensanschauung in Frankreich,* 2 vols. (Halle/Saale: Niemeyer, 1927, 1930); *Philosophische Anthropologie* (München & Berlin, 1934), French version: *Anthropologie philosophique* (Paris, 1952); *Mythes et portraits* (Paris, 1947); A. O. Lovejoy, *Essays in the History of Ideas* (Baltimore: Johns Hopkins Press, 1948); *The Great Chain of Being* (Cambridge, Mass.: Harvard Univ. Press, 1933); *The Reason, the Understanding and Time* (Baltimore: Johns Hopkins Press, 1961); *Reflections on Human Nature* (Baltimore: Johns Hopkins Press, 1961); *The Thirteen Pragmatisms and Other Essays* (Baltimore: Johns Hopkins Press, 1963). For an interesting recent book on Dilthey's work, see Kurt Müller-Volmer, *Towards a Phenomenological Theory of Literature: A Study of Wilhelm Dilthey's "Poetik"* (The Hague: Mouton, 1963), and for a recent discussion of Lovejoy's method-

apparent in the work of A. O. Lovejoy. Lovejoy had immense learning and an indefatigable power to understand the logic of ideas, including religious ones, in their development through history. He also had a great distaste for ambiguities and confusions of thought, and yet he felt that most writers are ambiguous or confused, often expressing conflicting ideas or incongruous feelings on a single page of their writing. Lovejoy's attitude toward Western history was a bit like that of a positivistic anthropologist collecting the strange myths and beliefs of the aborigines. This detachment is apparent in his habit of separating the statement of a "unit-idea" from its living context in the thought of a writer and presenting it in cold isolation where it can be subjected to his merciless power of logical analysis. This analysis puts in question both the idea that there is a unity in the culture of a period and the idea that there is a unity in the thought of an individual man. Examples of this are Lovejoy's fragmentation of romanticism and his discrimination of sixty-six different senses in which the idea of nature was, in antiquity, connected with "norms."[17]

Neither objective description of historical facts nor sympathetic recreation of the life-forms of the past can be a self-sufficient end in itself. A twentieth-century inheritor of historicism, Wallace Stevens, recognizes this when, in "The Noble Rider and the Sound of Words," he rejects Plato's image of the charioteer of the soul and Verrocchio's splendid equestrian statue of Bartolommeo Colleoni.[18] They are of little interest to us now, he says, if they are no more than outmoded forms of the past, a stage set which has been taken down and carted away. The study of the supreme fictions of history has value only if it is related to our search for the supreme fictions of today. Dilthey himself, at the end of *Die Einbildungskraft des Dichters,* an essay of 1887, affirms that though there is something universal about the work of the greatest poets, nevertheless even they are creatures of history. This means that the poets of the past can never move us as they did their contemporaries. The poets of most value to us are the poets of today, those who can speak to us of our own

---

ology, see Maurice Mandelbaum, "The History of Ideas, Intellectual History, and the History of Philosophy," *The Historiography of the History of Philosophy,* Beiheft 5 of *History and Theory* (The Hague: Mouton, 1965), pp. 33-42.

[16] See, e.g., the end of his speech on the occasion of his seventieth birthday, in *Die Geistige Welt,* Part 1, *Gesammelte Schriften,* v, 9.

[17] See "On the Discrimination of Romanticisms," *Essays in the History of Ideas,* pp. 228-253, and the Appendix to A. O. Lovejoy and G. Boas, *A Documentary History of Primitivism and Related Ideas* (Baltimore: The Johns Hopkins Press, 1935).

[18] See *The Necessary Angel: Essays on Reality and the Imagination* (New York: Alfred A. Knopf, 1951), pp. 7, 9.

experience.[19] The study of literature cannot be justified in the same way as scientific research can. Each new scientific fact builds up man's picture of the universe and may have practical applications in the great technological civilization he is creating. The student of literature, quite properly, wants to know what's in it for him, and a pure historical relativism, to the degree that it answers that there's nothing in it for him, reduces the study of literature to triviality. Homer's work, or Dante's, or Hardy's must be more than just one way of looking at things among innumerable others, and yet the consequences of assuming this involve the difficulties I discussed earlier.

No doubt in practice a good critic can reconcile his religious convictions with catholicity of taste and wide-ranging sympathy for many authors, but still he must be on guard against the dangers of unwittingly making works of literature over in his own image, or of unjustly condemning them, or of failing to take them seriously enough to put in question the authenticity of their religious themes. The tension between dispassionate objectivity and engagement is in the nature of literary study and must be lived by each critic as best he can.

II

Even if the critic interested in the religious aspects of literature makes his peace with this tension, a new set of problems faces him when he considers the external context of a poem or novel. I said at the beginning that a poem embodies its meaning. This is true, but words are not, after all, like notes in music, meaningless except in their relation to one another. They have a complicated cultural history. The notion of intrinsic meaning is not incompatible with the idea that each poem draws into itself all those connections it has with its various contexts. It is often useful to have those connections identified, not only for their own sake, but for the light they may shed on meanings which are there in the words of the work. Such investigations may show how a certain text draws its life from similar passages in other works by the author, or from books read by the author, or from the social and historical milieu in which it came into existence, or from the tradition to which it belongs.

But where does the context of a poem stop? Its relations to its surroundings radiate outward like concentric circles from a stone dropped in water, and it may be extremely difficult to give a satisfactory inventory of them. Moreover, this investigation tends to disperse the poem into the multiplicity of its associations until it may become little more than a point of focus for the impersonal ideas, images, and motifs which enter into it. Instead of being a self-sufficient entity, it is only a symptom of ideas or images current in the culture which generated it.

If the critic rejects this implication of contextual study and returns

[19] *Die Geistige Welt*, Part 2, *Gesammelte Schriften*, VI, 241.

to the poem itself, another danger awaits him. The more completely he cuts the poem off from its mesh of defining circumstances, the less, it may be, he can allow himself to say about it. The poem means only itself, and any commentary falsifies it by turning it into something other than itself. Fearing the heresies of paraphrase and explanation, he may be reduced to silence, or to repeating the poem itself as its only adequate commentary.[20]

No doubt there is validity in both these views of literature. Each authentic poem is something altogether individual, and even other poems by the same writer are more or less irrelevant to its self-enclosed integrity. On the other hand, the insights gained by study of a poem's context may help the critic in many ways in his attempt to understand this particularity.

The problem of the proper focus to choose for the interpretation of a given work or author has, however, special difficulties in relation to the study of religious themes in literature. How is the critic to treat these? Is he to hold that each religious poem has a meaning which is peculiar to that poem alone? If this is the case then there is, for example, one religious view of things for Gerard Manley Hopkins' "The Windhover," another for "God's Grandeur," another for "Spelt from Sibyl's Leaves," another for "The Wreck of the Deutschland," and so on. In each case the religious meanings must be developed solely from the words of the particular poem, and this means that each religious poem will have a unique religious meaning. A strict "new critical" approach to Hopkins' work would follow this path, and in fact many of the essays on "The Windhover" assume that it can be understood more or less in isolation from the rest of Hopkins' work.

Obviously, however, there are echoes, resemblances, fraternal similarities between one poem by Hopkins and the others. Nor are his letters, notebooks, essays, and devotional writings without relevance to an understanding of his poems. Each poem lives in a context which includes everything Hopkins ever wrote. Should the critic therefore attempt to show how that circumambient milieu is a complex harmony of related themes?[21] But then, once more, the individual poem is in danger of losing its integrity and becoming a node in a web of connections or a moment in a spiritual history which transcends it.

On the other hand, why should the critic stop with Hopkins' own writings? The poet was a nineteenth-century Jesuit and a graduate of Oxford. His reading in Scotus, Ignatius, and Suarez, his knowledge of

[20] Jean Starobinski has eloquently described this paradox of criticism in *L'Œil vivant* (Paris: Gallimard, 1961), pp. 24-27

[21] As, e.g., I have tried to do in my chapter on Hopkins in *The Disappearance of God: Five Nineteenth-Century Writers* (Cambridge, Mass.: Belknap Press of Harvard Univ. Press, 1963).

the Bible and of Catholic liturgy, the influence of his tutor at Oxford, Walter Pater, his readings in Greek philosophy as an undergraduate, his place in the Oxford movement or in the general history of Victorian religious experience—none of these associations is irrelevant, and yet their investigation tends, as it proliferates, to dissolve Hopkins into what influenced him, to make his work no more than a "product" of its time.

Certainly all three focuses of criticism are valid, the study of the individual work, the study of all the works of one author, the study of the ideas or sensibility of an age, but each tends to imply a different notion of the way religious themes are present in literature.

The contextual problems in the interpretation of religious literature are especially apparent in the scholarship on medieval and Renaissance poetry. A complex body of learning—traditional topoi, subtle methods of allegory, many-layered symbols—may be hidden in an apparently simple lyric of these periods. For an educated man of the Middle Ages or Renaissance, it is argued, all literature, philosophy, and theological writing from Greek times to the present form a single tradition which should determine the shape and content of any authentic poem. This tradition was taken for granted by a contemporary reader of Chaucer, Spenser, or Milton, and guided his understanding of their poems. The twentieth-century reader must labor to recover the context permitting a just interpretation of such writers, just as a reader of the twenty-fifth century will no doubt have to labor to recover what he needs to know in order to read Faulkner, Camus, or Beckett, not to speak of Eliot or Joyce. To understand Dante, Chaucer, or Donne, or at least to understand them in relation to the traditions in which their work participates, the scholar must steep himself in these traditions, know Greek and Latin literature, classical philosophy, medieval encyclopedias, Biblical commentaries, and so on. Admirable work has been done in this way by scholars as different in their methods and commitments as E. R. Curtius, Erich Auerbach, D. C. Allen, C. S. Singleton, Morton Bloomfield, and D. W. Robertson, Jr.[22]

[22] See E. R. Curtius, *Europäische Literatur und lateinisches Mittelalter* (Bern, 1948), English trans. Willard R. Trask (New York: Pantheon, 1953); Erich Auerbach, *Mimesis* (Bern, 1946), 2nd ed. (Bern, 1959), English trans. Willard R. Trask (Princeton, N. J.: Princeton Univ. Press, 1953); *Literatursprache und Publikum in der lateinischen Spätantike und im Mittelalter* (Bern, 1958), English trans. Ralph Manheim (New York: Bollingen Foundation, 1965); "Figura," *Archivum Romanicum,* xxII (1938), 436-489; "Typological Symbolism in Mediaeval Literature," *Yale French Studies,* No. 9 (1952), pp. 5-8; D. C. Allen, *The Harmonious Vision: Studies in Milton's Poetry* (Baltimore: Johns Hopkins Press, 1954); *Image and Meaning: Metaphoric Traditions in Renaissance Poetry* (Baltimore: Johns Hopkins Press, 1960); C. S. Singleton, *An Essay on the Vita Nuova* (Cambridge, Mass.: Harvard Univ. Press, 1949); *Dante Studies* (Cam-

Critics still differ, however, about the proper way of interpreting medieval and Renaissance literature. Their recent disagreements have often had to do with the question of the way religious meanings inhere in secular literature. C. S. Singleton and R. H. Green, to cite one example, have argued about whether *The Divine Comedy* is to be considered allegory of the poets or allegory of the theologians.[23] The question at issue is whether or not it is proper to read Dante's poem strictly on the model of the four-level allegorical interpretation which was applied in the Middle Ages to the Bible. The answer to this question will determine what is meant when *The Divine Comedy* is called a religious poem.

Quarrels about context arise as much or more from disagreement about which is the important context for a given poem as from disagreement about whether or not a given poem can be understood in isolation. Even though all scholars would probably now agree that *Beowulf* is a Christian poem, still the poem changes magically if it is moved from the milieu of the Bible and Latin literature of the Middle Ages to the milieu of Germanic heroic poetry. On the other hand, a secular lyric of the Middle Ages or Renaissance may appear innocent of religious meaning when it is looked at in isolation, but when it is set against texts from the Bible, St. Augustine, St. Gregory, Rhabanus Maurus, and so on, images which seemed realism or decoration take on another meaning and reveal themselves to be symbols of transcendent truths. Who is to say that this symbolism is in the text itself and has not been installed there by the legerdemain of the learned critic? Only the tact born of long immersion in the literature of the period can tell, but the long immersion produces different results in different cases. A consensus among critics in these areas is an ideal to be worked toward rather than a goal yet attained.

III

The problem of context is associated with another problem, the last of the issues involved in the relation of religion and literature which I shall discuss. Exactly what does it mean to say that religious meanings are pres-

---

bridge, Mass.: Harvard Univ. Press, 1954—); Morton Bloomfield, *The Seven Deadly Sins* (East Lansing: Michigan State College Press, 1952); *Piers Plowman as a Fourteenth-Century Apocalypse* (New Brunswick, N. J.: Rutgers Univ. Press, 1962); D. W. Robertson, Jr., and B. F. Huppé, *Piers Plowman and Scriptural Tradition* (Princeton, N. J.: Princeton Univ. Press, 1951); D. W. Robertson, Jr., *A Preface to Chaucer: Studies in Medieval Perspectives* (Princeton, N. J.: Princeton Univ. Press, 1963).

[23] See C. S. Singleton, "Dante's Allegory," *Speculum,* xxv (1950), 78-83; "The Other Journey," *Kenyon Review,* xiv (1952), 189-206; "The Irreducible Dove," *Comparative Literature,* ix (1957), 129-135, and Richard Hamilton Green, "Dante's 'Allegory of Poets' and the Mediaeval Theory of Poetic Fiction," *Comparative Literature,* ix (1957), 118-128.

ent in a poem or a play? It may mean the following: The poet belonged to a certain culture. Among the elements of that culture were religious beliefs. These were part of the world view of his age, and naturally they enter into his poems, since all men are subject to the spirit of their times. To take this view is to accept that historicism which, as I argued earlier, tends to turn religious themes in literature into something other than themselves. Of what religious interest are such themes in Dante's poems, or George Herbert's, or T. S. Eliot's if they are accidents of a certain time and place, determined horizontally, as it were, by the influence of other men and their books? Religious themes in literature are without religious significance unless they spring from a direct relationship between the poet and God, however much they may take a form dictated by the age. If human history is made by men alone, then religious elements in culture have only a human meaning. For Ludwig Feuerbach and other such humanists religious ideas are symptoms of the way men lived together at a certain time. Religion for Feuerbach or for George Eliot is the cement of culture, a collective belief which holds people together.[24]

A similar transmutation of the religious import of literature is implicit in an exclusive commitment to either of the other focuses of criticism I have identified. If, as the structural linguists and some "new critics" tend to assume, the meanings of a work of literature are entirely intrinsic, generated by the interaction among its words, then the symbolizing process predominates over what is symbolized, and literature is in danger of becoming a play of words mirroring one another vacantly. In such a case, religious themes will not be different in kind from any other themes in literature, since poetry on any subject does no more than demonstrate the power of language to develop complex symbolic structures. To such a view of literature a man interested in religious themes in poetry could make the same reproach Paul Ricœur directs against the anthropological structuralism of Claude Lévi-Strauss. Ricœur sees in Lévi-Strauss's work "an extreme form of modern agnosticism." "For you," he said to Lévi-Strauss in a public discussion of June 1963, "there is no 'message,' not in the cybernetic sense, but in the 'kerygmatic' sense; you give up meaning in despair; but you save yourself by the notion that if human beings have nothing to say, at least they say it so well that one can subject their discourse to a structural analysis. You save meaning, but it is the meaning of meaninglessness, the admirable syntactic arrangement of a discourse which says nothing. I see you at that point of conjunction of agnosticism and an acute understanding of syntaxes."[25]

[24] See Ludwig Feuerbach, *Das Wesen des Christenthums*, Bd. 7 of his *Sämmtliche Werke* (Leipzig, 1849), English translation by George Eliot (London, 1854), also available in Harper Torchbook series.

[25] *Esprit*, 31ᵉ année, No. 322 (novembre 1963), pp. 652, 653: "Je penserais plutôt que cette philosophie implicite entre dans le champ de votre travail, où

The same kind of restriction may limit that form of criticism which takes as its goal the comprehension of the mind of an author as revealed in the ensemble of his works. If each writer's mind is autonomous, the sole originator of the meanings which are expressed in his works, then any seemingly religious themes in those works will have a human rather than a divine meaning. They will be nothing but a part of the pageant of human history.

Any method of criticism which presupposes that meaning in literature is exclusively derived from the interrelations of words, or from the experiences of a self-enclosed mind, or from the living together of a people will be unable to confront religious themes in literature as such. Only if some supernatural reality can be present in a poem, in a mind, or in the cultural expressions of a community can there be an authentic religious dimension in literature. Only if there is such a thing as the spiritual history of a culture or of a person, a history determined in part at least by God himself as well as by man in his attitude toward God, can religious motifs in literature have a properly religious meaning. The scholar's position on this issue will follow from his religious convictions, which returns me to the assertion that the religious commitment of the critic, or lack of it, cannot be considered irrelevant to his work.

In the relation of the critic to the work criticized and in the relation of the work to its context there are methodological problems which take especially difficult forms when the connections of religion and literature are in question. Though there is no easy way to solve these, no golden mean which will allow a happy steering between extremes, there is an attitude toward literary study which will escape some of its dangers. The scholar-critic must be as learned as possible, not only in literature itself, but in history, philosophy, theology, the other arts, and so on. Only in this way can he avoid egregious errors caused by ignorance. Nevertheless, the end of literary study is still elucidation of the intrinsic meanings

---

je vois une forme extrême de l'agnosticisme moderne; pour vous il n'y a pas de 'message': non au sens de la cybernétique, mais au sens kérygmatique; vous êtes dans le désespoir du sens; mais vous vous sauvez par la pensée que, si les gens n'ont rien à dire, du moins ils le disent si bien qu'on peut soumettre leur discours au structuralisme. Vous sauvez le sens, mais c'est le sens du non-sens, l'admirable arrangement syntactique d'un discours qui ne dit rien. Je vous vois à cette conjonction de l'agnosticisme et d'une hyperintelligence des syntaxes." See also, in the same number of *Esprit*, the essay by Paul Ricœur entitled "Structure et herméneutique" (pp. 596-627). Ricœur's essay is an excellent discussion of the relation between the objectivity proper to structuralism and that form of interpretation from within which he calls, after Dilthey and others, "la compréhension herméneutique." The latter he sees as most appropriate for reaching, by way of sympathetic participation in a tradition, religious meanings in literature and in other cultural forms.

of poems, plays, and novels. In the effort toward such elucidation the proper model for the relation of the critic to the work he studies is not that of scientist to physical objects but that of one man to another in charity. I may love another person and know him as only love can know without in the least abnegating my own beliefs. Love wants the other person to be as he is, in all his recalcitrant particularity. As St. Augustine puts it, the lover says to the loved one, "Volo ut sis!"—"I wish you to be." If the critic approaches the poem with this kind of reverence for its integrity, it will respond to his questioning and take its part in that dialogue between reader and work which is the life of literary study.

The metaphor of lover and beloved will also indicate what tone the critic should take with *his* reader. I may tell you what the man or woman I love is like, but this is no substitute for your direct confrontation with that person. Criticism too is only a preliminary to the reader's own dialogue with the work. In the end criticism must efface itself before the texts, stand back, having done the work of interpretation, to let the works show themselves forth as they are. Only in this way will those religious meanings which are in the work and not in the beholder's eye be made visible.

Literature and Music

By Bertrand H. Bronson

Epigraph

Mr. Chromatic professed himself astonished that a gentleman of genuine modern taste, like Mr. Milestone, should consider the words of a song of any consequence whatever, seeing that they were at the best only a species of pegs, for the more convenient suspension of crotchets and quavers. This remark drew on him a very severe reprimand from Mr. Mac Laurel, who said to him, "Dinna ye ken, sir, that soond is a thing utterly worthless in itsel, and only effectual in agreeable excitements, as far as it is an aicho to sense? Is there ony soond mair meeserable an' peetifu' than the scrape o' a feddle, when it does na touch ony chord i' the human sensorium? Is there ony mair divine than the deep note o' a bagpipe, when it breathes the auncient meelodies o' leeberty an' love? It is true, there are peculiar trains o' feeling an' sentiment, which parteecular combinations o' meelody are calculated to excite; an' sae far music can produce its effect without words: but it does na follow, that, when ye put words to it, it becomes a matter of indefference what they are; for a gude strain of impassioned poetry will greatly increase the effect, and a tessue o' nonsensical doggrel will destroy it a' thegither. Noo, as gude poetry can produce its effect without music, sae will gude music without poetry; and as gude music will be mair pooerfu' by itsel' than wi' bad poetry, sae will gude poetry than wi' bad music: but, when ye put gude music an' gude poetry thegither, ye produce the divinest compound o' sentimental harmony that can possibly find its way through the lug to the saul."

Mr. Chromatic admitted that there was much justice in these observations, but still maintained the subserviency of poetry to music. Mr. Mac Laurel as strenuously maintained the contrary . . .

T. L. Peacock, *Headlong Hall,* Ch. xiii, "The Ball"

Formerly, in the person of Apollo, the arts of poetry and music were inseparable. But since his day, their functions have been specialized, and it is notorious that since about the time of Shakespeare, when they were still, at farthest, on a footing of sister and brother (see Barnfield's sonnet "If music and sweet poetry agree"), they have been growing less and less familiar, and are content to live independent lives. The older union has persisted in conventional collaborations, though songs without words no longer occasion surprise, and songs only to be read are far commoner than songs made for singing. It seems to be the case, generally speaking, that what poets nowadays most want to express has little use for a tune, and indeed would be hampered by musical accompaniment of any sort; and that, conversely, music aspires to be self-sustained and free from the contamination of foreign ideas, or from dependence upon a language with commitments outside the limits of pure tonal sense. But whenever the separation approaches absolute divorce, with music forsaking melody and poetry forgetting lyrical, rhythmic statement, it is at least to be feared that the loss on either side will be palpable. "Musick and Poetry have ever been acknowledg'd Sisters, which walking hand in hand, support each other; As Poetry is the harmony of Words, so Musick is that of Notes: and as Poetry is a Rise above Prose and Oratory, so is Musick the exaltation of Poetry. Both of them may exist apart, but sure they are most excellent when they are joyn'd."[1] To argue the case is unnecessary here. Moreover, as already implied, it is irrelevant to the bulk of evidence, which for the past two thousand years or more until yesterday has exemplified the junction, not the separation, of words and music. And it would appear axiomatic that where marriage is perfect, each partner fulfills and enhances the other. It is the nature and possibilities of this relationship, therefore, that constitute our proper subject matter. The question of relative dominance, upon which Mr. Chromatic and Mr. MacLaurel were so obstinately opposed, has a long history and is ultimately inescapable; but we have all known blessed moments of felicity when it ceased to be—or better, did not come in consciousness. *Moments* they were, because, as with other marriages, an ideal realized within time is brief and miraculous; so that most experiences of this transcendent kind have probably occurred in the smaller, lyrical forms. But there are so many degrees and kinds of collaboration, combination, relation, interpenetration, and imitation that we shall have to limit ourselves to fleeting glances at selected parts of a very wide spectrum.

There is, however, an aspect of the divorce mentioned above that may best be discussed before we proceed to consider the relationships just now adumbrated. Granted the divorce, and the consequent divergence of paths between the arts, the question arises whether music has

[1] Henry Purcell, Dedication of *Dioclesian* to Charles, Duke of Somerset, 1691.

developed, on its independent course, techniques that might be service-
able or suggestive to literature or to literary analysis. What have the musicians to teach or to lend the writers, either creative or critical, that
might illuminate the latters' practice?

The answer, I fear, is: less than one might have imagined or hoped.
To perceive that both arts exist in an aural medium, and therefore in a
temporal dimension, is of course to set them off against the spatial arts
of architecture, painting, and sculpture, and also to infer a whole series
of analogies, appeals, and devices implicated in those aural and temporal
facts, such as sonal similitude and contrast, repetition, development and
pace, allusion backward and forward (hence irony), climax, suspense
and surprise, rhythm and metre, and other inherent elements common to
both. But to assume that the verbal arts can adopt and exploit the formal
patterns and technical devices of music, even in their simplest states,
with the same or similar effects, is to be beguiled by the specious logic of
a shared terminology. Identical aesthetic effects do not follow, in the two
arts, from apparently identical means. Even where the device is most
nearly duplicated, our reactions are likely to be quite different. Take for
example the case of simple repetition. First, our tolerance for musical
repetition is far greater than for verbal repetition, explain the fact who
can. Moreover, meaning accrues from musical repetition by allusive interplay, analogous to, but far subtler than, the verbal reversions of triolet
or rondeau. A folk song will serve for illustration:

The four phrases of this tune, repeated in pairs, take on new significance
by being repeated, like an image under a succession of varicolored
lenses. Phrase (a), when it follows (b) in the repeat, has a plaintive insistence it did not have the first time it was heard; and similarly with the
rest. The cadence of (b), identical with that of (d), gets a fourfold repetition within this narrow space; but the first halves of those phrases (b)
and (d) address each other across the intervening notes, and this marked-
ly alters the sense of the conclusion. At the recurrence of (b), the reference is only to (a)'s rejoinder, in a *quasi* "nevertheless"; while, as the end
of (d) at (d)'s first occurrence, the cadence shows a strong thrust to continue discussion. But when (c) flags on repeating itself, (d) catches, both
from (b) and (c), a sort of assurance that it will not be further chal-
lenged, and ends with a quiet finality not heard before.

If we turn from this miniature musical colloquy to bare words with a corresponding repetitional pattern, we find that, as soon as we have grasped the sense, and learned the refrain, the repetitions do nothing to enhance the total meaning of the statement. The words are as follows:

> *Babes, O babes, I wish you were mine,*
> > *Down by the green wood sidey,*
> *Babes, O babes, I wish you were mine,*
> > *Down by the green wood sidey,*
> *I'd dress you all in silk so fine,*
> > *Down by the green wood sidey,*
> *I'd dress you all in silk so fine,*
> > *Down by the green wood sidey.*[2]

The brooding speaker, a woman, conveys little added conviction by repeating. She neither raises a doubt of her sincerity nor adds pathos; and if we do not appropriate the refrain to ourselves as our own bewildered commentary, she may in her katatonic state arouse pity but little sympathy. Dreariness is intensified, and boredom is ready to set in if things go on like this. Now, of course, if we are aware of the situation here, the lines become charged with a melodramatic *frisson*. What evokes the words is the fact that this mother has murdered, and secretly buried, her own babies, and does not realize that these naked revenants are her own dead children. Her heart goes out to them in maternal, and remorseful, yearning. But it remains true that the electric shock of this event could hardly be conveyed in a more listless manner. Without the music, the repetitions deaden, instead of animating. There is little to choose between them and Calverley's ballad-parody:

> The farmer's daughter hath soft brown hair
> > *(Butter and eggs and a pound of cheese)*
> And I met with a ballad, I can't say where,
> > Which wholly consisted of lines like these.

If, then, in so minute a scale as a four-phrase tune such profound differences of effect are manifest when repetitive verse is compared at the same level, it should be apparent that in larger and more complex forms the contrasts are geometrically multiplied and magnified. Except as suggestive analogy, comparison is impossible, and it should not surprise that Calvin S. Brown's interesting *Music and Literature: A Comparison of the Arts,* 1948, arrives at generally negative conclusions. Brown shows exhaustively how very seldom a successful interchange has

---

[2] *English Folk-Songs from the Southern Appalachians,* collected by Cecil J. Sharp, ed. Maud Karpeles (London, 1932), I, 61.

occurred. We can see, for example, that the *aria da capo* form, ABA, could never be adopted for narrative texts, although conceivable for lyric within narrow limits. The forms that make use of lyrical repetition need music to sustain them, and indeed were born *of* music. Sonata form—unless the author who borrows and adopts it in a literary work confides his intention to the reader—is unlikely to be perceived in a work of any complexity. When the "development" section is reached, the reader will probably conclude that the author has lost control of his materials; and to perform in any purely literary medium the counterpart of what happens in a musical "recapitulation" is a feat that could seldom be justified by the nature of the matter in hand. The writer of the present paper was once guilty of such an experiment in a critical essay, having been struck by the fact that the "second subject," though opposed, could really be assimilated with the first, when looked at against a changed social context. But, so far as he has learned, no reader by himself ever discovered what he was up to! The sole profit of the experiment was that it stimulated the author's imagination. It is *a fortiori* obvious that any musical form involving the simultaneous introduction of more than a single voice, in counterpoint or fugue or whatever kind of combination, is impossible to imitate effectively in a verbal scheme. Analogues are so distant as to beggar comparison.

There is, however, a sort of analogy between literature and music which is more deeply suggestive. It is that, as Rabkin points out in his studies of plot in Shakespeare's great plays, e.g., *Julius Caesar* and *Troilus and Cressida,* one part or plot-line of the play may operate over against another in such a way as to compel contemplation of both simultaneously, so that the effect is *quasi* contrapuntal and mutually illuminating.[3]

There is also the possibility of a recurrent theme or motif, woven into the texture of a long poem or narrative like a returning melodic idea, producing episodic parallels of contrast or similitude—echoes that serve to bind the parts into a closer and more suggestive unity. Calvin Brown finds a telling example of this technique in Whitman's slow-wheeling, ever-enriched recall of the three symbols, hermit thrush, evening star, and lilac, in his great ode, "When Lilacs last in the dooryard bloomed."[4]

Where music combines with a text to control and guide associational reception, it can of course do much in the way of pointed comment.

[3] Norman Rabkin, "Structure, Convention, and Meaning in *Julius Caesar,*" JEGP, LXIII (April 1964), 240-254; and "*Troilus and Cressida:* The Uses of the Double Plot," *Shakespeare Studies,* ed. J. Leeds Barroll (Cincinnati, 1965), pp. 265-282.

[4] Calvin S. Brown, *Music and Literature,* pp. 178-194.

Bertrand H. Bronson

Growing out of medieval cosmological theory, which assigned semantic significance to the modes, and attributed metaphysical import to tonal structure, and which still echoed faintly in the baroque feeling for diatonic scales and key-systems and for metrical patterns, music had developed a rather complex language conventionalized to express correspondence with verbal ideas and emotional states. Tonalities came to be associated with specific emotions, as can often be observed in Handel's practice. Thus, F major is a pastoral key, D major a martial. Meaning of this sort was not inherent but the result of consenting tradition. Keys come to seem, by cumulative precedent, appropriate to particular moods. It is normal that Beethoven's "Spring" sonata for violin and his "Pastoral Symphony" are both in F major. Of course, a tradition can (always) be broken for particular or idiosyncratic reasons. For example, the contralto solo in "Messiah," "He shall feed his flock," is in F major, but the "pastoral symphony" in the same work is in C, either for the *tessitura* of the violins or because of contrasting keys before and after. But it is important to know what we should be looking for, whether the expectation is flouted or satisfied: there is an added meaning either way. Thanks to continued associations with dancing or other forms of concerted motion, certain rhythms still carry strong ideational potency, though the choice of alternative possibilities of significance depends always upon the context, verbal and situational.

But the translation of ideas into musical notes is more difficult, and by the theorists of the seventeenth and early eighteenth centuries was carried to extremes. Johannes Mattheson, the boyhood friend of Handel, carried the elaboration of musical tropes to the point where he could speak of *Klangrede,* or tonal speech, and declared that musical notes in rhythmic order should strive to convey sense so as to excite the passions as effectively as the most accomplished orator. In his view, the technical resources of music should subserve the ends of describing or painting the passions objectively.[5] Such a language, intended to raise musical meaning to a level of parity with philosophical and literary thought, depended of course on general agreement as to the aural signs employed, and it may as well be admitted that the pitch of absurdity was easier to achieve than to arrive at so exact an equivalence. But the allegorizing impulse behind the so-called *Affektenlehre* is thoroughly characteristic of baroque art generally, and the effort to objectify the emotions so as to rationalize and in a sense bring them under intellectual ordering is an ancient and honorable ambition, going back through *maniera, musica re-*

[5] See Johann Mattheson, *Der vollkommene Capellmeister* (1739); M. Bukofzer, *Music in the Baroque Era* (New York, 1947); Herbert M. Schueller, "Imitation and 'Expression' in British Music Criticism in the Eighteenth Century," *Musical Quarterly,* xxxiv (1948), 544-566.

servata, the *camerata,* and *nuove musiche,* in keeping with the conviction that

> From harmony, from heav'nly harmony
> This universal frame began;

and that rightly conceived the realm of music extends from the physical to the metaphysical. Hear Sir Thomas Browne: "For there is a musicke where-ever there is a harmony, order or proportion; and thus farre we may maintain the musick of the spheares . . . for even that vulgar and Taverne Musicke, which makes one man merry, and another mad, strikes in mee a deepe fit of devotion, and a profound contemplation of the first Composer, there is something in it of Divinity more than the eare discovers. It is an Hieroglyphicall and shadowed lesson of the whole world, and Creatures of God, such a melody to the eare, as the whole world well understood, would afford the understanding. In briefe, it is a sensible fit of that Harmony, which intellectually sounds in the eares of God."[6]

In their endeavor to find a fit and comprehensible speech so as to match ideas with musical counterparts, the great composers seldom went to extremes. The simple expedients of "high" and "low" notes to suggest analogies either literal or metaphorical (heaven, hell; "depth of pains and height of passion"; "the blushing flow'rs shall *rise*") had long been familiar. Imitation of sounds in nature, of wind and water, of living creatures (barnyard noises, buzzing bees, humming gnats, barking dogs, clucking hens) were elementary, as were suggestions of motion swift or sluggish, abrupt or smooth. Vivaldi's *Seasons* is full of this mimicry. Handel depicts the plagues of Egypt with similar directness, and examples of such description can be found everywhere in his work. But the way in which Vivaldi suggests a world numb with winter's cold, or Handel conjures up a slope all white with sheep: these are greater wonders. Handel's *L'Allegro ed Il Penseroso* is crowded with English landscape painting, inspired by that immortal text. A striking example of a more technical kind is Handel's illustration of Dryden's "jarring atoms" by means of a succession of diminished triads. Chromaticism to express disorder was an old resource. More complicated are some of Bach's involutions, such as the cantata wherein, Bukofzer shows us, he interweaves five allegorical ideas, all imperceptible to the uninitiated.[7]

A little later, Mozart was to demonstrate in one seven-league stride of genius how all these and other translatable resources could be put to dra-

[6] *Religio Medici* (1643), pp. 164-165 (Section 9).

[7] Manfred Bukofzer, "Allegory in Baroque Music," *Journal of the Warburg Institute,* Vol. III, Nos. 1-2.

matic use in the portrayal of character in social interchange. *Le Nozze di Figaro* is Mozart's own inspired invention: as Kerman says, the drama is "not Beaumarchais's or Da Ponte's. Music here does not merely decorate what playwright or librettist had designed; Mozart's music creates a drama that they never suspected."[8] In and through the musical revelation, he transformed and even universalized the characters, giving them a depth and humanity and emotional range entirely missing from the verbal script. Thus, a musical phrase parodies, melodically or rhythmically, its use in an earlier context or by another character and thereby becomes pregnant with psychological implication, whether for wit, irony, pathos, or sudden illumination. Or the mutual attitudes of two characters may be implied in the key relation of their juxtaposed musical statements. The social level may be hinted in the quality and rhythm of phrase, and of course there is a continuous description of temperament in the musical utterance of the contrasting personalities. Occasionally the music may mock the plain sense of the words to which it is set, be it in a numerical jest on degrees of the scale, or a clumsy progression or frustrated expectation introduced where the singer supposes himself astute but proves himself imperceptive or deceived. Mozart was not averse to a private joke that was yet not an inviolable secret. In the ensembles, the disarray of conflicting emotions and divergent thoughts is yoked in reluctant harness with brilliantly dramatic effect.

There is no verbal sequence, prose or verse, that cannot be "set to music," or be given tonal and rhythmic statement, by a composer who chooses to accord it that distinction. Plain chant is a vast and inexhaustible demonstration of the fact. Children's taunts and chants are also perennial proof. And for the last three hundred years, in opera and oratorio and other large forms, recitative of various kinds has been providing continuous exemplification of the same truth. A late and spectacular instance of the buxom submission of prose to music occurs in the use of a passage, set in repeated six-phrase stanzas for choral singing, from Thomas Jefferson's Declaration on taking up arms in 1775: *"We fight not for glory or for conquest. We exhibit to mankind the remarkable spectacle of a people attacked by unprovoked enemies, without any imputation or even suspicion of offense. They boast of their privileges and civilization, and yet proffer no milder conditions than servitude or death."*[9] The *stanzaic* treatment of this is certainly a *tour de force*. But of course English speech is rhythmed by its natural accents, and on becoming impassioned aspires instinctively to the condition of chant. Besides, there are always private factors subtly at work. We all would acknowledge, though we seldom give it heed, that some speakers live closer to

[8] Joseph Kerman, *Opera as Drama* (New York, 1956), p. 108.
[9] Randall Thompson, *The Testament of Freedom* (Boston, 1943).

the level of singing than others, and articulate more musically, whether
by a wider range of speaking tones or accentual emphasis, or because of
livelier dynamics of temperament:

> *When you speak, sweet,*
> *I'd have you do it ever: when you sing,*
> *I'd have you buy and sell so, so give alms,*
> *Pray so; and, for the ordering your affairs,*
> *To sing them too.*   (*The Winter's Tale* IV.iii.136-140)

As these lines show, spoken English is so close to blank verse in its normal iambic rhythm that with little effort it becomes metrically regular.
From verse to music is but a step higher; and indeed, from this point of
view, blank verse can be thought of as in itself a rather strict *recitativo
secco*. On the other hand, because of its closeness to prose rhythm it is
probably the least lyrical of English metres, and is commonly felt to
need the help of rhyme to raise it to the level of singing. But, granted the
resources of rhyme and pause, the possible transformations of iambic
pentameter are almost infinite. Caesural pauses become held notes or
rests in musical translation, and these may be reinforced by internal
rhyme or by phrasal repetition. With such simple aids, two couplets from
Pope's pastoral, "Summer," have been turned into the most famous *aria
da capo* in English: "Where'er you walk," in Handel's *Semele*. The setting is even-paced, stately; the composer has taken full advantage of the
caesuras and given a smooth deliberation, almost spondaic, to the metrical feet, so that the articles, auxiliaries, and conjunctions all acquire a
magnified and unhurried dignity and amplitude in their elevation.

To drop from the sublime to the ridiculous in illustration of the lim-
itless flexibility of this metre, suppose we take another well-known cou-
plet of Pope and set it, with no more coaxing than Handel's, to an equally familiar tune, not *andante* this time but a brisk waltz:

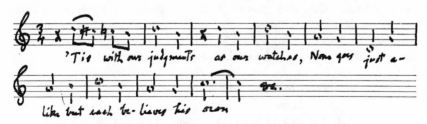

The caesural pauses of this metre, commonly employed for variety,
can be equally fascinating when made invariable, or when a rhyme is
substituted for the pause. When the line is disguised by breaking for
print (not for the ear), other possibilities leap to light. Two examples
may be cited from Herrick:

> *Though Clock*
> *To tell how night drawes hence, I've none,*
> *A Cock*
> *I have, to sing how day drawes on.*
> *I have*
> *A maid (my Prew) by good luck sent,*
> *To save*
> *That little, Fates me gave or lent.   &c.*[10]

> Both you two have
> Relation to the grave:
> And where
> The *Fun'rall-Trump* sounds, you are there.

> I shall be made
> Ere long a fleeting shade:
> Pray come,
> And do some honour to my Tomb.[11]

It is obvious, on a moment's inspection, that both these patterns, superficially so different, are basically iambic pentameters, oddly divided. Herrick was a careful metrist and we shall return to him later. But in his practice, he contrasts in striking ways with the generation of lutenist songsters that just preceded him, whose work fills the first quarter of his century. Had his verses been set by the musicians of that school, his neatest effects would have been spoiled, for he demanded more subservience than they chose to give.

It is doubtful that the union of poetry and music was ever closer, more mutually compliant—in English, at least—than it was in the work of these composer-poets. Although their verses have often been anthologized and can be read with delight for their own sufficient beauty, it is yet fair to say that they cannot be fully experienced apart from their proper musical settings. Most of the songs are in normal metres and simple stanzaic patterns. But not all: it is not at all clear how, for example, the following verses are to be read. The notes are essential:

> *Never may my woes be relieved,*
> *Since pity is fled;*
> *And tears and sighs and groans my weary days*
> *Of all joys have deprived.*

[10] Robert Herrick, *Poetical Works*, ed. F. W. Moorman (Oxford, 1915), p. 246.

[11] Ibid., p. 111.

> *From the highest spire of contentment*
> *My fortune is thrown;*
> *And fear and grief and pain for my deserts*
> *Are my hopes, since hope is gone.*
> *Hark! you shadows that in darkness dwell,*
> *Learn to contemn light.*
> *Happy, happy they that in hell*
> *Feel not the world's despite.*

This is the latter half of Dowland's "Flow, my tears," one of his most celebrated songs. In Shakespeare's lifetime its popularity was a byword; it gave no trouble in singing.[12]

But its irregularity is of an unusual kind. The *typical* surprises are not apparent on the surface of the texts. We may take Campian as example both for the high level of his poetry and because we know that he set it himself; also because some acquaintance with it may be taken for granted. Campian was a student of classical verse, studied syllabic quantity, and was a subtle metrist. He greatly liked changing and interchanging the stress-pattern, often alternating iambic with trochaic lines, as in "Follow thy fair sun, unhappy shadow."[13] A brilliant example of this kind is the song beginning:

> *Kinde are her answeres,*
> *But her performance keeps no day,*
> *Breaks time as dancers*
> *From their own Musicke when they stray.*[14]

Another song, "Break now, my heart, and die," closes each stanza with a metrical shift from iambs to dactyls.[15] But these points are superficial. The real subtleties come in the mating of words and notes. Often, the music imposes a contrary rhythm, or exploits metrical ambiguity, as in the familiar, "Come, Phyllis, come into these bowers."[16] Continually, the notes transform the phrase by prolonging syllables and exaggerating speech rhythms. A good example of such interplay is "Her rosy cheeks," of which a full stanza is needed to show it off:

[12] John Dowland, *Second Booke of Songs or Ayres* (London, 1600), Song 2.

[13] Philip Rosseter [and Thomas Campian], *A Booke of Ayres* (London, 1601), Song 4.

[14] Thomas Campian, *The Third Booke of Ayres* (London, c. 1618), Song 7.

[15] Ibid., Song 10.

[16] Thomas Ford, *Musicke of Sundrie Kindes* (London, 1607), Song 6.

> Her rosy cheeks, her ever-smiling eyes,
> Are spheres and beds where love in triumph lies.
> Her rubine lips, when they their pearl unlock,
>   Make them seem as they did rise
>   All out of one smooth coral rock.
> O that of other creatures' store I knew
>   More worthy and more rare;
>   For these are old, and she so new,
>   That her to them none should compare.[17]

These basically iambic lines of varying lengths Campian sets to triple time, which yet is denied wherever the natural emphasis requires. Thus, in the second line, the underlying musical count would put the stress on *Are, beds, in,* and *lies.* But of course the triple beat is overlaid with the plain duple rhythm of the natural accents on every alternate syllable. Against this, however, regular triple time is maintained by the accompaniment. And these contradictions persist in lines 3, 5, 6, 7, and 8. In the first line, the triple time is clearly established by giving three full beats to *cheeks,* making it equal to the time of the first three syllables combined. Over all, the effect is of a supersensitive responsiveness and flexibility of rhythmical interplay, which description plods after in vain. Though Campian was by no means the most gifted musician of the school, the freedom of his melodic line is the more surprising because as a poet he was so clear in his verbal patterns. Since one must suppose that these came first, one would have expected them to be restricting. Probably his experiments in classical metres, promoted in the little tract *Observations in the Art of English Poesie,* 1602, contributed to free him; for his awareness of syllabic length, delicately exemplified in "Rose-cheekt Laura," and in the less successful sapphics of "Come, let us sound," is nearly everywhere a distinctive mark of his work.[18] An especially felicitous conjunction of all his gifts is the song, "Harke, al you ladies," in the Rosseter book, of which the first of five stanzas is the following—and it might have sweetened the imagination of Chaucer's Merchant, could he have known it:

> Harke al you ladies that do sleep,
>   The fayry queen Proserpina
> Bids you awake and pitie them that weep.

---

[17] Thomas Campian, *The Second Booke of Ayres* (London, c. 1613), Song 20.

[18] Rosseter, Song 21.

> *You may doe in the darke*
> *What the day doth forbid,*
> *Feare not the dogs that barke,*
> *Night will have all hid.*[19]

But such freedom and mutual flexibility is characteristic of all these lutenists—most notably, of course, the greatest of them, John Dowland; and it is hard to limit discussion to a few illustrations. It must at least be evident now why Herrick's typographical displays would not have survived such handling.

But it is unjust to charge Herrick with typographical trickery. It is true that some of his most characteristic pieces make a sharper impression when seen as they lie on the page than through the ear. But this is because they need close inspection, as we bring a cameo nearer to the eye for full appreciation. If he relies on spatial devices, he also exploits them for valid aesthetic ends and makes them serve, not dominate, his purposes. We hear the rhymes but we also hear the rests. The eye affects the ear in odd ways. An example will clarify better than generalization here. The old tune of "Flying Fame" was used for the ballad of "Chevy Chase" and in time became a ubiquitous vehicle for ballad quatrains or street verses on any subject in common metre (CM) throughout the seventeenth and eighteenth centuries.[20] Its suitability for such service is evident when used with the Percy MS copy of "Chevy Chase,"

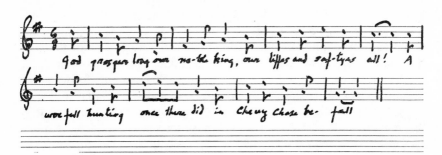

> *To drive the deere with hound and horne*
> *Erle Pearcy took the way:*
> *The child may rue that is vnborne*
> *the hunting of that day!*

[19] Rosseter, Song 19.

[20] William Chappell, *Popular Music of the Olden Time*, 2 vols. (London, 1855-59), I, 198-199.

Now, there is a poignant set of verses by Herrick, called "Comfort to a youth that had lost his Love." It runs as follows in the first two stanzas:

> *What needs complaints,*
> *When she a place*
> *Has with the race*
> > *Of Saints?*
> *In endless mirth,*
> *She thinks not on*
> *What's said or done*
> > *In earth:*
> *She sees no teares,*
> *Or any tone*
> *Of thy deep grone*
> > *She heares:*
> *Nor do's she minde,*
> *Or think on't now,*
> *That ever thou*
> > *Wast kind.*[21]

It would be unlikely to strike the reader that Herrick's poem is metrically kin to "Chevy Chase" and could be sung to the same tune. For in setting his lines down on the page in short, rhymed units, Herrick has contrived to seize control of our reading and make us give extra time, by hold and pause, to the last syllable of each line. This works even better on the mind's ear than it does with the best spoken reading, for when the sense runs over as in lines two and three, six and seven, what we feel is equivalent to a held note in music that does not affect the sense; but in reading aloud, the sense is disturbed by so long a pause. It might prove no easy matter to set the poem to a music that would preserve the carved, inscriptional quality of Herrick's art. A typical CM tune would do violence to it.

Yet it is an odd truth that in the unconscious operations of tradition in British-American folk singing, there is a rooted instinctual tendency to linger on certain syllables of the ballad quatrain elsewhere than on the normal pauses at the end rhymes of the second and fourth lines. The result of this, metrically, is to transform the duple scheme of 6/8 or 4/4 into a triple scheme best written as 3/2. This impulse is evident in a widely familiar form of the folk ballad "Barbara Allen." Appalachian variants abound. E.g.:

[21] Herrick, *Poetical Works,* p. 314.

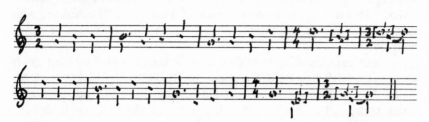

It will be seen that Herrick's verses conform precisely to this metrical scheme and could be sung to it without wrenching. (The feminine cadence is unnecessary here and would be for the nonce simply left out, as suggested in the alternative readings above.)

How Herrick arrived at this pattern is as uncertain as to fathom the instinct of the folk. But the parallel is undeniable, and it is not improbable that the poet evolved his scheme from the simple one of tradition. He was a student of country pastimes and popular ways. Many of his happiest verses are in straight ballad metre ("The Mad Maid's song")[22] or with added, sometimes feminine, double rhymes. "Gather ye rose-buds while ye may" is such a one (p. 84). "To Anthea, who may command him any thing" is in straight ballad quatrains with alternate rhyme (p. 108). He was a tireless and delicate experimenter with this basic pattern, often cutting the lines in two at various points, introducing additional rhymes for fresh effects. (See "To Musique, to becalme his Fever."—p. 95.) Sometimes he achieves great intricacy by inserting a single additional rhymed foot, as in "To Daffadils," where two ballad quatrains are woven into a complicated stanza by breaking every other quatrain's first line into two unequal rhymed segments and running in, next, an extra foot that rhymes with line three (p. 125). He is fond also of a form containing frequent dactyls, basically in 6/8 metre, the first and third lines rhyming internally and divided in two, the second often with feminine double-rhyme. Autolycus' song, "Jog on, jog on" (cf. Herrick's "Upon [Mrs. Southwell] her feet"), is the normal scheme without extra rhymes. Typical of Herrick's use of the form are "To Electra" (" 'Tis Ev'ning, my Sweet"), "The May-pole," "Ceremonies for Christmasse," "Twelfe night," "To his angrie God."[23] We observe that most of these are seasonally festive, and folklike in spirit. This would tend to confirm the conjecture that Herrick, for all his fastidious classicism, was in familiar touch with the popular singing tradition. It is noteworthy that in Moorman's edition of Herrick's *Poetical Works,* there is record of not more than a dozen of his pieces having been put to music. Three quarters of these were set by

[22] *Poetical Works*, p. 156.
[23] Pp. 194, 195, 239, 263, 317, 353.

Henry Lawes, and he adventured on none of the more intricate patterns but kept by preference to the short couplets. He set also the two famous lyrics, "To the Virgins, to make much of Time" and "To Anthea, who may command him any thing" (pp. 84, 108); and two pieces in heroic couplets.

Later composers seem seldom to have been tempted by Herrick. It is not surprising that Purcell was not, for Purcell never looked back for lyrics. Unlike Henry Lawes, that enigmatic genius was not particular about texts, and took what fell to his professional lot without complaint —knowing, perhaps, that he could transfigure anything he touched. Dryden gave him tasks that contained the most literary merit, and Dryden wrote a good deal expressly for music. But it is not always literary excellence that a composer needs, and it is unlikely that Dryden warmly welcomed suggestions from a mere musician. He could turn out lyrics as deftly as any; but in his Odes he seems to have had no confidence in a composer's imagination, and to have felt that if he himself did not supply all the specifications, including the phrasal repetitions, e.g.,

> *And sigh'd and look'd, sigh'd and look'd,*
> *Sigh'd and look'd, and sigh'd again—*

and all the changes of metre and line-variation required and stipulated at the appointed places, nothing but disaster could ensue. Like a fussy Bottom, because no one else would do them right, he would play all the roles: and did, with remarkable success.

The primary purpose of these remarks will have been fulfilled if they stimulate the reader to develop his own latent interests, or to satisfy his special curiosities, by congenial research in particular areas of a country inviting delightful exploration. The examples cited are such as have attracted the attention of the writer, not as paradigms of method— although similar lines of inquiry are certain to be discovered in any cultural history of any western nationality—but as cases intrinsically interesting of themselves. Limitations of space and private knowledge preclude a systematic and encyclopaedic survey and in the concluding pages one can only touch on a few striking features of inter-relationship during the last three centuries in England, and point to opportunities for further investigation. Any reader naturally drawn to the subject, albeit in another language and literature, will soon find his own analogies.

The eighteenth century has been called the age of music because music then attained a height never equalled before in Western history, whereas such a claim could not be made for any other art in that age.[24] It has also been called the century of divine song, by an Englishman

---

[24] Hugo Leichtentritt, *Music, History, and Ideas* (Cambridge, Mass., 1954), pp. 134 ff.

thinking of the flood of sacred songs that carried the evangelical revival on a crest of popular melody set to words that not seldom reached high literary quality.[25] The century's title to be considered one of song in a more inclusive sense might easily be defended. Besides the many thousand Methodist hymns, there was a secular outpouring still larger, from beginning to end, in songbooks, in ballad-operas, in the pleasure-garden concerts of Ranelagh, Vauxhall, and elsewhere;[26] in new settings for Shakespeare's songs; in theatrical entertainment of every kind, from opera to pantomime. The musical side of pantomime, which must have done much for the productions, would bear investigation. There were, too, the convivial musical societies for the singing of catches and glees, which gave annual prizes, and for which hundreds of pieces were written. It is safe to say that the printed collections of such things number well over a hundred: the Noblemen's & Gentlemen's Catch Club alone produced thirty-two volumes. This territory has never been thoroughly explored, either as to the individuals concerned or for the whole product. The elegancies of social singing are abundant in mid-century engraved anthologies like Bickham's *Musical Entertainer, Calliope, Clio and Euterpe.* The urban popular at the level of D'Urfey and Ramsay appears early in the century, and the rural popular at the level of Burns at the end. The decades between could be filled with a long list both of collections with tunes, like the early *Musical Miscellany* of Walsh and Watts, and Ritson's late English and Scottish anthologies, and of wordbooks culled from Garden concerts and elsewhere. These, too, are largely unstudied today. The musical average is tame enough but not without surprises and charms, as many competent musicians made contribution. Most of the still favorite Shakespeare settings belong to this period.

The folk tunes of Scotland were discovered early, and indeed Burns's lyric achievement is inconceivable without that tradition in the forefront of his mind. His metres, his stanzaic patterns, his refrains; the lines framed to the short musical phrases, the "O" endings to fit the phrasal cadence, the undramatic and unvaried level from stanza to stanza: all these refer to a fixed and unchanging melodic unit and assume the note-for-syllable habit of his tunes.

> *I rue the day I sought her, O;*
> *I rue the day I sought her, O;*
> *Wha gets her needs na say she's woo'd,*
> *But he may say he's bought her, O.*

[25] John Sampson, "The Century of Divine Songs," British Academy Warton Lecture, 3 March 1943. *Proceedings,* Vol. xxix (1943).

[26] See Warwick Wroth, *The London Pleasure Gardens of the Eighteenth Century* (London, 1896); Mollie Sands, *Invitation to Ranelagh* (London, 1946); Peter Warlock, *Songs of the Gardens* (London, 1925).

Beyond the choice of a suitable air (and Scottish tunes are surprisingly accommodating in temper), there can be no *particularizing* of words to notes for expressive effects, nor, of course, of notes to words. Where, say, Dryden could count on Purcell's playing with a verbal image in melodic illustration, Burns must accept the bare vehicle as his rule and conform to it in metre and mood. It is amusing to imagine what Purcell might have done in the way of pictorial description[27] if he had been confronted with a text like "John Anderson my Jo": "Now we maun totter down, John, And hand in hand we'll go, And sleep thegither at the foot"! But it is rather startling to reflect how inviolate Burns's lyrics have proven to later composers: a convincing proof of the inseparable bond between his words and their own wedded music.

The nineteenth century may also rightly be called a century of song. But here, with the advent of romanticism, a new sensitivity is engendered between words and music, an individualism emerges that makes each new song a personal declaration of feeling; the *aria da capo* and the strophic form tend to grow tiresome with the development of the Lieder *durchkomponiert*.

> *Poesie ist tiefes Schmerzen,*
> *Und es kommt das echte Lied*
> *Einzig aus dem Menschenherzen,*
> *Das ein tiefes Leid durchglüht.*
>
> (J. Kerner)

Thanks mainly, perhaps, to the patriotic fervor and impact of Burns, Scottish folk song was too firmly entrenched to be neglected. But England had shown no such pride nor passion to preserve the traditional heritage, and abjectly capitulated with hardly a murmur to the art song and folk song of the Continent, convinced that native folk song was virtually nonexistent. At the mid-century, men like Petrie and P. W. Joyce began to collect and preserve the rich treasure of Irish melody; but there were no field-workers to do the same for England; and the best showing was that of William Chappell, who sought the national music in old library books and manuscripts of the preceding centuries.[28] It took the zeal and faith of a small band of dedicated spirits, about the beginning of the twentieth century, to reveal the fact that the stream of native English melody had been running clear and full all through the nineteenth, and, as its pre-harmonic modal character proved, steadily and unbroken at least since the days of Elizabeth. But for the Victorians the hue was not the wear, and they did not recognize it when they heard it but apologized

---

[27] See, e.g., A. K. Holland, *Henry Purcell* (London, 1932), pp. 115-131.

[28] See n. 20. See also Claude Simpson, in Bibliography following.

and hurried to buy German collections, Schubert and Mendelssohn and Schumann, for whom their own song writers were no match. In our century the scene has been transformed and the reproach of English unmusicality can be laughed out of court. The strength of this renascence stems not only from the revelations of the English Folk Song Society, which enlisted the efforts, before the First World War, of Cecil Sharp, Vaughan Williams, Gustav Holst, and other gifted men, but from the renewed historical study of the Tudor and Stuart composers, and the growing realization and inspiration of their greatness.

It would be a comfortable and tidy procedure to order the multifarious interconnections of literature and music according to the closeness of their mutual dependency. Thus, at one extreme would come forms united continuously throughout, of which either half was created with the other in mind and never intended for an independent existence: Opera of which the "book" was written for music (e.g., *Dido and Æneas*); Oratorio; ideally, Odes; certain kinds of songs and ballads with choral elements. Next would be set forms intended for intermittent combination, as masques, opéra comique, operetta, musical comedy, some sorts of cantata, of which Burns's *The Jolly Beggars* would be a shining example. At the opposite extreme, perhaps, would be set Imitations: verbal structures strongly suggestive of music but not demanding it; musical structures distilling or re-creating specific literary works, as overtures and tone poems and ballets (Tchaikowski's *Romeo and Juliet,* Vaughan Williams' *The Wasps*, Elgar's *Falstaff,* Prokofief's ballet *Romeo and Juliet*).

The trouble with this scheme is twofold. In the first place, many finished and self-sufficient literary works have been chosen by composers for musical collaboration of one kind or another. Thus, hundreds of song texts have been set that were never so conceived. Randall Thompson's *Frostiana* Suite for chorus, Samuel Barber's *Dover Beach,* Benjamin Britten's *Serenade for Tenor and Strings* are contrasting modern instances. In such cases, the question how essential the collaboration is depends largely on the degree of success an auditor feels that the composer achieved.

But even in cases where the text presupposes its musical fulfillment, as a libretto, the author has to anticipate that completion without knowing precisely how it will be realized. There is perhaps never such a thing as a twin birth, even when the author unites in himself the faculties of poet and composer. The work of the poet must precede that of the composer (even in Wagner's or Campian's case), though the text may be subjected to modification in the course of its musical elaboration, before it becomes known and classic. In the ideal marriage of an art song, however, the vast majority of texts are pre-existent works of art, the virtual inviolability of which the composer must honor. Indeed, their beauty was what originally attracted him. His own contribution, even if it enhance and exalt the text, has of course no independent life. Where the text has this celebrity, especially in larger forms, as when Handel set Dryden's great Odes for St. Cecilia's Day, the preoccupations of criticism will inevitably be musical. It is very unlikely that the literary critic will learn much from such criticism that will illuminate the precedent literary work as such. The danger is that he will fail to adjust his insights to the new birth. The critical challenge will be to show, without retreating to a separate judgment of each partner, how and why a deeper or richer value inheres in the collaborative union.

But the other of the two obstacles indicated above is that from the beginning of its history, drama has found it necessary or highly advantageous to call in the services of music in numberless ways and in varying degrees. Overtures and entr'actes and incidental songs, interludes, and masque-like episodes are ponderable elements in many a dramatic exhibition, sometimes essential to the integrity of a work and sometimes detachable without organic loss. By virtue of his universal appeal, Shakespeare over the span of four centuries provides illustration of nearly all possible associational involvements of poetry with music.

There are many books and essays dealing, wholly or in part, with music in relation to Shakespeare's work. The subject is so vast and ramified that it cannot be said that any of them is either commensurate with the work or exhaustive of the aspect chosen for study.[29] But ideas and information can be gathered from them all. Probably the most valuable is the next to last; at least it is the most useful and comprehensive biblio-historical survey. This is the series of four essays, each by a different authority and edited by Phyllis Hartnoll, *Shakespeare in Music*. The collection contains an essay by John Stevens on the music in the plays on Shakespeare's stage, which discusses intelligently the mutual interaction of music and drama in Shakespeare as it appeared in contemporary performance; an essay by Charles Cudworth on song and part-song settings from Shakespeare's day to the present; an essay by Winton Dean on Shakespeare in opera; and an essay by Roger Fiske on Shakespeare in the Concert Hall. Fiske discusses in review the good or ill success of overtures, entr'actes, incidental music, symphonic poems, and ballets based on the plays. Dean's is a brilliant critical survey of scores of

[29] The following may be mentioned: E. W. Naylor, *Shakespeare and Music*, 2nd ed. (London, 1931); G. H. Cowling, *Music on the Shakespearean Stage* (Cambridge, 1913); Christopher Wilson, *Shakespeare and Music* (London, 1922); Richmond Noble, *Shakespeare's Use of Song* (London, 1923); J. S. Manifold, *Music in English Drama: From Shakespeare to Purcell* (London, 1956); F. W. Sternfeld, *Music in Shakespearean Tragedy* (London, 1963); Phyllis Hartnoll, ed., *Shakespeare in Music* (London, 1964). Winton Dean, "Shakespeare in the Opera House," in *Shakespeare Survey*, No. 18 (1965), pp. 75-93.

attempts to turn Shakespeare into opera. He lists an astounding number
of these in his bibliography: some 180, of which he says about eighty
have been published either in full or in vocal scores. He notes that all
but two of the plays (*Titus Andronicus* and *Two Gentlemen of Verona*)
have sired operas. As would be expected, the histories have been attempted least frequently. Even as this essay was passing through the press,
a star-bespangled *Antony and Cleopatra* by Samuel Barber was ac-
claimed at the opening of the new Metropolitan Opera House, with
libretto by F. Zeffirelli from Shakespeare. Well worth study in this conec-
tion are the sections on Verdi's *Falstaff* and *Otello* in Joseph Kerman's
Opera as Drama, mentioned earlier. The early and late comedies are the
most lyrical of the works, and one might expect monographs focussing on
the importance in them of the musical element but no critic seems to have
confined himself to this relatively limited field, though many touch on it.
There is a highly speculative discussion of the role of music in *Twelfth
Night* in John Hollander's wide-ranging book, *The Untuning of the Sky,*
pp. 153 ff., and in *Sewanee Review,* 1959, pp. 220-238. In connection
with the first performance of Benjamin Britten's recent opera, *A Mid-
summer Night's Dream,* at Aldeburgh in 1963, there was a great deal of
critical writing in the current journals. In Wilfrid Mellers' recent book,
Harmonious Meeting, there is a suggestive chapter on *The Tempest.*
That any opera based on a play of Shakespeare is a satisfactory surro-
gate for the original will hardly be maintained, but it is always possible
that it may be a great work in its own terms. Verdi's two Shakespearean
operas, for example, with libretti by Boito which do not dishonor the
original text, are undeniable masterpieces. It is not, however, easy for
the literary critic to concede the right of such a work to be itself and to
grant the music the privileges to which as an equal partner it is
entitled.[30] To discriminate between the multitude of pretenders and
blood royal is the task of the true critic.

The opportunities are abundant and inviting: there is plenty of
room for research. We need better studies of some of the greatest poets
against the background of the music that they knew. The musical literature of the late Middle Ages and Renaissance is becoming available in
print and (far more important) on records for repeated hearing; and
upon familiarity with the sounds to which—let us say—Chaucer was accustomed, we should begin to understand what music was to him as a
physical experience and an imaginative resource. It is not a mere matter
of compiling statistics from household accounts about the number and
sorts of instruments available or of the players and their salaries; nor a
faithful collecting of all the musical references in the poet's work, though

[30] See B. H. Bronson, "The True Proportions of Gay's *Acis and Galatea.*"
PMLA, LXXX (1965), 325-331.

these investigations are a valuable check on a soaring imagination.[31] Until very lately, music has been under a heavy handicap: it has had to be limited, as living experience, to the knowledge, skill, and lucky opportunity of very few persons. Occasions to listen have been rare and unlikely to recur. Whereas many artistic monuments—cathedrals, sculpture, brasses, windows, illuminated manuscripts, textiles—have survived for immediate and intimate enjoyment and study, music has had to be re-created every time it could be appreciated. It is symptomatic, and deplorable, that in the handsomely illustrated, and well informed and instructive, anthology, *Medieval England,* 2 vols., Oxford, 1958, music receives three paragraphs, under the heading, "Minstrelsy," in the general editor's chapter on Recreations! But, thanks to enterprises like the Archiv Production of the Deutsche Grammophon Gesellschaft, it is already possible to hear and possess fine recordings of some of the music Chaucer may well have known: Adam de la Halle, Troubadour and Minstrel music and—most important—secular pieces by Machaut, as well as his great Mass of Our Lady.

We need studies of forms poetico-musical, with equal attention to both sides wherever possible, and of individual examples of such forms: masques, operas and oratorios, odes, songs. We need readable studies of musical theory and musical history. We need musical criticism written responsibly but with a sense of style, for the non-professional reader. In England there have been a fair number of critics so qualified: Bernard Shaw, Ernest Newman, D. F. Tovey, E. J. Dent, Wilfrid Mellers, Winton Dean, for example. But in America there have been precious few who combined musical scholarship and literary flair. And finally, we could do with more, and more scholarly, biographies both of musicians and literary men with a strong musical concern. Two notable examples are Jacques Barzun's *Berlioz,* Boston, 1950, and Roger Lonsdale's recent biography of Dr. Charles Burney, Oxford, 1965. But the problems and tactics of this type of biography are not different from those of men and women in other walks of life, and we may leave them to be discovered by those inspired by affection, knowledge, and ambition to worthwhile effort.

[31] See C. C. Olson, "Chaucer and the Music of the Fourteenth Century," *Speculum,* xv (1941), 64-91; Gustave Reese, *Music in the Middle Ages* (New York, 1940).

Bibliography

The following brief list is self-explanatory and will be found variously useful. It supplements titles already given above.

Arundell, Denis. *Henry Purcell.* London, 1927.

Arthos, John. *On "A Mask Presented at Ludlow-Castle."* Ann Arbor, Mich., 1954.

Baskerville, C. R. *The Elizabethan Jig and Related Song Drama.* Chicago, 1929.

Bontoux, Germaine. *La Chanson en Angleterre au temps d'Elisabeth.* Oxford, 1936.

Bukofzer, Manfred. *Music in the Baroque Era.* New York, 1947.

—— *Studies in Medieval and Renaissance Music.* New York, 1950.

Dean, Winton. *Handel's Dramatic Oratorios and Masques.* London, 1959.

Dent, E. J. *Foundations of English Opera.* Cambridge, Eng., 1928.

Duckles, Vincent. "The Gamble Manuscript as a Source of *continuo* Song in England." *Journal of the American Musicological Society,* I (Summer 1948), 23-40.

—— "The 'curious' Art of John Wilson (1595-1647): An Introduction to His Songs and Lute Music." *Journal of the American Musicological Society,* VII (Summer 1954), 93-112.

—— "John Jenkins's Settings of Lyrics by George Herbert." *Musical Quarterly,* XLVIII (Oct. 1962), 461-475.

Geiringer, Karl. "Haydn and the Folksong of the British Isles." *The Musical Quarterly,* XXXV (1949), 179-208.

Evans, Willa McClung. *Ben Jonson and Elizabethan Music.* Lancaster, Pa., 1929.

—— *Henry Lawes.* New York, 1941.

Fellowes, E. H. *The English Madrigal Composers.* Oxford, 1921.

—— *The English School of Lutenist Song-Writers.* 2 series. Stainer & Bell.

Kerman, Joseph. *The Elizabethan Madrigal: A Comparative Study.* New York, 1962. (American Musicological Society.)

Mellers, Wilfrid. *Music and Society.* New York, 1950.

—— *Harmonious Meeting.* London, 1965. [Cf. especially Part II, on Shakespeare, Purcell, and Handel.]

Musique et poésie au XVIe siècle. (Centre National de la Recherche Scientifique. Colloques Internationaux, 5.) Paris, 1954.

Orgel, Stephen. *The Jonsonian Masque.* Cambridge, Mass., 1965.

Pattison, Bruce. *Music and Poetry of the English Renaissance.* London, 1948.

Reese, Gustave. *Music in the Renaissance.* New York, 1954.

Sachs, Curt. *Rhythm and Tempo: A Study in Music History.* New York, 1953.

Simpson, Claude M. "Tudor Popular Music: Its Social Significance." *Huntington Library Quarterly,* V (1942), 176-179.

Bertrand H. Bronson

—— *The British Broadside Ballad and Its Music.* New Brunswick, N. J., 1966.

Sternfeld, Frederick W. *Music in Shakespearean Tragedy.* London, 1963.

Stevens, John. *Music and Poetry in the Early Tudor Court.* London, 1961.

Tovey, D. C. *Musical Articles from the Encyclopaedia Britannica.* London, 1944.

Tuve, Rosemond. "Sacred 'Parody' of Love Poetry, and Herbert." *Studies in the Renaissance,* VII (1961), 249-290.

Notes on the Contributors

James Thorpe is Director of the Henry E. Huntington Library & Art Gallery. He has written several kinds of studies, including literary criticism, bibliography, literary history, and textual criticism.

Rosalie L. Colie holds appointments as Professor of History and as Professor of English at the University of Iowa. Her most recent book is *Paradoxia Epidemica: The Renaissance Tradition of Paradox;* her special interest is in literary aspects of intellectual history.

Northrop Frye is University Professor at the University of Toronto. His most influential book is probably *Anatomy of Criticism.* He is generally thought of as the leading exponent of myth criticism.

Leon Edel is Henry James Professor of English and American Letters at New York University. His contributions to the art of biography have been both to its theory (*Literary Biography*) and to its practice (the life of Henry James).

Frederick C. Crews is Professor of English at the University of California in Berkeley. He is the author of books on Henry James, E. M. Forster, and Nathaniel Hawthorne. He has been using modern psychological insights to illuminate writers and their work.

Leo Lowenthal is Professor of Sociology at the University of California in Berkeley. His books include two sociological studies of literature: *Literature and the Image of Man,* and *Literature, Popular Culture, and Society.*

J. Hillis Miller is Professor of English and Chairman at the Johns Hopkins University. His work has been concerned with writers of the nineteenth and twentieth centuries; his two most recent books are *The Disappearance of God* and *Poets of Reality.*

Bertrand H. Bronson is Professor of English at the University of California in Berkeley. His literary studies have centered on Chaucer and the eighteenth century; his major musical study is *The Traditional Tunes of the Child Ballads.*